Sex and Scandals *in* Georgian England

This book is dedicated to my parents Stewart and Penny, my wife Morgan and our two children Ryan and Gage.

SEX AND SCANDALS IN GEORGIAN ENGLAND

JOHN RANKIN

PEN & SWORD
HISTORY
AN IMPRINT OF PEN & SWORD BOOKS LTD.
YORKSHIRE – PHILADELPHIA

First published in Great Britain in 2025 by
PEN AND SWORD HISTORY
An imprint of
Pen & Sword Books Ltd
Yorkshire – Philadelphia

ISBN 978 1 03610 636 2

A CIP catalogue record for this book is available from the British Library.

Typeset in Times New Roman 11.5/15 by
SJmagic DESIGN SERVICES, India.
Printed and bound in the UK by CPI Group (UK) Ltd.

The Publisher's authorised representative in the EU for product safety is
Authorised Rep Compliance Ltd., Ground Floor, 71 Lower Baggot Street, Dublin
D02 P593, Ireland.
www.arccompliance.com

For a complete list of Pen & Sword titles please contact
PEN & SWORD BOOKS LIMITED
George House, Units 12 & 13, Beevor Street, Off Pontefract Road,
Barnsley, South Yorkshire, S71 1HN, England
E-mail: enquiries@pen-and-sword.co.uk
Website: www.pen-and-sword.co.uk

or

PEN AND SWORD BOOKS
1950 Lawrence Rd, Havertown, PA 19083, USA
E-mail: uspen-and-sword@casematepublishers.com
Website: www.penandswordbooks.com

Contents

Introduction

During the Georgian period (1714–1837), British people held complex and often contradictory views towards extra-marital affairs.[1] While in the modern age, 'cheating' has numerous forms and connotations, in the eighteenth and nineteenth centuries, an affair was a term applied to married individuals who had a sexual relationship with anyone other than their spouse. Similar to today, marriage in the eighteenth and early nineteenth centuries was the norm; most Britons married during their lifetime.[2] As Jane Austen and numerous other writers of the period demonstrated, the question of who, not if, one married occupied a central role in the minds of not just marriageable youths but their parents as well. Even Emma, Austen's heroine who professed that she had no desire to marry, fell in love and ended up walking down the aisle.[3] Not all marriages had such a happy ending.

This work analyses the Georgian elite to better understand their attitudes towards marriage and adultery. It is guided by a series of questions, including: can a modern-day reader penetrate the decorum and double-talk to gain a better understanding of the role that extra-marital affairs played within both the Georgian state and society? What were the recognised rules for having an affair? What were their expectations concerning fidelity, and how, during the Georgian period, were extra-marital relations framed, managed and understood? How were extra-marital affairs accommodated, and what were the punishments for those who broke the rules of having an affair? As a central institution of the Georgian state, marriage secured property, formulated and fomented alliances, encouraged the propagation of legitimate children, and was considered the foundation of good and proper government. So why did those entrusted with wealth, power and responsibility believe marriage to be necessary but did not equate matrimony with love or happiness?

This work will also shine some light on a few of our modern assumptions about normative behaviour while connecting today's 'scandal ridden' society with the past. In a world where politicians, athletes and celebrities are under a microscope and are often criticised for their private behaviour, including extra-marital affairs, how were similar issues dealt with in the past? Why is it, just like during the Georgian period, that some people are celebrated for their infidelities while others shamed and forced into social exile for what appears, on the surface, to be similar behaviour?

This evaluation uses well-known vignettes in narrative form to explore the contradictions and rules of having an affair in Georgian England. Many individuals included in this study will be familiar to the reader: George IV, Horatio Nelson, the Lennox sisters, Georgiana, Duchess of Devonshire. To date, while numerous historians and biographers have studied Georgian peoples and society, little attempt has been made to understand affairs as a cultural phenomenon, and less still to understand why some individuals were punished and others praised for their 'indiscretions'.[4] Through the examination of the rules of a particular society, in this case as it relates to having an extra-marital affair, we can gain important insights into what people in the past valued, their outlooks, and ultimately better understand the world they constructed and occupied.

Sandwiched between two distinct periods, Georgian England preceded the Victorian period (1837–1901), an era remembered today for its strict modes of behaviour and morality. Queen Victoria and her husband, Albert, set the standard for the day, and through their careful guidance, they modernised, stabilised and reinvigorated the monarchy. Victoria and Albert consciously distanced themselves from what they perceived to be the permissive morality that had characterised aristocratic culture and behaviour during the Georgian period. They chose instead to adopt the middle-class values of frugality, hard work and family. Until Albert's death in 1861, the queen and her consort set the example of what constituted a good marriage. They were faithful, involved in their children's lives, and supportive of each other. They also made good use of the marital bed; Victoria gave birth to nine children.

The Restoration Era, which celebrated the return of the Stuart dynasty to the throne, preceded the Georgian period.[5] Charles II ascended the throne during a period fraught with religious and political tensions. His father, Charles I, had lost both his crown and his head. After the execution of Charles I in 1649, England officially became a republic. Oliver Cromwell emerged as the central power and, from 1653, ruled as the Lord Protector. Basing his government on Puritan values, Cromwell set out to remake England. Cromwell would rule until he died in 1658. Cromwell's new world order barely survived him, and in 1660 the monarchy would be restored as Charles I's son Charles II became king of England. While few mourned the end of Oliver Cromwell's strict Puritan government, Charles II needed to manage the strong religious sentiments that defined the Restoration Era.

An era dominated by court culture, the Restoration was a time of courtiers, famous rakes and glamour. King Charles II set the standard for the period by fathering numerous illegitimate children with a host of women. His daughters married into aristocratic houses while he ennobled many of his sons. Some of the loftiest and most important aristocratic houses, including the Dukes of Grafton, the Dukes of St Albans, the Dukes of Lennox and Richmond, and the Dukes of Buccleuch originated with an ennobled illegitimate son of Charles II.[6] Not to be outdone, his younger brother and future king, James, Duke of York, had several illegitimate children of his own.[7]

While his numerous children born out of wedlock testifies to Charles II's ability to father children, he and his wife Catherine of Braganza did not produce a legitimate heir, as Catherine suffered at least three miscarriages. Some urged Charles II to divorce her and to marry a princess capable of providing him with legitimate children.[8] Not only were royal children necessary for keeping a dynasty alive, their betrothals and marriages helped cement important political alliances. In a period of religious, social and political turmoil, not having royal children to seek, secure and solidify alliances put Charles and England at a disadvantage.

Encouraged by his brother, who believed marriage would be good for him, James married Anne Hyde in 1660. As the daughter of the important courtier and advisor Edward Hyde (shortly thereafter made the Earl of Clarendon), Anne was a commoner. Her lowly birth and the fact that she was already pregnant with James's child generated much gossip and further supported the notion that the Stuarts played by their own rules. While the union would produce six children, only two of their children, Mary (b. 1662) and Anne (b. 1665), survived into adulthood. Encouraged by both his wife and what he witnessed during his exile in France, James converted to Catholicism in 1668 or early in 1669.[9] James's conversion, coupled with Charles's religious policies, prompted some of his more stridently Anglican subjects to worry about what they perceived to be Charles's Catholic sympathies. Anne Hyde died in 1671 from what appears to have been breast cancer. Mary and Anne were both raised and would remain dedicated Protestants.

Having been criticised for his Catholic sympathies, Charles wanted James's daughters to marry Protestant husbands.[10] He proposed that James's eldest daughter Mary wed William, the head of the powerful and, more importantly for Charles, Protestant Orange-Nassau family. William and Mary married on 4 November 1677. Not happy with her perspective spouse, Mary cried during the ceremony while the unemotional William did not crack a smile.[11] In 1683, James's youngest daughter, Anne, married Prince George, a Protestant and younger son of Frederick III, king of Denmark. Charles hoped that having his nieces marry Protestant husbands would quell rumours of a 'Catholic plot' while securing important political allies both within and outside of England.[12] Charles spent much of his reign trying to re-establish monarchical control and, having failed to produce legitimate children, to ensure that the throne passed to his brother James, Duke of York.

Two years after his first wife's death, James married Mary of Modena, an Italian Catholic nearly thirty years his junior. Not happy with the prospect of having to live in England or her upcoming nuptials, Mary begged to be allowed to enter a nunnery instead.[13] Her future husband did not cut the most dashing figure as he had significant scarring from smallpox and a pronounced stutter or delay. Unable to hide her disappointment when her mother left her in England with James, she cried for many days.[14] Over time, she came to love him. James, in his way, loved Mary as well, although he continued to have numerous affairs with women his brother, the king, described as 'ugly trollops'.[15] Not known for her looks, Catherine Sedley, one of James's many mistresses, wondered at the Duke of York's attraction to her. 'It cannot be my beauty because I haven't any and it cannot be my wit because he hasn't enough of it to know that I have any.'[16]

With the death of Charles II in 1685, James became king. He struggled to work with parliament, and his preference for Catholics and French-style absolutism worried the political elite. Frustrated with James and concerned about the creation of a Catholic dynasty, many leading Englishmen hoped that James and his queen would not produce an heir. Their hopes were dashed when, on 10 June 1688, Mary of Modena, after a series of miscarriages, stillbirths, or children dying in infancy, gave birth to a healthy boy whom they named James Francis Edward Stuart. The birth of an heir meant that Protestants either move to unseat James or accept the establishment of a Catholic dynasty. Anne, who had a complicated and often fraught relationship with her mother-in-law, had questioned the pregnancy from the beginning, telling her sister Mary that the queen had a 'false belly'.[17] This led to the creation of a popular and, for William and Mary, convenient myth that the 'prince' had been smuggled into the birthing room by Jesuits as part of a Catholic plot to re-establish England's ties with Rome. James's decision to only invite Roman Catholic members of the court to witness the birth did little to suppress the rumours.[18]

Worried about the creation of a Catholic dynasty, James's religious policies, and his preference for French absolutism, leading members of the English establishment discussed ways to remove James from the throne. A few weeks after the birth of James Francis, several political leaders took the momentous step of inviting William, Prince of Orange, the husband of James II's eldest daughter, Mary, to launch an invasion to take the English throne on behalf of his wife. An invasion appealed to William; not only would it protect his wife's interests but William desperately wanted England to aid him and his native Holland in its struggle against France.[19] Having been invited to take the throne, William assembled a large army and set sail for England. Worried about being viewed as an ambitious conqueror who took advantage of his father-in-law, William asserted that his actions were that of a husband doing what he could to protect his wife and her birthright.

Although the warm and kind Mary and the cold and rational William seemed, at first glance, an odd pairing, they had made a happy life together in Holland. Nearly twelve years her senior, prone to long and loud coughing fits, hunchbacked, and preferring the company of attractive young men to women, William would have swept few women off their feet.[20] Mary had been warned of William's preference for male company and may have had some sympathy for her husband, for in her youth the person she most idealised was her childhood friend Frances Apsley. From about the age of 9, Mary had exchanged letters with Frances, the daughter of the courtier Sir Allen Apsley. These were passionate letters, full of praise for Frances, that were, at least at first, enthusiastically received. However, as the girls matured, Frances may have seen the letters for what they were and tried to make the relationship more platonic. Mary accepted this turn and, by the time of her marriage to William, viewed Frances as a close friend and confidante.[21]

William landed in England on 5 November 1688. Before the battle began, James II suffered a desertion of a number of his officers, including the talented commander Lord Churchill. James would eventually flee to France. Divorced from his kingdom, the deposed king would never sit on the English throne again. William had won what would be known to history as the Glorious Revolution.[22] After some wrangling with parliament over William's position and power, William and Mary were acknowledged as joint monarchs. Although by law and tradition, all power should have rested with Mary, she was happy with the joint monarchy for she believed that a husband should not be forced to follow the dictates of his wife.[23] Having risked so much to become king, William worked hard to ensure that the marriage between England and the House of Orange was a happy and stable one. With the death of Mary in 1694, William became the sole ruler of England. William died in 1702 and was succeeded by Mary's younger sister, Anne.

Queen Anne and her husband, Prince George of Denmark, genuinely loved one another. Having had one happy marriage, Anne pursued another. Political in nature, this 'union' would wed Scotland and England by uniting the countries into a single political entity. Offered bribes, payments and the promise of further wealth, including access to England's burgeoning overseas Empire, Scottish elites, on 16 January 1707, voted for union.[24] Such a vote ended a separate Scotland and its distinct political system, including the Scottish parliament itself. The wedding of the two countries gave birth to Great Britain.

From a private, public and dynastic perspective, the biggest issue was the royal couple's inability to produce healthy heirs. Anne had miscarried or delivered stillborn at least a dozen times, and none of her children reached adulthood.[25] This put the Glorious Revolution in a perilous position and encouraged parliament to pass a series of Acts that barred Catholics from the throne. Over fifty candidates for the English throne were judged unsuitable as they were either Catholics or married to a Catholic.[26] Parliament settled upon Sophia of Hanover, the daughter of James I and VI's eldest daughter, Elizabeth, who had married Frederick, Elector of Palatine. In addition to her Protestant faith, Sophia could add stability to the Crown, for she already had five surviving children and three legitimate grandchildren. Crucially, her eldest son, the future George I, already had a son and heir. When the Act of Settlement named her heiress presumptive, few actually thought that Sophia, aged 70, would ever sit upon the English throne. Yet despite a thirty-five-year age difference, Sophia almost outlived Anne and, had she done so, would have been, at that point in history, the oldest person to ascend to the British throne. Following the death of Anne, George became king of Great Britain on 1 August 1714.

Not happy with the prospect of leaving his beloved Hanover for his new kingdom, George understood it was his duty to become king of England as it would enhance his family's reputation and power. Like many grooms during this period, his chief motivation for marriage was to please and protect his family. The English populace was also apprehensive about the match, for the new king of England could be described as being full-bodied, dull, and physically unappealing. He brought with him a mistress, or two, having locked his wife in a castle for an alleged infidelity.[27] If one was looking for an example of the extremes that could be found in what would later be termed the sexual double standard there are few better choices than a man who is rewarded with a kingdom (and shows up with his mistresses in tow) while his wife is punished for her presumed adultery by being placed under virtual house arrest for the remainder of her life. Although one supposes it could have been worse: his wife's lover had almost certainly been murdered.[28] Such contradictions did not seem to worry George; he was king, and his rule was law. Or at least that is how he thought it worked. Parliament quickly showed the new king that in this marriage, both partners, the Crown and parliament, had to work together.

The Georgian period began with this unhappy marriage. The English needed a king, and George proved the most suitable spouse. He had the right breeding, education and religion. But the list of positives ended there. The political marriage between the House of Hanover and the British people mirrors and represents the marriage of many aristocrats during the period. Happiness, contentment and satisfaction with one's spouse often proved elusive. For those not happy with the Hanoverians, there was always the awe-inspiring Stuarts whose grace, self-confidence, and kingly dispositions offered, for some, an attractive alternative. Both George I and George II would have the Stuarts and their supporters rise up to divorce them from the English throne. Despite the efforts of the Stuarts to regain the throne, most notably in 1715 and again in 1745, the Hanoverians held firm. For better or for worse, for richer, for poorer, in sickness and in health, the English people were wed to the House of Hanover.

The coming of the German monarchs was not the only change experienced by England, for, in the eighteenth century, England entered into, and began to profit from, the Industrial Revolution. While still very much an agricultural society, cities, particularly London, were growing at an astronomical pace. When George I ascended the throne in 1714, London had a population of around 600,000. By the end of the Georgian period, there were nearly 2 million people living in London.[29] Every day, people flocked to the capital from the countryside, looking for opportunities and a chance to better themselves. Although London contained much finery, including ornate gardens, grand houses and royal palaces, it also housed much poverty and squalor.

While tremendous inequality existed between rich and poor, a new group, the middling sort, began to grow in size and power. Made up of small merchants, shop owners, skilled artisans, factory supervisors, surgeons and the like, the middling sort embodied hard work, honesty and fidelity. This often put them at odds with the aristocracy and the first two Hanoverian monarchs, who displayed much different values. Aristocrats were the living embodiment of the exception to the rule. Often above the law, their wealth and power meant that they eschewed the rules that governed everyone else. Georgian aristocrats insisted that they had their own moral code and refused to be held to what they saw as the base morality of common people.[30] Aristocrats were clear: they had little need nor a desire to follow the dictates of those that they believed they were born to govern.

Members of the middling sort hoped that when George III became king in 1760, he would break the mould of his forebears by instituting policies aimed at reining in aristocratic culture and excess.[31] Young, handsome and idealistic, George III wanted to be a patriot king beloved by his people and represented in parliament by men of virtue. Believing that an individual's private behaviour mattered and that if the governing elite lacked morality, so too would the government they operated; George III attempted to align himself with men of sober values, ones he believed would set a fine example.[32] George concluded that if Great Britain was to prosper, he needed his nobility to be respected, virtuous, and loyal to the Crown, their commitments and their families.

George III wanted England to be led by what today would be called a family man. The king hoped that he and his growing brood of children (he would have fifteen) would set an example for morality and sober values. George's pleasure came from acting righteous and spending time with his family. Unlike the two previous Hanoverian monarchs and nearly every English king since the Norman Conquest, George III never took a mistress. The same could not be said of his sons. Christopher Hibbert has estimated that by 1817 George III had some fifty-six illegitimate grandchildren.[33] Despite his best efforts, George III could not convince his sons or the aristocracy to adopt his more upright standards, forcing him to rely upon men who held more permissive values.

Previous to the Georgian period, love was rarely considered an important part of aristocratic marriage. Marriage was about securing property and producing children, not seeking emotional fulfilment or a life partner. The desire to marry for love during the Georgian era came mainly from the younger generation, who saw first-hand the unhappiness caused by their parents' political marriages, which, more often than not, forced two poorly matched people together.[34] This could cause tension between those who wished to follow their hearts and families that insisted their children make prudent matches that protected and enhanced their family's wealth, power and property. There certainly was much at stake as Georgian marriages were meant to be for life.

For those who were unhappily married, getting a divorce in Georgian England was a difficult, rare and expensive process that required the approval of parliament. Up until 1857, when responsibility for divorce passed to the judiciary, parliament had only dissolved 311 marriages.[35] Only 4 of these 311 divorces were granted to female petitioners.[36] One could also seek a separation from one's spouse in an ecclesiastical court. While an ecclesiastical court could grant a separation of bed and board, which permitted a married couple to physically and financially separate, this was not a divorce and did not allow for remarriage so long as their spouse lived. For the Church of England, marriage was and must remain until death do us part.

The growing acceptance that love should play some role in the selection of a spouse gave rise to one of the biggest conundrums of the age: should marriage be for love or for the good of the family? Many clung to the belief that love was not necessary for a successful marriage, as the point of a good match was to enhance a family's status and reputation, produce children, and to ensure that property transitioned from one generation to the next. Unsure of love's place in selecting a spouse, aristocrats might heed the accepted wisdom of an old English proverb: 'Who married for love without money has good nights and sorry days.'[37] Indeed, the Lennox sisters, granddaughters of Charles II's illegitimate son Charles Lennox, 1st Duke of Richmond and Lennox, were so wary of love as a foundation for marriage that Caroline wrote to her sister Emily stating that she was pleased that their sister Sarah was getting married to Charles Bunbury, a man she did not love. In her words, 'happily for her she is not the least in love with him'.[38] The Duchess of Brunswick had a similar perspective asserting that, 'I seldom see love matches turn out well, love does make such havock.'[39]

Given its importance, marriage was primarily a family decision with parents or the acknowledged heads of the respective families planning the match. These individuals had their role strengthened in 1753 when parliament passed an act prohibiting minors from marrying without parental consent.[40] Those determined to ignore their elders still had the option of travelling to Guernsey or the popular Gretna Green just over the border in Scotland where the 1753 Act had no force.[41] Sir William Temple, a man who failed to convince his family to allow him to follow his heart, concluded that due to 'men's avarice, and greediness …', that English 'marriages are made just like other common bargains and sales by the mere consideration of interest or gain, without any love or esteem, of birth or of beauty itself, which ought to be the true ingredients of all happy compositions of this kind'.[42] Despite the experiences of William Temple, individual preference, whenever possible, was taken into consideration when making marriage decisions; the Georgian period saw a growing awareness that suitability in habits and temperament, if not love, should play some part in choosing a mate.

The notion that love should play some role in marriage engendered new questions about adultery. Whereas it may have been unfair to blame two ill-suited people, thrown together by a political match, for looking for love and physical fulfilment outside their marriage, what about couples who largely selected their own mates? Should those who chose their spouses be held to different standards from a person forced into a marriage based not on love but on the forging of alliances and the protection of their family's wealth and privilege? For most elites, the question of whether a love match changed how an extra-marital affair was understood remained largely unresolved, for Georgians cared less about the causes of adultery but rather that its participants follow the rules of having an affair.

Although class and rank were still very important during the Georgian period, they no longer had an absolute stranglehold on society. While dukes and duchesses continued to have tremendous power and social cache, attitudes had shifted, and rank no longer trumped everything. In the Georgian period, the way in which people carried themselves, the way they acted, and ultimately whether others saw them as fashionable had a much more significant impact upon their place among the social leaders of the period.[43] Known by a plethora of names, including the 'ton' and the 'beau monde', this group of fashionable people ruled the social calendar in Georgian England.

The Georgian world was a social one where people joined clubs, gossiped at the theatre, and went out to be seen. Aristocrats were constantly on the lookout for excitement, and this may explain the elite's love of gambling, horse racing, hunting and other heart-racing pastimes.

Affairs could be viewed as just another means of adding excitement to their lives. Most aristocrats felt, as long as one observed the rules that they and their friends set for themselves, there was little harm in seeking sexual satisfaction outside of one's marriage.

Georgian society offered numerous ways to engage in sex outside of marriage. One of the features of London society evident to all was the availability of prostitutes. Prostitutes could be found throughout London but tended to congregate around Drury Lane and Covent Garden. By 1725, the areas that made up Drury Lane contained no fewer than 107 brothels. Estimates vary, but by the late eighteenth century, about 50,000 women, comprising some one-eighth of the adult female population of London, worked as prostitutes.[44] Although it is difficult to know precisely how many men hired prostitutes, given the number of females engaged in the trade John Wade was probably correct in his assertion, made in the 1850s, that, 'there are few men who, in some period of their lives, have not dealt in mercenary love.'[45]

The sex trade in London varied immensely. On one end, there were women whose engagement in prostitution was temporary and needs based. Their involvement could be brief and used as a way to supplement their own or their family's income in times of desperation or as a temporary means to acquire items that were normally beyond their working-class incomes.[46] Prostitution for these women was a means to an end, not a full-time or permanent part of their lives. On the other end of the spectrum were professionals or full-time prostitutes who were organised in a variety of ways. The lowest and worst paid were the streetwalkers who had little protection or ability to demand much of a return.[47] They risked their lives and their health in an often-fruitless attempt to escape their conditions.

Rather than face the dangers of streetwalking, prostitutes could attach themselves to a bar or brothel. This provided more security, protection from the elements, and helped to attract clients. It provided a location for the transaction and meant that one could be certain of payment, although only after the establishment took its cut. These women would service a few men a day, trusting that sex with multiple partners meant that their customers' sperm would intermix, which was commonly believed to prevent conception.[48]

Prostitutes were part of a sophisticated system devised to cater to a wide variety of desires. To attract patrons and ensure little disappointment, manuals were constructed explaining exactly what men could expect from a specific prostitute. One of the most important and widely used manuals was *Harris's List of Covent-Garden Ladies*, which explained the physical appearance of prostitutes, where they could be found, and any sexual preference or abilities they may possess.[49] Brothels might even specialise in particular desires. Especially popular during this period were brothels that engaged in flagellation in which gentlemen who were used to being in control paid lower-class women to punish them physically.[50]

The growth of the sex trade, or at least its growing visibility in metropolitan areas, could be partially explained by the changing attitudes towards infidelity. Whereas before the Restoration, infidelity had been viewed as a sin against man and God, it was increasingly seen, at least among the aristocracy, as 'gallant'. Gallantry, to live life to its fullest, and to engage in numerous light relationships outside of one's marriage, became, for many leading Georgians, a way of life. Such relationships were not supposed to threaten the bonds of matrimony. If a relationship was perceived to have upset the delicate balance of society or threatened to supplant a spouse, the affair was deemed dangerous, and the participants were pressured to stop. Failure to do so breached the codes of gallantry and could lead to social exile. Thus, it may be best to view affairs as evolving from a sin that violated the laws of God to a potential social transgression in which one, by not adhering to the rules of having an affair, broke a civil understanding of proper behaviour.[51]

This work does not examine prostitution but rather focuses on affairs and the rules which governed sexual relationships outside of one's marriage. What follows is a guide of sorts comprised of not only the rules of having an affair but also an examination of the degrees to which adultery and extra-marital relations were accepted and accommodated by members of the Georgian elite. It seeks to better understand expectations of proper behaviour and decorum during an era of upheaval and social change. By drawing upon new developments in social and cultural history, this work challenges the notion of Georgian libertinism, demonstrating instead a complex, well-accepted, and strictly enforced social code of behaviour. This is important as historians have contrasted the 'wild' Georgians with the 'staid' Victorians for too long. Neither of these assumptions are true, nor are they borne out in a careful reading of history. By evaluating how Georgian elites viewed, perceived, engaged in and accommodated extra-marital affairs and by reconfiguring our understanding of the period to reflect actual lives lived, this work demonstrates that extra-marital affairs among England's elites fit within a rigid social, political and economic order. Examining the rules of having an affair during the Georgian period allows us to better evaluate many of the assumptions we make about marriage, the family and proper social, political and individual behaviour.

CHAPTER ONE

Making a Match: Marriage and Children

Although standards were changing, and fashion, good looks and talent could do much to help ambitious young men and women get ahead, it was still expected that young lords and ladies conduct proper marriages. While actors, poets, writers and other artists may become fixtures within an aristocrat's social circle, one did not marry such people. This was especially true for women. Men who hailed from the upper crust could marry a young beauty from the lower classes or a wealthy heiress not of aristocratic or even genteel birth, although this often came with its own set of difficulties. Daughters of the elite had much less freedom of choice and were expected to marry a gentleman, ideally one of aristocratic birth. From a young age, aristocrats were taught about their obligations to their family and lineage. After contracting an advantageous match, one of the most important responsibilities was to produce legitimate heirs to ensure that the family line continued. Since illegitimate children had no right to inherit, the future of the family rested upon producing legitimate children with their lawfully married spouse.

Living the life of the beau monde was very expensive. The pursuit of fashion, the upkeep of their various estates, losses sustained at the gambling table, and participation in other aristocratic pastimes drained the finances of England's leading families. In the Georgian period, many noble families borrowed heavily to make up for the shortfall between their income and the high cost of aristocratic life. Since most aristocrats could not or did not curb their spending, many families required a large infusion of capital with each new generation. This precipitated a shift in marriage as increasingly aristocrats, rather than marrying a member of their own class, looked for an heiress to rebuild their family's fortunes.

At the beginning of the eighteenth century, nearly 50 per cent of men with a father who held a title married an heiress. Three-quarters of these heiresses were not of noble birth.[1] In his study of England's highest-ranking peers, E.S. Turner noted that nearly all ducal families had profited at some point in their history from an opportune and financially prudent marriage.[2]

Sons of cash-strapped and heavily indebted aristocrats understood that they needed to marry an heiress in order to protect their ancestral property, dignity and birthright. Topham Beauclerk, son of the famous fortune hunter Lord Sidney Beauclerk, a younger son of the Duke of St Albans, followed in the family business of trying to secure a rich wife. He settled upon the very wealthy Miss Anna Maria Draycott, whose wealth and figure prompted one commentator to unkindly suggest that her large figure matched her enormous dowry. Two days before their wedding, she threw Beauclerk aside to marry the Earl of Pomfret. As Carola Hicks has pointed out, by marrying Beauclerk, she would have, like nearly every other married woman in the country, been a Mrs, but after marrying the earl, Draycott would be called countess.[3] This example suggests that wc should not view the union of a peer to a wealthy heiress as the well-born preying on the naivety of an heiress but that both parties were trying to gain as much as possible from their social or economic capital and that aristocrats, heiresses, and their respective families understood the finer points of the so-called 'marriage game'.

Topham's notoriously bad hygiene may have influenced Draycott's decision. Although regular bathing and general cleanliness eluded many Georgians, most of whom were in a state of near-constant filth, Topham's lack of hygiene was exceptional. Indeed, Lady Mary Coke tells us that ladies attending a Christmas party at Blenheim Palace complained to Topham that he was spreading lice. Unconcerned, Topham admitted that he 'had enough [lice] to stock a parish'.[4] Topham certainly was not the only filthy member of his class. Charles Howard, 11th Duke of Norfolk, was nicknamed the Dirty Duke. His servants had to wait until Charles, as he was known to do, passed out dead drunk so that they could finally wash the filthy duke.[5] Although the Duke of Norfolk and Topham are extreme examples of the neglect of hygiene, cleanliness certainly was not the norm, as even the richest and most fashionable in England rarely washed anything other than their hands, feet, neck and face.[6]

English women were widely considered to be less concerned and pay less attention to hygiene and general cleanliness than those on the continent. Comparing English women to Italian ones, physician John Shebbeare stated that, 'the parts concealed are more neglected than among the regions of Italy.'[7] Mary Wollstonecraft, an advocate for women's rights, also lamented the state of female cleanliness, stating in 1792 'that regard to cleanliness … is violated in a beastly manner'.[8] Given that both sexes seemed to lack what we would consider today to be the dictates of good hygiene, it is difficult to determine the degrees to which cleanliness influenced the choice of sexual partners. Renowned for her cleanliness, Diana Spencer married the lice-ridden and filthy Topham Beauclerk in 1768. Unfortunately for Lady Diana, whose first marriage was marked by sadness and ended in divorce, her second marriage would also be largely unhappy.[9]

Desperate for money to help fund their expensive lives, some men took the acquiring of an heiress to the extreme. While still married to the aforementioned Lady Diana, the heavily indebted Frederick St John, 2nd Viscount Bolingbroke, began planning a second marriage to salvage his financial life. Neither compatibility nor mutual affection mattered to the viscount; he cared only about her money. Indeed, he had few nice words for his chosen heiress, calling her a 'rich monster'.[10] Mrs Curtis, Bolingbroke's chosen target, reportedly was worth some £43,000. Bolingbroke failed to win over Mrs Curtis or any heiress, and two years after falling out with his 'rich monster', Bolingbroke lost his mind.[11] While Bolingbroke's approach leaves much to be desired, he understood that he needed money to preserve his family's status and dignity. He would not be the only one. Notorious rake and man of the town, Sir Francis Blake Delaval, married Isabella Paulett in an attempt to fix his finances. There was little to recommend Paulett to Delaval other than her money; she was not considered attractive, good company, or to be very intelligent.[12] With the help of his friend Samuel Foote, Delaval attempted to trick Lady Isabella into marriage as a means of securing her fortune. Knowing Isabella's fondness for fortune telling, Foote acquired knowledge of Isabella's tastes and habits from one of her servants and then supplied this information to a fortune teller. Agreeing to be a part of this scheme, the fortune teller used this knowledge to garner Isabella's faith in her abilities, and after proving her credibility, she informed Lady Isabella that she would soon meet, fall in love, and marry a man with the exact same physical description as Delaval. Delaval then ensured that he came to Isabella's attention. Convinced that Delaval was the man that she was meant to marry, Isabella agreed to become his wife. The joke, however, was ultimately upon Delaval because the real trick was that much of 'her' money had been placed in trust for the benefit of her daughter.[13] This meant that all his scheming had backfired as he was left with a wife he did not much care for and still remained in a rather precarious financial position.

Failure to marry well could be disastrous for a family. The 2nd Viscount Bolingbroke's unsuccessful attempts to marry a wealthy heiress coupled with both the 3rd and 5th Viscounts marrying for love rather than money (both the 3rd and 5th Viscounts married twice, and on all four occasions, their partners had little money or assets) hastened and later confirmed the family's decline including having to part with their family seat, Lydiard House.[14] This contrasts with the experiences of aristocratic families who married well. The Bedfords, for instance, buttressed their family's holdings when the Marquess of Tavistock married Elizabeth Howland, the daughter of a very wealthy London merchant.[15] During the Georgian period, trading a title for wealth was an accepted and increasingly necessary action.

Sir Richard Worsley, 7th Baronet, also set his sights upon winning the heart of an heiress. Although he had inherited a fortune and had a respectable income, his desire to increase his family's social and political power encouraged him to search for a wife who could help bankroll his ambitions. Descended from a distinguished family, the Worsleys had once been important courtiers (Henry VIII had visited their home). Increasingly, however, they had eschewed national prominence, preferring the comfort of the countryside on the Isle of Wight to life at the royal court.[16] As a baronet, Sir Richard was a commoner and not a member of the aristocracy, which meant that he did not have the right to sit in the House of Lords. Sir Richard believed that if he played the good parliamentarian and always supported the politically minded George III, he would be rewarded with a peerage.[17] Worsley hoped that a wealthy and fashionable wife would increase his profile and help him achieve his move from the Commons to the Lords.

Before he could even contemplate gaining a wealthy and well-bred wife, Worsley needed to be educated in the ways of being a gentleman. Just as young girls were expected to be accomplished in singing, dancing, needlework and other appropriate activities and preoccupations, young men were expected to know how to shoot, hunt, ride, dance and be capable of presenting themselves as cultured men of good breeding. This often involved expensive lessons and an extended trip to the continent, known as 'The Grand Tour'. Grand tours sought to introduce young men to continental culture and history, especially that of France, Italy and ancient Rome. They also exposed travellers to the fashions, arts and manners of a proper European gentleman.[18] A grand tour and the culture gained (supposed or actual) served as another method of separating aristocrats from the rest, helping to maintain the aristocracy's social, cultural and political dominance.[19]

While the duration and the specific destinations included within a grand tour varied, Wolsey went to the continent for what became a multi-year tour of France, Switzerland and Italy.[20] Such trips not only sought to inform but also gave the traveller a host of stories while also marking the transition from boy to man. Worsley gained much from his time on the continent, acquiring a genuine appreciation of the classics and a lifelong interest in ancient art forms. Upon his return, Worsley hoped that he could attract a wealthy wife capable of providing him with the money necessary to expand his growing art and antique collection while helping to finance his political ambitions.

Potential suitors looking for an heiress had to play the part. This meant being, or at least appearing to be, the perfect gentleman. Although fortune hunting was accepted in aristocratic culture, a certain degree of restraint was expected. Good manners dictated that a suitor avoid directly discussing or inquiring about the exact sum of money that would be received from an heiress's dowry. This could lead to conversations laden with innuendo, suggestion and allusion, as potential suitors tried to determine, without directly asking, the precise worth of their potential bride. While families may hint at how much, and society often gossiped and guessed at the extent of an heiress's fortune, the exact amount would usually only be settled after an engagement.[21]

Sir Richard set his sights on Jane Fleming, the eldest daughter of Sir John Fleming. A career soldier, Fleming had his life changed when his friend and commanding officer, William Hargrave, left his estate to Fleming rather than to his blood relations. Made a baron after his friend's death, Fleming needed a wife to produce a son who would hopefully inherit both his new fortune and title. His new wealth and position allowed him to gain the attentions of and subsequently marry Jane Coleman, a relation of the Duke of Somerset. Five children (one boy and four girls) followed, but only two daughters, Jane and Seymour, survived into adulthood. After Fleming's death in 1763, the wealth bestowed upon Jane and Seymour meant that both daughters were likely to marry into the upper echelons of Georgian society.[22]

Knowing that he must play the part of the perfect gentleman, Sir Richard purchased new clothes, a new carriage, and all the finery likely to impress not only Jane but also her socially conscious mother, who expected a good match for her daughters. Trusting in his education and knowing that he had his grand tour as proof of his class and refinement, Sir Richard expected to make a good impression and to win Jane's hand in marriage. Unfortunately for Sir Richard, despite his best efforts, proper training and background, Worsley managed to impress neither Jane nor her mother.

Sir Richard's significant outlay was not entirely in vain. Jane's younger sister, Seymour, who was 14 years old when Worsley had tried to win Jane's hand in marriage, appeared to have had a better impression of Sir Richard than the rest of her family. When Seymour and Sir Richard met three years later during the 1775 York Races, she certainly seemed happy to resume his acquaintance. Pleased with what he saw, Sir Richard decided to pursue Jane's younger sister. Quite taken with one another, Seymour and Sir Richard moved quickly and, if one source can be believed, within a week they had agreed to marry.[23]

Although the conclusion of this example might suggest that finding an heiress and proper spouse was easy, we must remember that Sir Richard had been searching for a wife for more than three years and, unlike many of his peers, he possessed significant financial assets, looked poised to have a successful political career, had no scandal or stain on his reputation to contend with, no famous mistress he needed to hide or break with, or really anything that would raise doubts about his suitability. The only knock against Worsley was that he lacked a peerage. Nonetheless, Seymour would be entitled to be known as Lady Worsley, and both Seymour and her mother would have considered that Sir Richard had all the attributes of a man on the rise and might soon be granted a peerage.

As convention and prudence dictated, both families hired lawyers to negotiate the marriage contract. A long and drawn-out process, marriage negotiations could prove stressful and frustrating to young couples anxious to enjoy the pleasures of matrimony. Negotiations could be conducted in bad faith, as one family not approving of the match might purposely draw matters out, hoping to offend the other party, prompting them to cancel the engagement. Unhappy with the prospective match, some families may have hoped that a long, contentious and drawn-out marriage negotiation would afford ample opportunity for the prospective bride or groom to have a change of heart. Even if conducted in good faith, it was a confrontational process with both sides trying to secure the most advantageous contract. In this case, both families had much to gain from the marriage and successfully concluded the negotiations.

When negotiating a marriage contract, an heiress and her family's main concerns were securing a healthy and independent allowance, negotiating what they would get in case they were widowed, and ensuring that any property brought to the marriage would return to the family if there were no children. The goal for the husband and his family was to extract as much of a dowry as possible. Sir Richard would receive some property and cash totalling £52,000.

Nearly £20,000 of this money would be spent buying land buttressing Worsley's Appuldurcombe estate. Almost another £5,000 went towards the purchase of a London townhouse. Both of these investments were meant to increase Worsley's social and political power and to help him gain a peerage.[24] That nearly half her dowry had already been committed before they wed suggests that an heiress's family could have much input into how their money was spent. That the money went to secure assets that would help increase Sir Richard's importance and move him closer to his goals is not surprising since both families had much to gain from Sir Richard becoming a peer.

Sir Richard and Seymour wed on 15 September 1775. Despite what novels, television and movies try to tell us, weddings during the Georgian period for both the aristocracy and the gentry remained small, unassuming occasions usually only involving a few friends and immediate family.[25] Many of the traditions modern readers associate with a wedding, including that a bride wears white, were developed later.[26] Within months of their marriage, Seymour became pregnant and in 1776 gave birth to a healthy son and heir. Despite a fine start to his life, having secured a wealthy wife, fathering a son and heir, and holding some prominent government positions, including being made a Privy Counsellor and Governor of the Isle of Wight, Worsley would be disappointed by both his marriage and in his efforts to be made a peer. The birth of a son did little to fix the relationship, and despite the 'good match', the marriage would not be happy, proving that even the 'most perfect' social and political matches could lead to much unhappiness.

Fathers often played a pivotal role in helping their sons and daughters select an appropriate spouse. Stephen Fox-Strangways, Earl of Ilchester, certainly expected his daughter Lady Susan to make a good match by marrying a man of good birth. Susan, however, had other ideas: she had fallen in love with the well-known Irish actor William O'Brien. Sensing the threat, her family warned her away from O'Brien. Susan relented, and her family took her at her word that she would no longer see him. Drawn to the actor, Susan could not, or would not, stay away. The two grew closer and eventually married in 1764. The union engendered widespread shock that the daughter of an earl would be allowed to marry a penniless actor. Commenting on Susan marrying an actor, Horace Walpole stated: 'Even a footman were preferable – the publicity of the hero's profession perpetuates the mortification.'[27] While society blamed Susan for her imprudence, they also blamed her family for failing to prevent such an inappropriate union from occurring.[28] The far-reaching condemnation of improper marriages prompted whole aristocratic families to become involved in guiding young adults into suitable marriages.

Family members, especially parents, were expected to stop youthful dalliances from developing into a serious relationship before one of their children did anything that might hurt their own or their family's reputation. There were numerous methods aristocrats could employ to encourage the other party to end the relationship. For instance, aristocratic families could use their wealth and power to threaten the other person, bribe them to go away, or ensure that a suitor gained a promotion that required them to move. Wishing to break his son's relationship with the famous courtesan Margaret Cuyler, the Earl of Haddington paid her to no longer see his son.[29] If paying off the love interest did not work, they could always send their child away, hoping that this would bring an end to the relationship. For instance, after years of trying to get his son and heir Lord Worcester to break with the famous courtesan Harriette Wilson, the Duke of Beaufort asked Wellington, who was stationed in Spain at the time, to make his son an aide-de-camp, knowing that his son would have to accept the position or else be branded a coward – something he knew his son would not risk.[30] These are just a few of the many examples of fathers or families stepping in to prevent an inappropriate relationship from going too far. Because aristocrats held such power over their children and had the money and power to buy off or chase away an unsuitable potential spouse, it was judged inexcusable when their children married the wrong person.

As a means of saving face and to show their collective disapproval, the Earl of Ilchester and his family levied a severe punishment on Susan and O'Brien. The couple was not just banished from society, provided with a small 'cabin' in the country while the scandal blew over, but at her family's insistence, Susan and O'Brien were also exiled across the Atlantic. They tried to make a life for themselves in a variety of venues, including New York, Philadelphia and Quebec. After several years of exile, believing they had endured their punishment long enough, the couple returned to London. They hoped that their lengthy stay abroad, coupled with Susan's good name, would allow them to re-enter society. This did not happen. Her family refused to welcome her back, and society followed her family's lead.[31] There were too many aristocratic families with young daughters who must have feared that any leniency shown towards Susan would have given their own children the wrong impression. While affairs could be tolerated, marriage to the wrong person rarely was. Only those who were persistent and held the highest of titles could hope to marry below their dignity without being shunned by the rest of society.

Emily FitzGerald's (née Lennox) second marriage tells us much about the importance of position and rank and how such privileges could allow for more flexibility and forgiveness when violating the rules of having an affair. By the time of her husband's death in 1773, Emily, widowed wife of James FitzGerald, Duke of Leinster, had developed a very close relationship with her children's tutor, William Ogilvie. A woman of noble birth was not supposed to conduct an affair with a man of common birth. While it was normative for men to have intimate relations with lower-class women, such relationships upset the convention of male dominance and power, as Emily's birth and position meant that she should be in control. To be seen as submissive to a man of lower birth challenged the hierarchical order of society and the absolute importance of rank.

Furthermore, while men might sleep with their employees (her husband had even impregnated one of them), this was not proper for a Lady and certainly not for a woman with royal blood. That an aristocratic wife might give birth to a common baby meant that such relationships were considered wholly inappropriate and even dangerous. Aware of the risks, Emily had been discreet, and, when alive, her husband, the premier Duke of Ireland, had tolerated the relationship, and this meant that others had to as well.[32]

Emily and Ogilvie's difficulties began with the duke's death in 1773. Emily had lost the protection of her permissive husband, and now that she could marry Ogilvie, the relationship went from inappropriate to a threat to noble privilege, her family's reputation, and her children's inheritance. Emily knew that if she continued with Ogilvie, it would mean scandal, but she refused to end her relationship with him. While Ogilvie's presence produced a torrent of gossip, Emily acted as if she was above it.[33] Emily's chief concern was not gossip but what would happen to any children she and Ogilvie might produce. Born in 1773, Emily's nineteenth child, Lord George, had almost certainly been fathered by Ogilvie but accepted by both her husband and society as the duke's. Emily knew that she would not send a child created from her relationship with Ogilvie away. Refusing to end her relationship with Ogilvie after the duke's death in 1773, the only other way to protect against illegitimacy would be to marry her children's tutor.[34]

In August 1774, Emily and Ogilvie married in secret. Before doing so, Emily warned her friends and family of her desire to marry Ogilvie. Her sister Sarah, in a letter to Lady Susan O'Brien (who, as we have just seen, had been punished for marrying below her dignity), said that those who were told of the likelihood of the marriage agreed 'that they could not *wish it*, but if she was happy, it was all they wished; and that she could not chuse a person they had better opinion of & had more regard for'.[35] Emily tried to explain her thinking to her friends and family, and according to Sarah, Emily prudently wrote to their brother stating that, 'I am content that you should call me a fool, and an *old fool*, that you should blame me, and say you did not think me capable of such folly.'[36] Emily pleaded with her brother, 'say what you please, but remember that all I ask of you is your affection & tenderness.'[37] Sarah believed that her sister's approach had worked, informing Susan that, 'I assure you my sister *gains* friends instead of losing any by her manner.'[38]

Despite flaunting the rules in such a spectacular way, Emily found acceptance and happiness in her second marriage. The couple would have a further three children. One of the reasons Emily maintained her position, despite flaunting convention and marrying a man well below her social standing, is that her son, the new Duke of Leinster, supported her, and his power and prestige meant that few would dare criticise his mother. By law, she was now known as Mrs Ogilvie, and while she no longer held the power of a duchess, or, after remarrying, that of a dowager duchess, she had a happy life with her new husband.[39]

Having married well below her station, Emily insisted on new rules for her second marriage. Emily desired a more egalitarian relationship than she previously had with the duke and, although she had tolerated the duke's numerous affairs, Emily demanded fidelity from Ogilvie. While Emily's better breeding and aristocratic grace and manners helped to equalise the power between the two, male dominance prescribed by law and tradition, coupled with Ogilvie's intellect, powerful personality, and her love for him, still gave him the upper hand in the relationship. The two forged a life together, and while Emily's new life would never be as grand as being a duchess, she was happy with Ogilvie.[40] Although the couple demonstrated that one could marry for love and that people of different classes could come together to make a happy marriage, most Georgians would have understood that Emily and Ogilvie were an odd exception and certainly were not the model to be followed. We must remember that Emily's marriage to Ogilvie was her second marriage and that she had already done her duty by producing healthy heirs, including the current duke. It is also important to remember that her son was the leading duke in Ireland and that he supported his mother, which encouraged others to do so as well. For those Georgian women of gentle birth and privilege, marrying a man from a lower class was a risky proposition that could lead to severe punishment, including being exiled from one's family and the fashionable. For most women who took this risk, their experiences were much more likely to resemble those of Lady Susan rather than Emily.

After contracting an advantageous marriage, leading Georgians were expected to produce legitimate children, and it was expected that a newly married woman would remain faithful to her husband until giving birth to a healthy son and heir. The notion that a wife remained faithful to her husband until an heir was born was so ingrained within the Georgian elite that Lady Melbourne's mother-in-law felt comfortable telling her that once she did her marital duty, she could do as she pleased so long as it did not embarrass the family.[41] Lady Melbourne listened well and after producing an heir she took on a string of lovers. Always concerned with discretion, Lady Melbourne famously coined the saying that 'no man was safe with another's secrets, no woman with her own'.[42] Although her eldest son, Peniston Lamb, had certainly been fathered by her husband, her other four children's parentage is less certain. It seems likely that her second son was fathered by George Wyndham, 3rd Earl Egremont.[43] The Earl of Egremont may also have fathered her youngest daughter, Emily. Her third son, Frederick, may have been the result of her relationship with Frederick, Duke of York and Albany, while the Duke of York's older brother and future king, George Prince of Wales, likely sired Lady Melbourne's fourth son.[44]

Aware of his wife's dalliances, Lord Melbourne mostly looked the other way, as he had his son and heir and his own string of affairs to deal with. The only real and lasting discord caused by his wife's extra-marital affairs occurred after the death of his son and heir, Peniston, in 1805. It is here that Lord Melbourne probably wished that he and his wife had practised the heir and a spare policy. After the death of his older brother Peniston, William, who had been fathered by another man, stood to inherit all. Frustrated with the situation, Lord Melbourne refused to give William, 'his' heir, the same allowance that he had afforded to his natural son. Having been pressured by friends and his wife to accept William, Melbourne eventually relented and gave William a stipend of £1,800 per annum.[45] Peniston had received an allowance of £5,000 a year.[46] Regardless of his questionable parentage, William inherited the viscountcy, became prime minister, and a confidant to a young Queen Victoria.

While convention dictated that married women remain faithful at least until after the birth of a healthy male heir, their husbands were not expected to exercise the same restraint. Men were, however, expected to make the time to father legitimate children. A husband owed it to his wife and family to not so thoroughly tire himself out with other women that he did not have the energy to mate with his wife. Although absolute fidelity was not expected, a married man without children who was seen too much with his mistress opened himself up to criticism, for he had a responsibility to his family, ancestors, and the aristocracy itself to ensure that he produced a male heir.

It was expected that leading Georgians would contract a proper marriage and that all Georgians of wealth and privilege would prioritise producing legitimate children, especially a male heir. Women who did not marry well could face stiff punishments, including being exiled from society. A woman owed it to her family and future children to find an advantageous match, one that improved the family's wealth and status. While not a Georgian innovation, the heir and a spare policy was a good one, for in cases like the Lambs having only one legitimate son and heir proved risky and could lead to another man's son inheriting all. Because of this, women were expected to remain faithful until a healthy male heir (or ideally heirs) had been produced, while husbands could conduct affairs from the start. Both leading men and women needed to consider that a failure to produce legitimate children would call into question not only their dedication to their family and its lineage but their virility (for men) and fertility (for women).

For the elites of England, marrying well during the Georgian period often had little to do with emotional attachment but with what a family could gain from a match. When considering whether a potential partner proved suitable, the question for Georgian elites was not whether their personalities aligned, or if they had an emotional connection, or even if they were attracted to one another, but whether their potential spouse had the right parentage, a title, and/or sufficient wealth and property. Basing the decision of who to marry on financial and/or social considerations often led to two people being joined for life who had little compatibility and were ill-suited to one another. These poorly matched partners could find themselves trapped in unhappy marriages, which prompted them to look outside their marriage for love, companionship and sexual fulfilment.

CHAPTER TWO

Flexible and Accommodating Marriages

Affairs were an established and important feature of elite Georgian culture, especially among the fashionable set that dominated the London scene. Given the frequency of extra-marital affairs among England's leading families, it was considered prudent for each married couple to discuss what kinds of affairs would be accepted within their marriage. There was little point and not much to be gained by insisting on fidelity. Certainly, some couples had monogamous relationships, but among the leading members of the beau monde, affairs were the norm and seen as a natural component of aristocratic culture. It was also widely accepted that a man who lacked access to his wife would engage in affairs. This included army or navy officers posted abroad and men unable to have intercourse with their pregnant or otherwise indisposed spouse. While many decried what they believed to be the moral decay of England's ruling elite, aristocrats believed that they were only beholden to their own values and that it made practical sense to come to an agreement on how they would handle extra-marital affairs to reduce the chance of misunderstanding, hurt feelings, or discord.

All couples needed to consider not only the rules of society but their own attitudes and comfort level before deciding whether adultery would be permitted within their marriage and, if so, how they and their spouse would conduct their affairs. As discussed, nearly all Georgians believed that it was advisable for a wife to remain faithful to her husband until giving birth to a male heir. Ideally, such fidelity would be maintained until the couple had produced multiple sons. This protected the family, ensuring (as much as one can) the continuation of the legitimate bloodline. Although generally free to have extra-marital relationships after producing a healthy son and heir, some husbands requested that their wives keep their affairs secret; they did not want their friends and the rest of society to gossip about their wives' behaviour. By keeping her affairs secret, a wife could protect her reputation and any future children from illegitimacy. Other men, although they may have preferred privacy, understood that hiding an affair was a difficult task and only wished their wives to act sensibly and not flaunt their affairs. Couples also had to determine what types of sexual partners would be acceptable. Attitudes on this differed. Almost all men demanded that their wives and, indeed, mistresses only have affairs with men of class and quality. This probably did not need to be discussed as all knew this to be one of the most essential and sacrosanct rules of having an affair. While some women appear to have placed no constraints on their husbands' sexual behaviour, others may have demanded that a husband be faithful or tried to guide a husband's sexual choices. They may have also simply asked that their husbands try to be discreet. While each married couple had its own rules, it was widely understood that having a flexible and accommodating marriage was the best and most realistic approach, especially considering the cost and difficulty of securing a divorce. Most marriages could accommodate extra-marital affairs, and so long as both husband and wife adhered to the rules that society set and that they negotiated, aristocrats tended to see little harm in seeking sexual satisfaction outside marriage.

Elite women understood that their husbands would conduct extra-marital affairs, and some prudently tried to control whom they might have relationships with. Although Caroline Fox (née Lennox), wife to the talented, if sometimes unscrupulous politician, Henry Fox, believed that extra-marital affairs were a natural part of marriage, she was concerned about the types of women her husband may have relations with. Fearing that a kept mistress would squander his money and time, Caroline preferred that her husband focused his attention upon serving girls and lower-class women. While extra-marital sex was healthy, normal, and to be expected, Caroline did not like the idea that her husband might form an emotional attachment, something she believed would be impossible for him to do with a woman from the lower classes.[1] Aristocratic women believed themselves to be superior to these 'low-bred' women who, while they might entice their husbands with their bodies, could offer them little else. They also were well aware of the power they and their husbands held over such women (especially those employed in the household) and knew that any lower-class women could be discarded, scared away, or bought off whenever either spouse no longer wished the relationship to continue. Given the class and power dynamics of Georgian society, aristocratic women were largely secure in the knowledge that their husbands' physical relationships with women from the lower classes would pose little threat to their marriage or happiness and thus were usually not worth worrying about.

Married couples that engaged or planned to engage in extra-marital affairs needed to discuss not only whom they may have sex with but also how much money they were free to spend on their lover. Leading Georgians could spend tremendous amounts of money on their mistresses, which could strain and sometimes even destroy the finances of leading families. This was also a worry for many parents whose sons wished to live the life of the beau monde but did not have the resources to be able to do so.[2] Indeed, more experienced courtesans, such as Harriette Wilson and Mary Robinson, specifically targeted rich young men knowing that they would most likely be able to extract valuable promises, annuities and payoffs.[3]

Married women may not have had the financial freedom possessed by their husbands but could still spend their 'pin' money on their lovers. Some may have even sold gifts they received from their husbands to purchase their lovers expensive presents. Affairs did not always have to be costly. In her memoirs, Harriette Wilson lambasts a number of aristocrats, including Lord Craven and Frederick Lamb, for what she sees as their cheapness and for leaving her to fend for herself.[4] As will be discussed later, a man who did not treat his mistress well could have his reputation questioned by other leading men. Georgian men could also profit from their wives or even their daughters engaging in affairs with rich and powerful men.

Margaret Stuart, the wife of James Archibald Stuart, did not worry if her husband conducted an occasional affair. Explaining her thoughts on the subject, she told the infamous rake James Boswell that 'she would not be uneasy at an occasional infidelity in her husband ...' although she would be concerned 'if he kept a particular woman ...' or 'if his infidelities were very frequent ...' Stuart concludes by saying that a passing interest in a girl, 'or being led by one's companions after drinking to an improper place, was not to be considered as inconsistent with true affection'.[5] Similar to Caroline Fox, the worry was not about the act itself, which was primarily seen as natural and a part of aristocratic culture, but that her husband might form an emotional attachment and develop a lasting relationship with another woman. For Emily and Margaret, an extra-marital affair could be solely conceived as a physical act that, especially if conducted with a woman who lacked their breeding and sophistication, should give them little cause for concern. In short, extra-marital affairs were natural and, if properly managed and conducted with the right people, were perceived to be little threat to them, their marriage, or happiness and were not seen as indicative of how their husbands felt towards them or their marriages.

Despite having reached an understanding with her husband, after a few years of marriage, Caroline Fox began to worry that her husband had been led astray. Henry seemed more distant, distracted, and clearly had less time for her. Given this change in her husband's behaviour, Caroline concluded that Fox had acquired a lover capable of competing for his heart and attention. Upset over this, Caroline took a preparation of medicine commonly believed to improve both health and mood. No medicine could change her situation, and after brooding over her relationship, she wrote to her husband in 1748, accusing him of falling out of love with her and allowing another woman to come between them. Caroline, who was on her annual visit to Bath, also suggested that Fox was glad of her absence for it allowed him more time and freedom to conduct his affair.[6]

In his response, Henry Fox vociferously denied any wrongdoing. He reminded Caroline of how much he admired her while professing his deep love and affection for her. Fox admitted to being preoccupied but not by another woman but rather by the demands of public office. As Secretary at War, Fox had tremendous responsibilities, and as a younger son of the relative upstart Sir Stephen Fox (himself the son of a yeoman farmer), he pushed himself to prove himself worthy of marrying the daughter of a duke. Fox's main ambition was to gain a peerage. His father had been offered one by James II on the condition he convert to Catholicism, but Sir Stephen had declined the offer (Henry Fox would be made a peer in his own right as Baron Holland in 1763). A trusted advisor to Charles II, Sir Stephen used his position and power to vastly enrich himself and his family, especially during his tenure in the newly created position of Paymaster of the Forces. Sir Stephen held this prestigious and lucrative position from 1661 to 1676 and from 1679 to 1680. Considered one of, if not the richest commoner in the land, Sir Stephen is well remembered for his role in creating the Royal Hospital Chelsea, an almshouse established for elderly or injured veterans. A talented and shrewd financer, Sir Stephen donated £13,000 to help establish the hospital. Still in operation today, the Royal Hospital Chelsea serves as a retirement and nursing home for hundreds of former British soldiers. These retired soldiers are known as Chelsea Pensioners.

While never fully forgiving Fox or Caroline for their marriage, the duke and duchess did eventually reconcile with them after Fox displayed his tremendous talents in both holding public office and in the House of Commons.[7] Fox not only became one of the leading lights of Georgian state and society but he had proven himself to be a useful ally to the duke and his family. He also continued in the family business by successfully leveraging his positions, especially as the Paymaster of the Forces (1757–1765), to amass a large fortune. He became a loving father, one notorious for indulging his sons. His son Charles James Fox would become one of the leading figures and politicians of the Georgian era. Henry Fox understood the rules of having an affair and that while he may have other sexual partners, he knew that his wife must come first and that she must never feel threatened by another woman or relationship. Although it took some convincing, Caroline would come to accept that her husband's lack of attention and time away was not the result of him gaining a new lover but the responsibilities of a busy and important man.

As already covered, Caroline's sister Emily accepted that her first husband, James FitzGerald, Earl of Kildare (later Duke of Leinster), would engage in extra-marital affairs. Like her sister, Emily believed that as long as his affairs were conducted without feelings or developing an attachment, such behaviour was normal and not worth worrying about. Writing to Caroline in 1751, Emily informed her sister that her husband had relations with a servant in their home and that the girl had become pregnant.[8] It is instructive that Emily felt no shame about this, openly told her sister who otherwise probably would never have known, and did not think this reflected poorly on her family or her husband. The often-pregnant Emily (she gave birth twenty-two times) even joked that maybe the house had something to do with the number of children fathered under its roof. It was often taken as a given that once a wife was unable or unwilling to engage in sex (some couples may have stopped having sex fearing that intercourse would harm the baby) that leading men would seek out sex elsewhere, as few Georgians expected a leading man to abstain from intercourse.[9] Musing about her husband's situation, Emily confided in her sister that she 'hoped that my turn for getting a lover will come in good time'.[10] We know that Emily would not only get a lover but would eventually marry her children's tutor. As discussed in the previous chapter, since her second marriage was based upon love and not socio-political or economic considerations, Emily expected mutual affection and fidelity, not the protection of rank and privilege, to be the cornerstone of her marriage to Ogilvie.[11]

Since many upper-class Georgians, especially those whose marriage was primarily based upon socio-political or economic considerations, expected neither love nor affection from their spouse, many Georgians practised what we might today refer to as an open marriage. George Carpenter, 2nd Earl of Tyrconnel, who, as we shall see, would encourage his wife to have an affair with Prince Frederick, Duke of York and Albany, allowed his friend and fellow peer John Bowes, 10th Earl of Strathmore (eldest son of infamous 'unhappy countess' Mary Eleanor Bowes) to carry on an extended relationship with his second wife, Sarah Hussey. Carpenter's first marriage to Frances Manners, a daughter of the Marquess of Granby, had been dissolved in 1777 after she had run away and eloped with her lover. Close friends Lord Tyrconnel and Lord Strathmore had much in common and would often pal around together, but at night Tyrconnel's wife could be found sharing a bed with Strathmore. Tolerated by both families, no one criticised the affair; Tyrconnel clearly approved of their coupling, and the two lovers did not seek to legitimise their relationship or to challenge Sarah's husband's authority.[12] This would have included Sarah seeking a divorce or no longer appearing in public with her husband.

As this chapter has shown, although the institution of marriage among the elite did allow for extra-marital relations, each couple needed to negotiate how and with whom their affairs would be conducted. While this may have cleared up any misunderstanding, it did not prevent jealousy, a spouse falling in love with their lover, or one or both spouses breaking the rules that society and their spouse set for having an affair. Such breaches, as we shall see, could lead to harsh and long-lasting repercussions, especially for women. Whatever their true feelings, married couples needed to maintain the veneer of a happy marriage. As long as they appeared to be happily married, aristocrats could have flexible marriages that allowed them to spend much of their time with a partner of their choice, providing that choice did not upset their spouse or transgress the rules of having an affair. This did much to lessen the burden of being pushed into a socio-political marriage and explains, in part, why so many suitors cared more about money, property and titles than suitability. One way of understanding affairs is to view them as a critical component in making political and social marriages palatable, which ensured that modern ideas like love and affection did not disrupt the nobility's ability to use marriage as a tool to cement and protect their power and control.

CHAPTER THREE

Having and Securing a Fashionable Mistress

Georgian men gave a variety of reasons for conducting extra-marital affairs. Justifications included being poorly matched, having little in common, finding their spouse unattractive or disagreeable, or simply because they could. It was also widely believed that sex was a medical necessity for men and that failure to expel sperm could leave one susceptible to illness. An unappealing wife, one who refused sex, was indisposed due to ill health or pregnancy, could not help a husband with this medical 'need', and a mistress was believed to be a better alternative than masturbation.[1] Leading Georgians were well aware that having a fashionable mistress was an expectation and that gaining and holding the attentions of a prized mistress would improve their standing with the leading members of society.

Believing that sex for men was natural and healthy and fearing that if their sons did not have an outlet for their sexual energies, they would turn to masturbation or homosexuality, some wealthy and influential parents suggested, or at least did not prevent, their sons from engaging in sex with servants or prostitutes.[2] In some cases, family members took matters into their own hands and helped arrange a younger family member's first sexual experience. For instance, George III's brother, William Augustus, Duke of Cumberland, arranged for his nephew, the Prince of Wales's first sexual encounter.[3] Upper-class men took pride in their sons' 'natural desires' and sought to explain to them the importance of virility.[4] On the matter of engaging in sexual activities, Henry Fox, 1st Baron Holland, who likely helped set up his indulged son Charles's first sexual experience, instructed his 19-year-old nephew Harry Digby: 'Whenever you can, whomever you can with safety; let that be your maxim.'[5] This encouragement was not extended to their daughters or female relations who were taught chastity and self-restraint.[6]

Although for the elites of England, sex with a prostitute or an evening in a brothel was, for the most part, an accepted activity (at least among their social peers), ultimately, what men of fashion really aspired to was to possess a famous mistress. A sign of more than just good taste, an elegant and happy mistress signified that the patron had a healthy mind and body while confirming his virility and sex appeal.[7] Known by a plethora of names, including paramours, courtesans and Cyprians, professional mistresses were not prostitutes *per se*. While a prostitute would accept nearly anyone willing to pay for their favours, a courtesan chose whom she did business with. Although the most successful paid close attention to financial considerations when selecting a patron, professional mistresses also factored in their own pleasure, including whether a potential suitor would be good fun.[8]

A sign of wealth, fashion and good taste, having a mistress was so important that even men who did not want one often acquired a mistress because it was expected of them. Rich and powerful men were supposed to have a public 'wife', and it did not do to bring your actual wife on a night on the town when all your friends were bringing a mistress. Fitting in mattered, and since numerous leading men had a public wife, including the Duke of Grafton, Lord Sandwich and Charles James Fox, to say nothing of the future George IV and nearly all of his royal uncles, if one wanted to rub shoulders with the leading lights of Georgian society a fashionable mistress was a necessity. In light of this fact, men who, under other conditions, might not have had a mistress obtained one anyway. This was true of the future George II, who had mistresses only out of the belief that it was expected of him.[9] On her deathbed, Queen Caroline told the king that he should remarry, but he said, 'Non, J'aurai des maîtresses (No, I will have mistresses).'[10] This probably came as no surprise to the queen, as she had been well aware of the king's activities.[11] According to Rebecca Fraser, Queen Caroline had, on an earlier occasion, prudently noted that his English mistress might 'teach him better English'.[12] George II would develop a reputation for not treating his mistresses well. Onc possible explanation for this is because, at least until the death of his wife, he really did not want to have them anyhow.[13]

For the Georgian elite, acquiring a fashionable mistress was not always easy and could prove both time-consuming and expensive. There were only a handful of leading women at any given time, and these women usually reserved themselves for fashionable men with deep pockets. Understanding that their exclusivity drove up demand, the most sought-after professionals would expect and receive only the best from any potential patron. Leading Georgians could spend a fortune trying to acquire a fashionable mistress. If successful, they would be required to spend another fortune to keep her.

Courtesans were well aware of the value of their reputations and were discerning with their attentions. As one of the leading professionals of the Georgian period, Sophia Baddeley certainly understood that most men desired what they could not have. Sophia did not simply give herself to the highest bidder but turned down men because she did not find them physically attractive or because they had an unfavourable reputation. For instance, she rejected the advances of Sir Cecil Bishop because she felt he was too old for her. His substantial wealth could not convince her to reconsider. When he sent her an invitation accompanied by a beautifully engraved silver plate worth around £100, she declined to meet with him and returned the plate.[14] Sophia understood that one of her most valuable possessions was her exclusive reputation. If she found herself with a man of taste and judgment, a man who garnered the respect of other men, she could expect frequent offers and see her value increase. Conversely, spending time with a man who lacked money and social cache might reduce her value. For this reason, the most desired courtesans were very particular with whom they spent their time.

Even the Prince of Wales, the most eligible bachelor in the realm, had difficulty securing a mistress. Not from the school of keeping a stiff upper lip, George Augustus let everyone know when he was displeased. The future king cried frequently and with much volume over a myriad of, to him, upsetting events. This included crying openly about arguments with other leading men of the day, his allowance, and women.[15] When Maria Fitzherbert refused to become the prince's mistress, George rolled on the floor in agony, crying and wailing profusely while simultaneously pulling at his own hair and striking his head against the floor.[16] The intensity of his reaction should not surprise us because men were expected to cry. Emotional outbursts were not perceived to be unmanly but rather drew admiration from their peers for displaying such depth of feeling and sensitivity.[17] For instance, when the prince had bestowed upon the famous and fashionable playwright Richard Brinsley Sheridan a sinecure that fetched £800 a year, Sheridan, who desired that it be given to his son instead, burst into tears.[18] Understanding the power of emotional outbursts, George refused to alter the sinecure.

The prince obsessively pursued Fitzherbert. A devout Catholic, Fitzherbert refused to become his mistress. Unwilling to give up, George wrote Fitzherbert several letters, including a forty-two-page love letter. In it, he professed his love for her while threatening to take his life if she would not be with him. When the letter failed to achieve the desired results, George went through the motions of a suicide attempt.[19] George's show of emotions and desperation impacted Fitzherbert, who eventually agreed to be with the prince but only after he married her, which he did, in secret, in 1785.[20] The marriage was not valid: The Royal Marriage Act of 1772 prevented George from marrying without his father's permission. Had the marriage been valid, the prince would have been ineligible to be king as no monarch could, since the Act of Settlement of 1701, be married to a Catholic. Content to call themselves husband and wife, most believed that Fitzherbert was nothing more than George's mistress, but they played along because of the prince's position and sensitive nature. Whatever his feelings or how he viewed the relationship, George, in 1794, 'officially' broke with Fitzherbert so that he could conduct a legal marriage. If the Prince of Wales had to go to such lengths to secure the company of a desirable woman, imagine how difficult it must have been for other men.

Displays of emotional strife, albeit not always as violent or public as those of the Prince of Wales, could aid elites in their quest to secure a leading mistress. The master of fashion, whose name is still given to young men of good looks and charm, George Bryan 'Beau' Brummell, well aware of the symbolic value of tears, explained to one of his romantic interests that he had 'yet sufficient command over my drooping faculties to restrain any tributary tears from falling over my farewell; you might doubt their reality; and we all know that they may be counterfeited upon paper, with a sponge and rose-water'.[21] Brummell understood the sensibilities of the period, spending hours getting ready and making sure he looked just right. Indeed, it was considered quite the honour to be invited to watch his routine as he readied himself for the day.[22] Brummell captured the spirit of the age, becoming the absolute arbiter of fashion and fashionable behaviour among the ton. He even won over the Prince of Wales, who hoped to trade on Brummell's reputation and elegance. Although still only a teenager, the prince asked Brummell to serve as his *chevalier d'honneur* (best man) when he married Caroline of Brunswick in 1795.[23] This confirmed Brummell's meteoric rise. Brummell had such a hold over George that the Prince of Wales, on one occasion, burst into tears after Brummell remarked that he did not like the cut of his coat.[24] Just having Brummell show up to a party meant that the gathering had been a success even if Brummell, as he usually did, stayed only a short while.[25] Despite being the son of a wealthy but relatively unimportant politician, Brummell had, until he had fallen out of favour with the Prince of Wales, supplanted members of the royal family as the most sought-after guest in the realm.

Living the life of the beau monde, especially if one had a fashionable mistress to support, was extremely expensive. A leading mistress's regular expenses might cost her patron upwards of £3,000 a year.[26] This figure did not include gifts or other rewards that a patron would be expected to provide.[27] It also does not account for the costs associated with securing a mistress. It would be a very rich man who could afford the exclusive rights to a fashionable mistress. One had to weigh these costs against the social prestige that could be gained by securing an exclusive and desired mistress.

Assuming that a potential suitor had already met the professional mistress with whom he wished to make an arrangement, how did he proposition her? One method included sending a gift which, as manners dictated, necessitated that a courtesan send a response. A gift opened negotiations and provided insight into how much a potential suitor was willing to invest in the relationship. While useful to know, some mistresses disliked this form of introduction as it brought to the fore that they traded their bodies for money, something that many of them preferred to ignore. Receiving gifts from men they barely knew seemed to emphasise the financial rather than the social side of these relationships. Certainly, not all courtesans stood on ceremony as Harriette Wilson once told one of her admirers that, 'a fifty-pound note will do as well as a regular introduction.'[28] An introduction from a mutual acquaintance was usually preferred as the person conducting the introduction would, in effect, be vouching for the potential patron. Peniston Lamb, Viscount Melbourne, first approached Sophia Baddeley through a friend who gave her over £300. This friend explained that the money was from Peniston, who wished to become her patron, 'in exchange for the possession of her heart'.[29] Sophia initially declined his proposal. After Melbourne increased his offer, Sophia agreed to his terms, starting, what would be a long-lasting relationship with Melbourne.[30] Another method of approaching a professional mistress involved hiring someone to make the introduction. Lord Halifax happily paid another man to help him attract the attentions of the famous courtesan Mary Ann Faulkner.[31] Employing an intermediary was not without risk. Some men may have preferred sending a gift as asking a friend or hiring an intermediary for an introduction would let their intentions be known. It is easy to see why men who guarded their reputations so closely would not want their friends and the rest of society to know if they were unsuccessful in acquiring their chosen mistress. A gift costs only money, but an introduction from a friend or intermediary, if rebuffed and subsequently this rejection became widely known, could cost them their reputation as a desired man of the town.

Georgian elites were not above advertising in the newspaper to try to acquire a mistress. In 1754, a London newspaper carried an advertisement from a 'Gentleman' looking to connect with a woman whom he had met 'at the last Masquerade'. To ensure that his meaning and sincerity were not missed, he let her know precisely what he would provide: 'A Coach and Six, and 7000 l. per Annum, at her Service' adding as long as 'she don't think the Gentleman too old'. If interested in his proposal, he instructed her to ask for, 'C.G. at the Cocoa-Tree in Pall Mall'.[32] Advertisements provided a relatively anonymous and low-stakes way to try and connect with a courtesan while making apparent precisely what the patron was willing to spend.

For professional mistresses, dealing with frequent proposals and claims of affection came with the territory. At the height of her power, Sophia Baddeley constantly had to ward off potential suitors. While she was serving as the kept mistress of Lord Melbourne, Hugh Percy, 1st Duke of Northumberland, sought exclusive access to her company. To win her favour, the duke promised to, 'present her with 1,000 guineas as an earnest of his esteem and to settle upon her an annuity of £500 a year' while still promising to pay all of her debts if she agreed to live with him or at least near him.[33] She also received an offer from Lord Pigot who desiring a wife and knowing that she had rejected other aristocrats who tried to pry her away from Melbourne, offered to pay for a formal divorce from her husband Robert Baddeley so that they could marry. He also offered her an annuity worth £600 a year. If she accepted as his wife, she would have been known as Lady Pigot.[34] In a period where a labourer needed £30–£40 a year to provide for their family, and a gentleman might support himself on £300, £600 per annum would be a significant income for the daughter of a musician.[35] Either of these two offers would have made Sophia secure and very comfortable, demonstrating that a sought-after mistress could be well provided for. Sophia rejected both proposals preferring to stay with Melbourne.[36]

Turning down a man of rank and power was no easy task. These men were willing to pay extraordinary sums for the things that they wanted.[37] Accustomed to getting their way, men of fashion did not always handle rejection well and, in a vein similar to the Prince of Wales, would continue to pursue the object of their affections hoping that their persistence would pay off.

Certainly, one of the worst aspects of being a leading mistress must have been the constant unwanted attention. Sophia Baddeley complained that not only was she continuously bombarded with proposals but that she had to deal with the same flirtations over and over again. Sophia explained that what she really desired was intelligent conversation, not professions of love.[38] Like many modern millionaires, aristocrats often believed that everyone had a price, and thus when faced with rejection, rather than humbly accepting the wishes of the woman they wanted to secure they just as often upped their offer.

Having been rejected by Sophia, the Duke of Northumberland increased his offer to £1,500 a year while still promising to clear her debts. For this sum, Sophia had to agree to be his exclusive companion.[39] Despite offering her a lavish and generous income while promising to cover most of her living expenses and pay off her extensive debts, Sophia turned down the offer. Although Melbourne could not offer nearly as much, he had been kind to her, and Sophia wished to stay loyal.[40] The Duke of Northumberland persisted. Hoping to buy his way into her company, the duke offered Sophia £500 if she would allow him to come for tea a couple of times a week. In doing so, he got much more. Not only did Sophia admit the duke into her presence but also her bedchamber. She regretted her mistake, telling a friend, 'I found my resolution give way, and I did what I now repent of.'[41] Sophia had made one of the greatest mistakes a courtesan could make. While £500 was a huge sum, Sophia, having let the duke into her bed, had passed up an opportunity for further gains from the wealthy duke.

Understanding the differences in wealth and power between themselves and their patrons, courtesans, for their own protection, could insist that legal agreements be drawn up which would spell out their relationship in clear, unambiguous language. Contracts detailed what their compensation would be and, to avoid confusion or misunderstanding, often included what patrons expected from their mistress as well. While not exactly romantic, such contracts probably helped relationships, ensuring that both parties were fully aware of what was expected of them. Anxious to secure Sophia's services, Lord Molyneux brought his attorney to the negotiations so that if they made an agreement, it could be signed that very day.[42] Presumably, Lord Molyneux did not want to give Sophia any chance to change her mind, or he may have hoped to get some of what he paid for without any delay. Sophia declined Lord Molyneux's offer.

Numerous Georgians went bankrupt trying to keep up with the expensive life of the beau monde. If your friends or relations were unable or unwilling to cover your debts, this meant either debtors' prison or exile to the continent where one was outside the jurisdiction of English bill collectors. This was a place of solace and final resting spot for not only bankrupt gentlemen like Beau Brummell (who most probably died of syphilis) but famous courtesans who had lost their suitors, money, and their looks. In one extreme example covered by Nicola Phillips, William Jackson, the son of a wealthy former East India Company clerk (also named William Jackson), driven by the need to act and look like a wealthy gentleman, turned to a life of crime, including forgery to raise money to fund his expensive lifestyle. He was eventually imprisoned for his crimes and, after losing the support of his father, transported to Australia, where he died living the life of a 'convict dandie'.[43] Many men hastened their descent into bankruptcy by chasing women, gambling, trying to win the admiration of their peers, purchasing the latest fashions, and by supporting a famous mistress. Ultimately, to claim the perfect mistress, one needed deep pockets (to avoid debt, exile, or even debtors' prison), the right clothes, social acceptance, and, sometimes, emotional blackmail, including a few tears, real or faked.

As we have seen, even for those with wealth, power and prestige, acquiring a desirable and sought-after mistress could still be rather difficult. It could be an expensive, frustrating, time-consuming, and, at times, humiliating process. Acquiring a fashionable mistress could become all-consuming and, for those without great wealth, could lead to bankruptcy and even exile. That said, a fashionable mistress enhanced a man's reputation while also offering a chance at companionship and sexual satisfaction outside of one's marriage. If a man could attract the attentions of a leading woman, their relationship could be formalised by a contract or reliant on trust and the norms concerning how a gentleman treated his mistress.

CHAPTER FOUR

The Purpose, Role and Treatment of a Mistress

Leading men expected that a professional mistress would enhance their reputation. Securing a fashionable and exclusive mistress confirmed that they were fashionable, desired, and a man of wealth, discernment and taste while also reinforcing their manliness and virility. In order to meet these aims, a professional mistress needed to look expensive and shine in the limelight. Expected to have an eye for fashion, a kept mistress would ideally not only wear the latest style but also determine what was fashionable. Setting the standards of good taste enhanced not only a mistress's own reputation but that of her patron as well. A professional mistress would also be expected to have a pleasant disposition, offer steady and fun companionship, be flexible, and accommodate her patron's wishes and desires while also offering comfort and support. In return for their time and company, professional mistresses demanded that they have all their bills paid, be provided a house in a fashionable part of town, and to be given gifts and spending money. Leading professionals could demand good money for their company, and the money spent on their jewellery, clothes and homes became widely discussed and gossiped about. Courtesans had influence over some of the most connected men in the country and could live like aristocrats. The power and notoriety achieved by these women meant that a patron who broke promises or did not treat them well risked having his reputation questioned by his peers. Men who did not live up to their obligations or promises could face stiff social consequences and lose access to the most sought-after professionals who would avoid any connection with a man who could not be trusted. Both courtesans and the men that paid them worried about their reputations.

The source of so much drama both on and off the stage during the Georgian period, the theatre proved an ideal location to show off one's mistress. Going to the theatre had less to do with the show and was more about meeting with friends, catching up on the latest gossip, and displaying one's finery and figure. Managers kept the house lights on because showing off and socialising was just as, if not more, important as seeing the play.[1] Lord Melbourne's long-time mistress, Sophia Baddeley, dominated the theatre first as an actress and then as a beloved theatre goer. Determined to maximise her visibility, Sophia occupied a stage box adjacent to the actual stage.[2] While it must have been an awful location for viewing the play, it was ideal for being seen. Beautiful and enchanting, Sophia must have, on occasion, stolen the show by upstaging the unfortunate actors.

It is fitting that Georgians placed such importance on being seen, as few activities during the Georgian period were enjoyed outside the company of others. A walk in the park would be a group activity and would necessitate frequent stops to converse with other members of society. Certainly, one of the most tiring aspects of Georgian life in general, but heightened for a kept mistress, was the lack of privacy, as when in public, they would be expected to mix with all appropriate company. Although she revelled in the limelight, even Sophia tired of the unceasing attention from both sexes. She complained to her long-time companion, chaperone and biographer, Elizabeth Steele, that, 'I declare to you, my dear friend, I often wish I was a hermit, and lived in a cave unnoticed by the world.'[3] While Sophia's desire for peace and quiet is understandable, the lives of leading members of society and professional mistresses were, by design, public ones that afforded them very little privacy or time to themselves.

Some men expected their mistress to not only be attractive and fashionable but to be a keen conversationalist capable of discussing the leading issues of the day. Equally desired for her beauty and conversational skills, Harriette Wilson was well-read and made sure to keep up with the latest political developments. Worried that she would not be able to hold her own while speaking with the leading men of the period, Harriette would commit to periods of extended study. Secluding herself in the country, she would wrestle with topics like Greek and Roman history while brushing up on her Voltaire, Rousseau and other influential thinkers.[4] A contemporary of Wilson, Harriet Powell was such pleasant company that men would pay just for the chance to play cards and converse with her.[5] Powell made such an impression on the Earl of Seaforth that the two would later marry. These examples prove that professional mistresses provided more than just sex and could be highly valued for their company and intelligence.

Patrons spent large sums of money to ensure that their mistress dressed in an attractive and impressive manner, as they expected their mistress to act as a visible representation of their wealth and grandeur. Professional mistresses certainly dressed in a manner to draw attention to themselves including wearing expensive jewellery purchased by either their current or a previous patron. Indeed, women like Sophia Baddeley must have sparkled from all the jewels she would wear on a given night and it was not missed by leading women that their own jewels may, in comparison, be worth less than those wore by leading courtesans. When a society hostess mentioned to the courtesan Sally Pridden that her jewels were finer than her own, Sally responded that, 'They had need be finer than yours, my Lady, you have but one Lord to keep you, and to buy you jewels, but I have at least half a score, of which number, Madam, your Ladyship's good Lord is not the most inconsiderable.'[6] On a given night, Sophia might wear her two diamond watches, each of her four diamond necklaces, her diamond-studded bracelets, and several diamond rings.[7] It has been estimated that the jewellery collected and worn by Sophia would be worth approximately £1.5 million today.[8] Despite the value of such gifts, Sophia, as did so many of the leading ladies of the period, ended her life in poverty.

While their wives were often concerned with fitting in, making sure to wear the appropriate clothes for whatever upcoming event or dinner party, professional mistresses were much freer in their choices and used this independence to push the boundaries of acceptable fashion. Ann Catley became so popular that numerous leading ladies copied the way she dressed and styled her hair.[9] Similarly, at the height of her power, whatever the famous courtesan Fanny Murray wore immediately became fashionable.[10] Men might also opt to style themselves in ways in which they knew met with a renowned courtesan's approval.[11] Given the large sums of money spent on their mistresses' attire, it is not surprising that leading men expected them to be much talked about, to set the fashions, and to ultimately bolster their reputations.

Patrons expected their mistresses to support them in all of their endeavours. Prince Edward (made Duke of Kent in 1799), the fourth son and fifth child of King George III, expected his mistress, Madame de Saint Laurent, to follow him wherever his duties took him. Worried about what he believed to be the inappropriate nature of his son's relationship; George III hoped to break them up by transferring Edward's army unit away from Saint Laurent. Initially, Edward refused to go. Worried that ignoring the order would reflect poorly on him, Edward eventually agreed to the transfer. Before he left Geneva, Edward devised a plan for Saint Laurent to meet him in Gibraltar. While waiting for her to arrive, Edward became rather despondent. Writing to his brother, the Prince of Wales, in 1790, Edward explained his need for companionship reminding the prince that he 'needed a partner for his leisure hours …' and that he 'despise every sensual enjoyment, which one might procure when the object of it is a prostitute, in short I look for a companion, not for a whore. I know, you will laugh at my strange out of the way ideas …'[12] When George III heard that the couple had reunited in Gibraltar, the persistent king sent Edward to Quebec in 1791; she also followed him there.

Despite all her loyal service, both in and out of the bedroom, Saint Laurent understood that she might be forced to step aside to allow Edward to marry and beget heirs. While royal dukes were expected to have a mistress, their relationships were not supposed to get in the way of marrying and producing heirs. Unhappy marriages coupled with various misfortunes meant that with the death of Princess Charlotte (the only child of the Prince of Wales (the future George IV) and his wife Caroline of Brunswick)) in November of 1817, there was not a single legitimate grandchild of George III. After the death of Charlotte, there was a genuine threat that the Georgian line might end despite George III having seven living sons. The threat to the future of the Hanoverian succession and the kingdom itself meant that George III's unmarried sons were expected to marry as soon as possible so that they could begin the process of fathering heirs. Without much delay, wives for the Duke of Kent and his older brother, the Duke of Clarence, the future William IV, were secured. In a double wedding held on 29 May 1818, the Duke of Kent married Victoria of Saxe-Coburg-Saalfeld, while the Duke of Clarence married Adelaide of Saxe-Meiningen. The Duke of Kent and his new duchess had one child, a daughter, born on 24 May 1819. Shortly after the birth of his daughter, Edward contracted pneumonia. Edward did not recover his health and died from the disease on 23 January 1820. His daughter, Victoria, would become queen in 1837.

Although she understood the need to end their relationship, Saint Laurent was nonetheless devastated. For twenty-seven years, she had been at Edward's side. Her relationship with Edward was much more than simply a financial one. Edward had long been concerned about Saint Laurent and what the future might bring. Rather than find another man to support her and begin the process once again, she retired to France. Worried not only about her financial situation but also that she be able to maintain the dignity and respect that she had received as a royal mistress, Edward had diligently put aside money for her future maintenance. Although he left her to marry, Edward thought about her often, wrote to her, and did his best for her financially. Ultimately, the money provided by Edward and, after his death, help from friends and the widowed duchess, who felt a responsibility to help support her husband's former mistress, ensured that Saint Laurent had a comfortable retirement.[13] Saint Laurent died in 1830.

Leading Georgians would seek out their mistress not just for sex but also for their company and as a temporary escape from the doldrums of everyday life. While the gentleman's club played a similar role in Georgian society, a professional mistress allowed leading men to experience female company without having to deal with many of the realities of everyday life. On one occasion, a weary and tired Lord Melbourne visited Sophia after a long day out with his wife. According to Melbourne, he had been 'prancing about all day with his Betsy a-shopping …'[14] Claiming he was 'tired to death', it is telling that

Melbourne came to find peace and quiet in the home of his mistress.[15] Married to a bright and forceful woman, Melbourne never had complete control of his wife, but with Sophia, he was mainly in charge (or so he believed). He literally paid for her company and expected his time with her to be light and pleasant. Regular life and marriage were not always that.

A professional mistress was expected to organise her life to accommodate their patron's plans, schedule and desires. One of the most onerous and tiring aspects of being a courtesan was the expectation that you always be available to your patron. While some might send advanced notice of their plans, many patrons expected to be able to stop by with no notice. Patrons also expected that their mistress drop everything (assuming that they did not believe that their mistress spent her day simply waiting for them to arrive) to attend to their wishes, whatever they may be. One of Sophia's biggest complaints about her relationship with Melbourne was his propensity to drop by without notice at inconvenient times.[16] Not knowing if or when their man might stop by meant that they had to be all dressed up just in case he did. Looking right could take hours. Some nights, a kept mistress might get ready, and their patron not come, or if he did, he might give her a quick peck on the cheek and head to bed having barely looked at her. In any case, patrons expected their mistress to be ready for any activity; no man could be expected to wait while she dressed. It was her job to be prepared to go out on the town at a moment's notice. On a day spent with their patron, a courtesan might change outfits numerous times. She might even alter her hairstyle and change her jewellery as well to ensure that she continued to hold his attention. She would, of course, have to make such changes without inconveniencing her patron. Ultimately, his wishes, be it to make it a night on the town, a quiet night in, sex, or simply to chat, dictated what, if anything, they did together that evening.

Courtesans looked for ways to increase their independence and to have time away from their patrons. We know from the writings of Mrs Steele that Sophia often tired of Melbourne and his expectations. Melbourne came and went as he pleased and, as discussed, expected her to drop whatever she might be doing so that she could completely focus on his wants and needs. The inability to set one's social schedule must have been rather restricting and exhausting. Although she adored Melbourne, Sophia, a sensual and vivacious woman, found little joy or fulfilment in their sex life and, on occasion, feigned illness to encourage Melbourne to take his attentions elsewhere. It is no wonder that when Melbourne was called away, Sophia viewed this relative freedom as a 'holiday'.[17]

Arrangements with mistresses varied. When the Duke of Northumberland tried to entice Sophia Baddeley to break with Melbourne and become his mistress, he expected her to be utterly devoted to his needs and to see no other men. Others were not as controlling, or lacked the deep pockets or the prestige to demand exclusivity and accepted that 'their' mistress may have other men who also paid for her attention. There were a few caveats. Most expected that these other affairs would be conducted in private, not get in the way of their enjoyment, would not threaten or supplant their relationship, and be conducted exclusively with men of quality. Because most patrons wanted their mistress to be at their beck and call, they expected her to arrange these rendezvous for times when they would be otherwise engaged. There would be sufficient opportunity for this. Leading men would go to the country to hunt, visit and look in on their other estates and would do so without taking their mistress with them, providing ample opportunity for other liaisons. Having taken London by storm, the alluring Fanny Murray had several lovers while under the protection of Sir Richard Atkins.[18] Despite these other relationships, Atkins would become more than just her patron as the two later married. While under the protection of Francis Delaval, Ann Catley continued to charge other men for the pleasure of her company.[19] Sophia Baddeley also had a string of lovers while having Melbourne as her patron.[20] The opportunity to make extra money on the side when their patron was away or otherwise engaged may be another reason why Sophia and other courtesans looked forward to occasions when their patron did not require their services.

A courtesan and her patron negotiated the amount of freedom she could expect. Because of the relative scarcity of exclusive companions and the prestige that came with securing one of these women, it would have been difficult for any patron to put too many restrictions or demands upon a desired woman's free time. Only those willing to spend vast amounts of money would be able to demand exclusivity from a sought-after courtesan. On the other hand, mistresses who were either young, naïve, past their prime, or not fully established had little bargaining power and could be placed wholly under the control of their patron.

The relationship between a patron and his mistress was governed by rules that left much to interpretation. This flexibility certainly favoured patrons who could ignore promises made to their mistress, especially after the relationship ended. That said, reputations very much mattered, and Georgian men often lived in fear of not being considered a gentleman. This is why they did all they could to pay their gambling debts and why men defended slights of honour through duelling.[21] In a society where honour was of great importance, not living up to the promises that one made to his mistress could negatively impact a leading Georgian's reputation. For instance, Prince Frederick, Duke of York and Albany, the commander-in-chief of the army, had his reputation questioned by his own brother after it broke that he allowed his mistress, Mary Anne Clarke, to sell army commissions for profit. George, Prince of Wales, was less upset with the apparent breach of security, trust and duty than he was about the testimony of his brother's mistress, who told the court that the Duke of York routinely failed to pay her allowance in full.[22] Not paying her the money he had promised was considered a truly dishonourable act and could brand a leading Georgian as a man without class or integrity.

For leading Georgians, failure to live up to promises not only hurt one's reputation but could also result in legal action. Maria Foote, a famous actress-cum-mistress, sued Joseph Hayne for breach of promise, alleging that he had failed to keep his pledge to marry her.[23] The prosecution argued that Maria, because of the promise to marry, did not seek employment in the theatre resulting in a loss of income. For lying and leading her on, Maria sought £10,000 in damages. Maria's lawyers successfully demonstrated that Hayne had repeatedly broken his promise to marry Maria and that his leading her on had caused her emotional and financial harm. For his treatment of her and breaking the rules of society and that of a gentleman, the jury awarded Maria £3,000 in damages.[24]

Professional mistresses expected that their patron would continue to care for them when their relationship ended, at least until they found another man willing to support them. A true gentleman left his former mistress with not only an annuity but also a cash payment to help support her until she found her next patron. If unable or unwilling to do so, at the very minimum, a gentleman ought to introduce his former mistress to a worthy and wealthy patron willing to cover such costs. It is in this way that many mistresses moved from one person to another. In the politically minded Georgian era, where social circles and outings were often divided along political lines, this meant that many mistresses might spend their whole careers tending only to men of a single party.[25] While many did hold strong political opinions, and may have preferred men of the same ilk, some of this party loyalty has to do with the fact that they mostly met and interacted with men from only one side of the House.

Any professional mistress without an annuity was vulnerable. This is why it was so important to negotiate an annuity before starting the relationship when a courtesan had more bargaining power. Time and again, a patron promised an annuity, but promises did not pay the bills. Leading men made assurances that, for one reason or another, they never fulfilled. For instance, although Lord Melbourne had always promised to 'take care of his dearest love for life', he never settled an annuity on Sophia, and when the relationship ended, Sophia found herself in a difficult situation having no income nor an annuity to fall back on.[26] On the lack of annuity, her biographer Mrs Steele stated that, 'I hope it will be a lesson to some of my young readers, to be upon their guard against the treachery and deception of man, and learn by the fate of Mrs Baddeley …' who is left, 'to lament her folly in bitterness, anguish and distress'.[27] Sophia had no wealthy husband or relation to pay off her significant debts and like so many professional mistresses, her family, especially her brother, leeched off her success.[28] As we shall see, this lack of an annuity and the steady income it would have provided left Sophia vulnerable and ultimately contributed to many of her later difficulties.

Since a mistress was in a vulnerable position and was subject to the whims of her patron, even the most successful and prudent professionals endured periods of financial worry and were well acquainted with the fear of being unable to pay their creditors. Ultimately, professional mistresses, especially those without a contract or annuity, had to trust that their patron would live up to his promises and, if the relationship ended, would provide them with enough funds to cover their costs until they found their next lover. The frenetic life, one of glitz and glamour, must be placed alongside the periods of worry and poverty when a kept mistress was without a patron. Although the life of a professional mistress offered wealth, power and freedom, courtesans occupied a precarious position that required them to trust that their patrons would play by the rules. Patrons who did not live up to their promises risked hurting their reputation, could be sued for breach of promise, and, as a result, could potentially lose access to the most fashionable and expensive mistresses. The expectations placed on a mistress made it a difficult and demanding job. Always expected to be at the ready and having, at least on the surface, little choice or say in how the couple spent its time must have been exhausting. Being a courtesan allowed some women a degree of social mobility, and during their careers, the leading professionals could live like aristocrats. Those who saved their money might achieve a comfortable life and retirement, but this required carefully managing their money, reputation and career.

CHAPTER FIVE

A Patron Can Shape His Mistress to Suit His Needs

Georgian men saw nothing wrong with altering their mistress's looks, behaviour and personality to better suit their preferences. This attitude towards moulding a partner could even be applied to prospective spouses. The Englishman Thomas Day remains the most infamous example of trying to create a perfect partner.[1] After numerous failed attempts to find what he considered to be a suitable wife, Day successfully acquired two girls from an orphanage in order to train them to be his ideal wife. Inspired by Rousseau's *Emilé,* his perfect wife would be a woman of intelligence, willing to shun much of society's conventions while living a life of rural isolation. She should also please Day physically, especially his preference for puffy white arms.[2] Day and other Georgian men believed young and vulnerable females were malleable and could and should be improved. Such attempted 'improvement' reflects Georgian attitudes towards women while providing insights into the attributes that leading men believed the ideal spouse would possess.

Day believed that the women he met were already tainted by society, and only by training a girl from a young age could he produce an ideal spouse. Missing that Rousseau's *Emilé* is allegorical, Day acquired two girls from an orphanage to train his ideal wife. He proceeded to educate the girls while also conducting a series of dangerous and harmful experiments with the aim of ensuring that his pupils did not fear nature. His lessons included burning hot wax on their skin, firing pistols near them, and forcing them into icy cold water.[3] Day believed that his 'true' wife would emerge during this rigorous process. He planned to place the other girl in a trade or help her attract a suitable husband by ensuring she had a sufficient dowry.[4] In the end, neither girl lived up to his expectations nor became his wife.

This attitude towards reform and creating an ideal partner was also in vogue among men looking not for a wife but a mistress. Georgians had great faith in reform, many believing that people and society could be quickly and radically transformed. A belief in personal transformation gave rise to institutions that sought to eradicate a plethora of social ills, including prostitution. Founded in 1758, the famous Magdalen Hospital strove to end prostitution through an intensive programme of reform. Called 'Magdalens', these former prostitutes caught the public imagination, who became interested in their daily living and efforts to reform.[5] Encouraged by this cultural milieu, some men wished to be personally involved in reforming women who possessed less than sterling reputations.

Knowing the difficulty of altering their wives' behaviour or temperament, leading men focused their reforming zeal upon their mistresses. Aristocratic women were raised from childhood to behave in a certain manner and were unlikely to bend to any husband who wanted to change their behaviour. On the other hand, courtesans understood that their ability to conform to their patron's wishes increased their desirability and purse. Some of the most successful mistresses of the period were chameleons capable of adapting and profiting from nearly any situation. One of the best-known tales is that of Amy Lyon (later Emma Hart and finally Lady Hamilton), who morphed from the daughter of a coal miner to (an alleged) prostitute, to a mistress, to Lady Hamilton, and back to a mistress again. Each time, she changed herself to better suit the needs of both her suitors and her situation.

The story of Emma (born Amy Lyon) is one that has been told and retold in a plethora of Victorian novels. In many ways, it is the classic story of a poor girl winning the affections of a gentleman and subsequently marrying into an old and distinguished family. However, her story of becoming Lady Hamilton is a bit more gritty and full of compromise and struggle than most rags-to-riches stories. Born in 1765 to a hand-to-mouth existence in Ness, Cheshire, Emma's father worked in the coal pits. He died when Emma was still a baby. After the death of her husband, Mary, with baby Emma in tow, fled Ness. Mary struggled to provide for her daughter in their new home of Hawarden in Wales. Marriage to another labourer was an option, but she had been so dissatisfied with that life that Mary entered into a relationship with a (likely married) man of some means willing to provide for her and Emma. This relationship supplied Emma and her mother with some money and allowed Emma a better education and a more comfortable upbringing than otherwise could have been expected.[6] Early in life, Emma had learned that by attaching yourself to a powerful man, you could carve out a comfortable life, regardless of your background.

Tired of country life and looking for something more exciting, Emma, around the age of 12, took a job in Chester as a maid. Realising that such work did not suit her, she packed up and moved to London in search of fame, fortune and a better life. Emma would not be alone: during this period, an estimated 8,000 young people flocked to the capital each year looking for opportunity and a better life.[7] London was a dangerous place for a young girl. Madams and pimps preyed on naïve girls from the countryside, tricking them into prostitution. They did this by pretending to care about the welfare of these new arrivals and offering protection to them. They provided food, lodging and clothing, all the while keeping a running tab well aware that their 'wards' lacked the money to repay 'their debts'. Eventually, these new arrivals would be told of their 'debt' and forced into prostitution to pay off the money they supposedly owed. For many of these women, their 'debts' would never be paid, and they would be forced to work until they could no longer turn a profit, and then they were discarded. Cast out with little or no money and few clothes, these unfortunate 'fallen women' had little prospects for a different life. For most, streetwalking became their only option. The least lucrative and most dangerous form of prostitution, streetwalkers had little protection from either their customers or the elements.

Having arrived in London, Emma found employment as a barmaid at a pub whose clientele were encouraged to go upstairs with prostitutes attached to the establishment. Such an arrangement was not unusual.[8] Whether Emma's job required or encouraged her to provide more than alcohol is unknown. Emma rarely spoke of her early life and asked the few people who knew her during her early years in the capital not to talk about her former life. This makes it difficult to know exactly what she did to survive in London.[9]

After leaving the pub in 1779, Emma may have worked at the so-called Temple of Health. Run by James Graham, the Temple of Health purportedly employed the latest scientific advancements to help infertile couples conceive. The most expensive treatment, costing £50 a night, involved an electrified bed that stimulated the areas needed for conception. Called the 'Celestial Bed', it contained a Latin inscription that stated: 'It is a sad thing if a rich man has no heir to his property.'[10] This is a sentiment that most wealthy-but-childless Georgian couples would have agreed with. Other stimulation – although of a different nature – was provided by scantily dressed young women who danced around the bedroom. Emma may have worked as one of these girls.[11]

The next significant development in Emma's life occurred after meeting Sir Henry (Harry) Fetherstonhaugh. Sir Harry, a young man intent on enjoying his privileged life to the fullest, hired Emma, aged 16, to serve as a 'hostess' to entertain him and his wild friends during an extended period of youthful revelry. He took Emma to his family's estate Uppark in Sussex, placing her in a nearby cottage. The entertainment she provided the 26-year-old and his friends included dancing naked on the dining-room table.[12]

Well aware of the effect she had on men and tired of moving from place to place and having to start afresh without having any money to her name, Emma hoped to use this 'opportunity' to attract a patron capable of providing for her. This would add some stability to her life. Her good looks and pleasant, easy-going nature won over Sir Harry, who took her as his mistress. Being a mistress, even to an unreliable and self-absorbed man, proved so much better than scratching out a living in London. Desiring to experience all that life had in store for a wealthy, unattached man with few responsibilities, Sir Harry did not seek a long-term commitment. Emma soon became pregnant and, in 1782, gave birth to a healthy girl, whom she named after herself. Wanting nothing to do with the child, Sir Harry decided to break with her.[13] Emma, lacking the means to support her daughter, left the child with her grandmother.[14]

Having lost the support of Sir Harry and having little money or prospects, Emma needed help. She wrote to friends of Sir Harry, hoping that they might be able to help repair their relationship, encourage Sir Harry to support her financially, or in the hopes that they might take pity on her and provide her with some much-needed money or support. One of the men she wrote to was Charles Francis Greville, a second son of the Earl of Warwick, who had seen her 'entertain' at Sir Harry's and liked what he saw. Intrigued by the idea of 'rescuing' the beautiful yet vulnerable Emma, Greville signalled his willingness to provide for her. Having few other prospects, Emma agreed to become Greville's mistress.

A patron could control much of his mistress's life if she had, or was convinced that she had, few other options. Although he liked to think of himself as a different man from Sir Harry, Greville, who was nearly sixteen years her senior, expected Emma to be completely reliant upon him for protection, friendship, love and companionship. In return for offering Emma financial security, something she had lacked since leaving home and trying to make her way in the world at the age of 12, he expected her to bend to his every demand. Greville hoped that by personally educating Emma, he could mould her into the perfect mistress.

Greville desired the beauty of Emma but wanted nothing to do with her past; he insisted that Emma distance herself from her earlier life. Greville expected Emma to stop associating with anyone that she had previously known, including her own child. He planned to completely remake Emma, and he did not want any of her old friends or behaviours to sabotage his project, although he allowed one exception: Emma could continue to see her mother. A proper mistress required a chaperone, and Greville, always short of money, probably viewed Emma's mother as a cheap alternative.[15] To help accomplish his task of transforming Emma, Greville created lessons where he explained to her the errors of her past life and the need for her to change her ways. These lessons not only sought to transform Emma but to preoccupy her while he went out on the town. Greville did not wish to share Emma with his friends; he wanted her to be utterly devoted to him and may have worried that her beauty would create competition for her attention.

Despite being born into a wealthy and connected family, Greville was always short of money. Although his income of around £500 a year should have been enough for a gentleman to live comfortably, Greville's spending vastly outstripped his income.[16] He passed his need for economy onto Emma, whose job it was to run his household. Like a good pupil, Emma did this well. Like many elites, Greville had little knowledge of the costs of household items, which allowed Emma to inflate prices and keep the difference for herself.[17] She had learned from her experiences with Sir Harry; having left the relationship with little money and no security, Emma began putting money aside to ensure that she never found herself in such a position again. As the leading professional mistresses of the period had learned, money provided independence. Despite Emma inflating household costs, Greville, all things considered, got her on the cheap.

Greville wanted Emma to establish and manage a house based upon sober thought and clean living. Although she was a social person, who loved being the centre of attention, Emma bent to Greville's demands, desperately trying to conform to his version of the perfect mistress. Whereas Sir Harry had encouraged Emma to act without shame or restraint, Greville desired a quiet and clean mistress, one that acted more like a middle-class wife. Impressing him with her adherence to his dictates, Greville proudly boasted that Emma did, 'not wish for much society' and, due to his efforts is 'totally clear from all the society & habits of kept women …'[18] Emma, who had once dreamed of a career in the theatre, had convinced Greville of her complete transformation. Her outward appearance had undoubtedly changed. She had gone from entertaining Sir Harry's friends scantily dressed, or wearing nothing at all, to donning very conservative clothes. Dressing to Greville's taste and specifications, biographer Kate Williams stated that Emma's daily uniform more closely resembled that of a nun rather than that of a kept mistress.[19]

While pleased with his progress with Emma, Greville wanted to marry an heiress or wealthy widow capable of funding his desired lifestyle. Greville explained to his uncle, Sir William Hamilton, that his desire to marry was based solely on economic considerations: 'If I was independent I should think so little of any other connexion that I never would marry.'[20] The difficulty here lies in the fact that Greville, neither dashing nor really that interesting, had little that could convince a wealthy father or his daughter that he would make a good husband. Rather than changing his ways (he saved his reforming zeal for others), Greville determined that in order to acquire an heiress, he must make himself appear to be an independently wealthy gentleman. The best way to do this and still make a good investment, he believed, would be to build an impressive home. Well aware that appearances mattered in Georgian England, Greville hoped his new home would make him look the part of a wealthy younger son of an important noble family. He planned to use the house to entertain wealthy fathers and their marriageable daughters, showing them the grand home and lifestyle that his wife would enjoy. After marriage, Greville planned to use his new wife's dowry to pay for the home.[21] Greville believed that the fashionable Portman Square would be an ideal location to build his new residence.[22]

While the building project would help, Greville also had other matters to deal with. He knew that no family would marry off an heiress without learning more about a potential suitor's habits and temperament and that such inquiries would reveal not only that he had a long-standing mistress but that he had a propensity for 'girls of the town'.[23] While Greville could do little about his past or his reputation, he could do something about his current mistress, and this realisation prompted him to reconsider his relationship with Emma. It appears that while proud of his achievements in transforming wild Amy into sober Emma, his interest in her began to wane. Is it possible that Greville was more interested in the project of transforming Emma than Emma herself? Had Greville, deep down, missed the fun and enthusiastic Amy, having grown bored of sober and sensible Emma? Whatever the case, Greville began spending less time at 'their' cottage, and increasingly he viewed Emma as a complication, one that threatened to upend his plan to marry a wealthy widow or an heiress.[24]

Despite the obstacles of his relative poverty, Emma, and his reputation as a man about town, Greville believed that he had made some progress in his plan to marry into wealth. In June 1785, after two years with Emma, Greville had set his sights upon 18-year-old Miss Henrietta Willoughby. Greville knew that Henrietta's eldest sister had provided her husband with a dowry of around £20,000.[25] He believed that if he could get his uncle, Sir William, to formally accept him as his principal heir, then he would be able to convince Henrietta's father, Lord Middleton, to allow him to marry his daughter knowing that Greville would eventually come into some wealth. After some wrangling and desperate pleas from Greville, Hamilton told his nephew that he could consider himself his heir. Greville wasted little time in showing this letter to Lord Middleton.[26] Having been confirmed as Hamilton's heir and believing himself close to achieving his dream of marrying a wealthy heiress, one that could provide him with the finances and lifestyle that he felt he deserved, Greville still had one task to complete: he needed to get Emma out of the picture.

While it was one thing for a man to acquire a mistress after marrying (and ideally after siring an heir), it was seen as poor form to start your marriage with a mistress already at your side. As discussed, even royalty, including both the Duke of Kent and his brother, the Prince of Wales, were expected to, and did, end long-term relationships before they married.

Knowing that when his uncle had visited England in 1783 that Sir William had been captivated by Emma's beauty, Greville wondered whether Hamilton might be willing to take Emma off his hands.[27] Knowing full well the hardships that she endured the last time she lost her patron, rather than just breaking with Emma, Greville planned to use his uncle as a soft landing for her. Greville believed that the best course of action for everyone would be to ship Emma off to Naples, where his uncle served as Envoy Extraordinary to the Kingdom of the Two Sicilies. There she could start a new life as Sir William's mistress.

Greville wrote to his uncle to inquire whether Hamilton would be interested in taking Emma off his hands. Hamilton wanted to help his nephew, and although intrigued by the offer, Sir William worried about having Emma with him in Naples. Concerned that Emma would give in to other men while under his protection and that he would be made to look a fool, Hamilton told his nephew that, 'I am not a match for so much youth and beauty.'[28] Desperate to be rid of Emma, Greville dropped the veil and wrote to his uncle that he should reconsider his stance towards Emma, asserting that a 'cleaner, sweeter bedfellow [does] not exist'.[29] Greville persisted in his plan, informing both Sir William and Emma that he intended to travel to Scotland alone in the hopes that removing himself from the situation would convince them to agree to his plans. He even encouraged Emma to write to his uncle, saying how much she looked forward to going to Naples.[30] Hamilton eventually relented and agreed to the visit. Greville never told Emma of the real reason she was being sent to Naples and let her think that he would be joining her there.

Whether Greville planned to re-establish his relationship with Emma after securing his bride is unknown. Perhaps it was an open-ended question with Greville waiting to see how he got on without Emma. If he missed her company, he might have tried to reclaim her; if not, he would leave her with his uncle in Naples, knowing that Sir William would care for her. Whatever his intentions once Emma left, Greville seemed happy in her absence and did not appear to miss her company. Having travelled north to look in on the lands that, since becoming Sir William's heir, would, if all went according to plan, one day be his, Greville must have been looking forward to his new life with his prospective wealthy heiress.

Greville had not shared his plans with Miss Willoughby as his discussions had been with her father, Lord Middleton, not his 18-year-old daughter. This was a mistake as Henrietta probably never considered him for a husband, for Greville had a reputation for being a bit of a bore without a sense of humour. In 1787, Henrietta married another second son, Richard Savile, son of the Earl of Scarbrough.[31] After the death of his elder brother in 1807, Richard inherited the title. Unaware of Henrietta's attitude towards him, Greville pushed on with his plan.

Busy trying to secure his potential bride, Greville thought about Emma less and less. Whatever his original plan, with each letter he sent to Emma, Greville appeared to move further and further away from her.

He even began to suggest to Emma that she seek a more permanent position with Sir William. Emma admitted to liking Sir William; he was good company and had treated her kindly, but she wanted to be with Greville. As his letters became more distant, Emma begged Greville to write to her as a lover would do. Realising that she had lost Greville's affection and that her former patron wanted her to 'take up' with Sir William, Emma tried to convince him that such an event could not happen. She explained to Greville that, 'Sir William is ever friend. But we are lovers …'[32] Dazzled by her beauty and charm, Sir William formed an immediate attachment to Emma; but Emma, in her way, loved Greville and begged him to come and collect her.

Although Greville's behaviour towards Emma may shock modern readers, other than hiding his true intentions, Greville had done little wrong in the world of eighteenth-century affairs. Admittedly, he had got rid of Emma by shipping her off to a strange country, but he did not abandon her and rightly judged that his uncle would care for her. This conformed to the rules of having an affair as a gentleman did not just drop his kept mistress but either bought her out with an annuity or made sure she found another patron; or both.[33] Lacking in money, Greville chose to 'give' Emma to his kindly uncle who would care for her. Compared to Sir Harry, who left her with no money and a child, in this instance, Greville played the part of a proper eighteenth-century gentleman.

Emma resisted Greville's plan. As Emma became increasingly aware that she was a pawn in Greville's larger game and that he had no intention of coming to retrieve her, Emma's letters became very angry. In one of her letters, she wrote: 'Oh, if you knew what pain I feil in reading those lines where you advise me to W[hore] nothing can express my rage, I am all madness.' Emma continued, 'if I was with you, I would murder you & myself boath.'[34] This threat probably had little effect on Greville. He wanted to attract a wealthy wife, and if this meant upsetting a mistress who he had grown tired of, then, for Greville, it was a price worth paying. Greville believed that he was to finally achieve the life he deserved, one in which he had a fashionable house and a wealthy wife capable of providing him with the money to pursue his interests. In this, Greville would be disappointed. Greville would fail to secure the hand of Henrietta or any other heiress, and the closest thing he had to children were his collections of antiques, rocks and plants, which he loved and nurtured with much care.[35]

By choosing to fight for their relationship, Emma threatened to upend Greville's plans. She told Greville that, 'it is not in your interest to disoblige me, for you don't know the power I have here. Only I will never be his mistress. If you affront me, I will make him marry me.'[36] This must have caused Greville some distress, for his whole happy life depended upon being Hamilton's heir. If Emma married Sir William and had a child, Greville would inherit nothing, and his entire future life and plans would be ruined. Greville refused to budge. He must have been fairly confident that Sir William would not risk his carefully cultivated reputation by marrying so far below his dignity. He would have also been aware that as a senior government official, Sir William would need the king's blessing to marry. Greville would have been fairly certain that his uncle would not risk his career by asking the Crown to permit him to marry his mistress, who happened to be a coal miner's daughter and may have been a former prostitute. Furthermore, Greville must have been aware of the rumours concerning Sir William's impotency (which, in the eighteenth century, commonly meant not a failure to form an erection but rather an inability to sire children) so a marriage, while improbable (since if the rumours were true it would most likely be childless) would not have been a disaster for him.[37]

Realising that Greville had shunted her aside and that she was stuck in a foreign country with no one to care for her other than Sir William, Emma eventually relented and became Hamilton's mistress. Emma revelled in the lax attitude of the court of Naples. No longer expected to act as a meek and 'reformed' woman spending her time cleaning and keeping accounts, Emma could now be more of her 'true' self. Despite this change, Sir William, like his nephew, also wanted to reshape Emma to suit his purposes and preferences. Unlike Greville, Hamilton did not want to keep Emma to himself but wanted an accomplished mistress that he could show off, and that would help him entertain both local and foreign dignitaries.

Hamilton believed that Emma needed instruction on how to behave to be certain that she best met his expectations. He began by purchasing her new clothes that ensured that she wore both what was fashionable at the court in Naples and would impress English travellers and officials. He also sought out and employed tutors who would help Emma learn a plethora of skills, including how to sing and dance. Proud of his pupil, Hamilton boasted about how quickly Emma learned her lessons.[38] These new clothes and lessons helped shape Emma into Hamilton's perfect mistress, one that could share the burdens of entertaining. Emma, ever the chameleon, once again appeared fully transformed.

Emma's ability to adapt allowed her to become one of Naples' most recognisable and celebrated figures. She had even caught the attention of the king. Worried that rejecting the king would hurt Sir William's position at court, Emma acted as if she did not understand the king's obvious overtones. This caught the attention of Queen Maria Carolina, the sister of Marie Antoinette, who, seeing her as a woman of quality and worthy of trust, admitted Emma into her inner circle.[39] Emma had become Sir William's perfect mistress, powerful, beautiful, and able to enhance his reputation and position at court. Having fallen madly in love with Emma, Hamilton risked his career by seeking permission to marry his mistress. After meeting with and securing the king's approval, Hamilton and Emma married in September 1791.

As the example of Emma has shown, Georgian men did not need to find the perfect mistress, for they could select a woman close to their liking and attempt to reform her to better suit their preferences. Professional women were expected to adapt to the wishes of their patron, including how to act and what clothes to wear. Leading Georgians saw nothing wrong with trying to 'improve' their mistress, and some men really enjoyed the process of reshaping a woman to suit their preferences. Success as a professional mistress relied, in part, upon being able to adapt and conform to your patron's desires and preferences. There is little doubt that, in addition to her good looks and engaging personality, Emma's chameleon-like nature contributed to her success as a mistress. Ever the actress, Emma could play any part, from wild Emma to Greville's lover/housewife and maid, to Hamilton's entertaining and captivating mistress, to the respectable Lady Hamilton. As we will see, Emma changed once more as she became the famous mistress of the naval hero Horatio Nelson.

CHAPTER SIX

An Affair Should Not Upset a Leading Georgian's Spouse or Hurt Their Reputation

Georgians were well aware that an extra-marital relationship must never threaten the viability of a marriage nor result in either spouse feeling slighted or pushed aside. When a man put his mistress before his wife, he committed a great crime, and both participants could be ostracised for their behaviour. A wife who put her lover above her husband or made him appear weak might find herself banished from elite society. As the bedrock of the Georgian state and society, marriage remained the best vehicle for passing wealth through generations, cementing family alliances, and producing legitimate lords and ladies. Not treating or at least appearing to treat your spouse well was considered a major social transgression, one that upset the delicate balance of aristocratic culture. For leading Georgians, an important aspect of treating one's spouse appropriately meant managing their extra-marital affair so that they neither hurt their spouse nor their reputation.

Some men could not or would not manage their affairs properly. Richard Brinsley Sheridan was one such man. A talented playwright and owner of Drury Lane theatre, Sheridan had fallen madly in love with Henrietta (Harriet) Ponsonby (née Spencer).[1] From the very beginning, Sheridan's relationship with Harriet had been improper. They both seemed too invested and lacked an awareness of how their relationship made their spouses feel. While the Sheridans had adopted the moral code of the beau monde (especially those of the leading Whigs of the period) and each enthusiastically indulged in extra-marital affairs, neither Sheridan nor his wife Elizabeth (née Linley) mastered the art of aristocratic indifference.[2] The intensity of Sheridan's relationship with Harriet worried Elizabeth, who begged her husband to end the affair. Hoping to appease his wife, Sheridan promised to do so but instead continued to 'visit' Harriet.

To make matters worse, Sheridan, who in the past had room in his life for both his wife and his mistress, no longer shared his wife's bed, breaking an important rule of having an affair.[3] No affair should displace a husband or wife or prevent them from appearing as a happily married couple. Although both she and Sheridan had been unfaithful, Elizabeth now felt as if something had changed, as Sheridan's affairs, especially his attachment to Harriet, had become more than just a harmless fling.[4] By neglecting the duties of a husband, Sheridan had made her feel as if her 'heart is entirely alienated from him, and I see no prospect of Happiness for either of us …'[5] Tired of being mistreated, Elizabeth left the family home.

Although he refused to break with Harriet, Sheridan did wish to mend his relationship with his wife. A few complications confronted Sheridan. His wife, not wishing to see him, had gone to stay with a friend. Unlikely to heed any summons to come see him, Sheridan resolved to travel to her. Unfortunately for Sheridan, Elizabeth was visiting Frances Crewe, a woman with whom Sheridan had previously had a relationship.[6] Despite the awkwardness, Sheridan judged that he should go to his wife and apologise for the scandal and embarrassment he caused. While pleading his case, Sheridan, who seemed to have lacked any restraint, took a liking to and subsequently pursued Crewe's governess. A few days into the visit, his wife stated that 'the whole house' had witnessed her husband 'locked up with her [the governess] in a bed chamber in an unfrequented part of the house'.[7] Sheridan sleeping, or trying to sleep, with the governess while there to apologise to Elizabeth for his indiscretions demonstrates a lack of regard for not only his wife but Harriet as well. Instead of participating in a bit of gallantry, Sheridan had become a remorseless rake whose actions hurt his reputation and trampled upon the dignity of others.

Frustrated with, and embarrassed by, Harriet's very public relationship with Sheridan, Harriet's husband, Frederick Ponsonby, Viscount Duncannon (in 1793, he became the 3rd Earl of Bessborough) threatened to seek a divorce. While some chose to ignore a wife's indiscretions and could act above such matters, for Duncannon it was clear that he did care and so his lack of control over his wife, and their growing financial difficulties (they both gambled more than they could afford to lose), made him appear weak and unmanly. Divorce would not only have rid Duncannon of a wife whose actions continued to embarrass him but would allow him to pursue an heiress whose dowry might ameliorate his money problems.

Worried that his sister-in-law's marital situation was distressing his pregnant wife and that a divorce would hurt his family's reputation, William Cavendish, 5th Duke of Devonshire, travelled from Brussels to England to save his sister-in-law's marriage. The duke was not the only concerned party. Despite how poorly Sheridan had treated her, Sheridan's wife, Elizabeth, worried that if Duncannon went forward with his plans her misbehaving husband would become, 'an object of Ridicule and Abuse to all the World'.[8] The duke believed the marriage could be saved, if he could get Harriet to agree to leave Sheridan. Although Harriet signalled her willingness to 'break' with Sheridan, getting Duncannon to reconcile proved more difficult. Desperate to keep the couple together and avoid scandal, Devonshire capitalised on Duncannon's deep love and respect for his father by suggesting that such a public fight might hasten the demise of his elderly father. Not wishing to upset or embarrass his father, Duncannon promised not to proceed with the divorce, at least while his father drew breath,. He even agreed to travel with Harriet and the duke to Brussels to demonstrate that a reconciliation had occurred. All involved hoped that such a public gesture would prevent any further gossip or speculation.[9] The duke's efforts largely held, and while Harriet would go on to have other affairs, most notably with Granville Leveson-Gower (later Viscount and then Earl of Granville), she remained married to Duncannon until her death in 1821. Duncannon, who survived Harriet by more than twenty-three years, never remarried.

Knowing the importance of having a good reputation, men of the middling sort accused of having an affair might go to great lengths to protect their names and reputations. Men were known to fight rumours about their alleged infidelities by taking out advertisements in the paper to publicly deny any impropriety in the hopes of restoring a besmirched reputation. Historian Joanne Bailey provides an example of a railway manager who, having been accused of having an affair with a married woman, took out an advertisement in the newspaper denying that he had engaged in relations with another man's wife.[10] This advertisement was not aimed solely at soothing his wife and a potentially angry husband but also to assure his customers and his employer that he had done nothing wrong and that he remained a trustworthy man and employee.

Arriving in Naples after his victory at the Battle of the Nile, Horatio Nelson became so besotted with Emma Hamilton that he failed to adhere to many of the rules of having an affair, and this would ultimately harm his reputation. Consumed by their love for one another, Nelson and Emma embarked on a long and very public relationship. Neither showed any discretion and, despite being married to other people, would flaunt their love for one another. As rumours of Nelson and Emma's relationship grew, his friends began to lament what they saw as Nelson's lack of sense and worried about its effect on his reputation and future career. The perceived age difference between Emma (born in 1765) and Nelson (born in 1758) did not help. Although only seven years older than Emma, Nelson's years at sea had prematurely aged him, giving him a rough and burnt appearance. Nelson had the use of only one eye, had lost many of his teeth, and his right arm. Cartoonists were keen to depict him as a blind old man salivating over the young and beautiful Emma.[11] Concerned about Nelson's behaviour and relationship with Emma, William Young, a Lord of the Admiralty, in a letter to Lord Keith, the commander-in-chief of the Mediterranean Fleet, wrote: 'that he was grieved that a man [Nelson] who on other occasions had done so well, should have exposed himself to ridicule and censure'.[12]

By not following the rules and flaunting their relationship, Emma and Nelson did much to open themselves to criticism. Charles Lock, Consul-General for Naples, criticised Emma's 'unbounded power' over Nelson and suggested that their relationship rendered Nelson 'the laughing stock of the whole fleet'.[13] Sir Thomas Troubridge, a man whom Nelson had once considered 'the very best sea officer in His Majesty's Service', also disapproved of Nelson's relationship with Emma and tried to remind Nelson of his obligations and the importance, especially for an active naval officer, of maintaining a good reputation.[14] Troubridge was right to be concerned: Nelson's lack of tact and unwillingness to abide by the rules of having an affair had made some wonder about his judgment and whether he could be trusted as a naval commander.

Georgian men were expected to always be in control, especially over 'their' women. This included their wives and mistresses. Unfortunately for Nelson and his reputation, he seemed powerless to control Emma. Lady Elgin believed that, 'Lady H. has made him [Nelson] do many very foolish things.'[15] The stark contrast in physical appearance may have been the first thing that one noticed about the couple, but for those who had spent time with Emma and Nelson it was their strikingly different personalities that really stood out. While Nelson ate little and rarely gambled, only doing so for small stakes and to be sociable, Emma ate much and gambled even more. Despite his best efforts, Nelson could not moderate Emma's behaviour. In failing to curb these appetites, Nelson could not uphold one of the rules of having an affair: a patron should always be (or at least appear to be) in control. Despite Nelson's frequent admonishments to follow him to bed, Emma would gamble into the early morning while Nelson either gave up and went to bed alone or, as happened on at least one occasion, after failing to convince her to come to bed but unwilling to go without her, he fell asleep at the table. Nelson could not control Emma's gambling, and, some nights, she would gamble away not only her own money but whatever monies Nelson had in front of him as well.[16] This did not go unnoticed. Worried about the gossip spreading, Troubridge warned Nelson, 'The gambling of the people at Palermo is talked of everywhere. I beseech your Lordship, leave off. Lady H_____'s character will suffer; nothing can prevent people from talking; a Gambling Woman in the eyes of an Englishman is lost.'[17] Nelson could not change Emma and once stated that because of her extravagance, out-of-control spending, and gambling that, 'when he was dead she would be a beggar'.[18] Nelson's failure to regulate Emma's behaviour and his obvious attachment to her violated important rules on how to properly conduct an affair which not only hurt his reputation but if some of his colleagues were to be believed, his career as well.

One of the greatest violations of the rules of having an affair was to enrich your mistress while impoverishing your wife. Despite his often-repeated claims of poverty and extensive efforts to increase his income, Nelson, although ignoring many of the rules of having an affair, understood the importance of continuing to pay for his wife's maintenance after falling in love with Emma Hamilton. Nelson ensured that Fanny received a quarterly allowance of £400 – half his yearly income. Nelson understood that paying for his wife's maintenance was an important, if only partial, measure in trying to protect his reputation as a gentleman. He may have also felt that since Fanny had done nothing wrong, she was entitled to the money.[19] He also allowed Fanny to remain at Roundwood, a home near Ipswich, which he purchased for £2,000 in 1797.[20] Because of his service at sea coupled with his desire to be with Emma and not Fanny, Nelson never spent a single night at there.[21]

While Fanny accepted the quarterly allowance, what she really wanted was her husband back. After receiving her first payment in January 1801, Fanny wrote her husband a note of thanks, and having heard that Nelson was suffering from a bout of eye pain caused by an old injury and aware that Emma was away, she offered to care for him. At its root, this extraordinary letter was from a wife seeking permission (she did not dare to show up unannounced) from her husband to tend to his wounds while his mistress was away. Nelson, who despised being reminded that he had a wife, responded coldly, telling her that whether he was blind or in perfect health that his well-being was none of her concern.[22] As Nelson tried to ignore the fact that he was married he stopped reading her letters and instructed his secretary that all future correspondence be returned to her unopened. On one occasion, in December 1801, when one of Fanny's letters was purportedly opened by accident, Nelson instructed his private secretary to write on the letter that it had been opened in error but had not been read.[23] The message was clear: Nelson wished neither to think about nor hear from Fanny, and it was best if they both ignored the fact that they were married. By attempting to supplant his wife with his mistress, Nelson broke a fundamental rule of having an affair, and this behaviour did not go unnoticed: his reputation as a naval officer and gentleman was negatively impacted.

Georgians understood that marriage was for life and that an affair should never challenge the centrality of marriage, make one's spouse feel neglected, or negatively impact one's reputation. If an affair threatened the bonds of matrimony, the participants were expected to stop, or they risked hurting their reputations. A wife's affair should not challenge her husband's authority, and a husband should never make his wife feel as if she had been pushed aside. If the couple had children (which, of course, was expected of all wealthy and privileged Georgians), the affair should not threaten the stability and tranquillity of the home or the passing of wealth and privilege from one generation to the next. If they did not have children, the propagation of heirs must come before any extra-marital activities. Ultimately, an affair should add and not detract from a marriage.

CHAPTER SEVEN

The Trouble with Getting too Attached

As a small and exclusive group tied together by shared interests, culture and class privilege, it was paramount that members of the Georgian elite got along. Friendships, patronage networks – and even the government – were held together by civility, and this meant that, as a group, England's elite must get on or at least pretend to. For this reason, members of England's ruling elite were expected to adhere to the rules of having an affair and accept the ending of any relationship with grace. It was a clear violation of the rules of having an affair to make the ending of a relationship impact society. It not only caused awkwardness but also suggested that a relationship had become more than a bit of fun and, for married individuals, indicated that the affair had violated another rule by threatening the bonds of marriage. Making a scene, acting the part of the scorned lover, allowing jealousy to upset the tranquillity of their affair, marriage, or causing a family dispute was in nobody's interest. Affairs certainly had their place, but ultimately an affair was supposed to be a bit of fun, not a lifelong commitment. Georgians who fell in love with their lover or allowed jealousy to take hold were on a dangerous path, one that could not only negatively impact their reputation and marriage but, by violating the rules of having an affair, could lead to them being ostracised by society.

One of the most important features of having an affair was to accept when it was over. No one profited from acting the part of the scorned lover whose outbursts only drew more attention to the relationship. Despite the importance of not making a scene, some men could not accept the ending of a relationship with grace. Richard Brinsley Sheridan was one such man. This should come as no surprise, as Sheridan was widely known to take anything that did not go his way poorly. As we have discussed, Sheridan had long cared for and had a previous relationship with Harriet Ponsonby. She had moved on; he had not. After Granville Leveson-Gower (later Viscount and Earl Granville) had been posted to Russia in 1804, Sheridan assumed that he would once again be the prime man in her life. Having outgrown the hard-drinking and increasingly bitter Sheridan, Harriet spurned his attempts to rekindle their relationship. Sheridan responded by secretly attacking her and her family via the press, with both the *Courier* and the *Morning Post* producing articles that hinted that Harriet's husband and her niece, also named Harriet, were romantically involved. Distraught over the attack in the press, Harriet demanded to see the anonymous letters to verify their existence and, if they did exist, on the off chance that she could recognise the penmanship. On seeing the letters, Harriet knew immediately that Sheridan had written them.[1] This strengthened Harriet's desire to avoid him.

Sheridan refused to give up and continued to try and re-establish his relationship with Harriet. In July 1805, the two attended the same ball. Angered and saddened by Sheridan's attack on her family and his refusal to accept that she did not want a relationship with him, Harriet chose to ignore Sheridan. Given the tight confines of Georgian high society, avoiding him completely was not possible. Rather than take the hint, Sheridan resorted to sitting across from Harriet and staring at her, hoping to elicit some sort of response. Uncomfortable and tired of his antics, Harriet decided to leave the ball. As she walked by Sheridan's table, he reached up and grabbed her by the arm, demanding to know why she no longer treated him as a friend. Baited into speaking to Sheridan, Harriet told him, 'his own sagacity might explain to him why I never would, and that his conduct tonight did not tend to alter my determination.'[2] Undeterred and driven by drink and desperation, Harriet reported that Sheridan loudly declared that, 'he had never ceased loving, respecting and adoring me, and that I was the only person he ever really loved.'[3] Astonished by Sheridan's behaviour, Harriet nearly fainted.[4] Sheridan had broken two cardinal rules. He allowed himself to fall in love and made himself appear rather foolish. Sheridan's pride and his wilful disregard of the rules ended up causing a scene and would create discord and hard feelings. Had he simply adhered to the rules of having an affair, no one would have been hurt. Sheridan never really gave up on Harriet, and his growing obsession prompted the sickly Sheridan to state that he hoped his ghost would haunt her. 'Because,' declared Sheridan, 'I am resolved you shall remember me.'[5] Having troubled her so much during his life, Harriet reportedly wondered why he wished to continue to do so in death.[6] Sheridan died three days after stating that he hoped to haunt Harriet.

Sheridan's jealousy caused him to lose all perspective, resulting in unnecessary emotional turmoil for not only Harriet but her family and his own wife as well. Jealousy is one of the most destructive sentiments within any relationship and since most members of the Georgian elite were married, everyone knew full well that their married lover had an open and liberal perspective when it came to practising monogamy. Jealousy not only undermined a marriage but could also detract from the pleasures of having an affair.

The correspondence between Emma Hamilton and Horatio Nelson provides insights into the ways in which jealousy could strain an extra-marital affair. Emma and Nelson struggled to align their passion and deep love of one another with their marital situations and his naval career, which often kept them apart. Nelson's intense passion for Emma while at home could present itself as jealousy when he was posted at sea. His deepest fear was that Emma would fall in love with a younger man, a fear that had once concerned her husband, Sir William Hamilton (evidently, rightly so). Nelson was twenty-eight years younger than Hamilton but still seven years older than Emma and with a much-aged appearance from his arduous times at sea. He worried, to the point of near insanity, that she would leave him.

In 1801, when Nelson heard that the Hamiltons were to host a dinner for George Augustus, a man who had previously shown an interest in Emma, a panicked and paranoid Nelson wrote letter after letter to Emma demanding that she not see the prince. As Nelson put it: 'DO NOT let the lyar come,' and 'Do not let the rascal in.'[7] He created multiple scenarios in which the prince would win over Emma. Nelson imagined that the Prince of Wales would sit next to her at the table, flirt with her trying to scheme a way to be alone with Emma. Nelson cautioned Emma not to fall for his flattery or protestations of friendship, warning her repeatedly that the prince fully intended to take her as his mistress. Nelson's anguish is evident when he wrote to Emma: 'Oh God! that I was dead' and that he has 'gone almost mad' over the situation.[8]

Nelson's letters accused Emma of being a fool for not knowing the prince's true intentions and predicted that she would give in to the prince. As Nelson put it, he did not believe that 'even Emma' could 'resist the serpent's flattering tongue'.[9] Nelson also worried that Emma's husband, Lord Hamilton, would encourage the affair as a means of gaining favour with the prince.[10] The son of a duke, Hamilton surely understood what an alliance with the prince could mean. Given his name, pedigree and service to the Crown, Hamilton would not have been wrong to think that befriending the future king might land him his own noble title. Driven to despair, Nelson could not prevent himself from writing threatening words that wished the prince ill. For instance, he wrote: 'God strike him blind if he looks at you.'[11] Nelson understood the risk he took by putting this to paper, pointing out that such utterances were 'high treason and you may get me hanged by revealing it'.[12] While cognisant that he should not commit such things to paper, Nelson seemed oblivious or simply not to care about the effect that such harsh words had on Emma. In response to Nelson's onslaught, a distraught Emma took to her bed complaining of headaches.[13]

Nelson's fears were such that they had an almost hypnotic or crazed effect upon him. Thoughts of losing Emma stalked him as he slept, engendering troubled dreams in which he acted violently towards her. After hours of disturbed sleep, Nelson wrote to Emma to inform her that, 'I dreamt last night that I hurt you with a Stick on account of that fellow [George, Prince of Wales] & then attempted to throw over [your] head a tub of hot water, I awoke in agony …'[14] One cannot be sure whether Nelson had such dreams or not but his decision to tell Emma suggests that he wanted her to know how crazed his love for her was and may have been an attempt to threaten her into remaining faithful to him.

Having considered his options, Sir William ultimately chose a happy home over ambition and cancelled the dinner with the prince, citing Emma's poor health. In an effort to sort out the situation with Emma's lover, Hamilton wrote to Nelson assuring him that he had nothing to worry about for he well understood the situation and 'the danger that would attend the prince's frequenting our house, not that I fear that Emma could ever be induced to act contrary to the prudent conduct she has hitherto pursued, but the world is so ill-natured that the worst construction is put upon the most innocent actions'.[15] This is an extraordinary situation in that a husband is writing to his wife's lover to assure him of his wife's faithfulness and love of him. Their interaction on this matter reveals the complicated nature of the relationship between Nelson, Sir William and Emma, while demonstrating not only the power and respect that could be afforded to an extra-marital relationship but also underscoring how flexible Georgian marriages could be. However, we should remember that despite such flexibility, the bonds of matrimony were to be respected. Emma had always been clear: she would not leave Sir William. While Nelson liked Hamilton, he occasionally voiced thoughts of Hamilton's death which, forgetting about his wife Fanny, in Nelson's mind, meant that he and Emma could get married. Nelson once wrote: 'If your uncle [code for Hamilton] would die, then he [Nelson] would instantly come and marry you …'[16] Nelson's passion for Emma knew no bounds and led Nelson to lose all perspective.

Emma also worried about Nelson's fidelity. Before becoming entangled with Emma, Nelson had been faithful to his wife in the tradition that was expected of a naval man. When he was posted at sea, no one really expected him to refrain from sexual activities.[17] It is said that in the past, Nelson had at least one dedicated mistress and would find other distractions while on shore duty.[18] This was the norm. We know from his friend Richard Bulkeley that Nelson had entertained women while posted in the Mediterranean. Anticipating Nelson's return to England after a long absence, Bulkeley wrote to his friend:

> For one part of the many things said of you, you may have some reason to be vain, for it has begot you the prayers & praises of the fair sex who *all* impatiently await your return, each hoping that she may be the one of the select

> few who are to become slaves to your amorous passion. I mention this that you may come back to us determined to gratify your own country women as much as you have by all accounts others in *your* Italian states.[19]

Despite such remarks, Nelson had always been more focused on finding love and a wife than looking for a good time.[20]

While quick to tell Emma all his fears and to share his concerns that she might leave him, Nelson would become angry when she revealed similar concerns to him. Nelson took any suggestion that he might not be faithful as an attack on his honour and dedication to her and would respond harshly. Responding, presumably, to her complaint that he too often and too fondly spoke of other women, Nelson claimed that it was normal for him to write about the other women he met and asked how his mentioning other women was any different from when she commented upon the appearance of other men. On one occasion, the frustrated naval hero wrote: 'Suppose I did say that the West country women wore black stockings, what is it more than if you was to say what puppies all the present young men are? You cannot help your eyes, and God knows I cannot see much.'[21] Nelson claimed that Emma had nothing to worry about and that his faithfulness and devotion to her was above reprove. Indeed, he once told Emma that he could be, 'trusted with fifty virgins naked in a dark room'.[22]

Since affairs were supposed to be just a bit of fun, those who developed deep feelings of affection could struggle to maintain their relationship and keep it within the rules of priority. Despite their feelings of insecurity, Emma and Nelson were utterly devoted to one another, but given the realities of their situation, including being married to other people coupled with Nelson's long absences and dangerous job, if they wanted their relationship to succeed, they had to trust in one another. Their difficulty in doing so impacted them both and caused frustration, worry and discord among much joy, love and mutual admiration,. This unresolved tension and jealousy detracted from the fun of having an affair.

Having fallen madly in love with the famous poet Lord Byron, Harriet Ponsonby's (née Spencer) daughter Caroline followed in her mother's footsteps by engaging in an affair that not only produced much gossip but would ultimately hurt her reputation. A dramatic and emotional person, Caroline, or Caro as she was often called, seemed determined to flaunt the rules of having an affair regardless of the consequences. When the relationship ended, Lady Caroline Lamb's refusal to acknowledge that the celebrated poet had moved on would, as we shall see, cause much upheaval and awkwardness. Her continued efforts to rekindle their relationship only served to further embarrass Harriet, her husband and her family and would ultimately ruin her reputation, resulting in an extended period of social exile.

Having married William Lamb in 1805, Caroline had become the daughter-in-law of the ambitious Lady Melbourne. A force of nature who closely monitored her family's interests, Lady Melbourne worked tirelessly to support the ambitions of her sons and would do almost anything to promote them. While the marriage to Caroline had been important to the relatively newly minted Lamb family, Lady Melbourne worried that Caroline's dramatic and volatile nature, her unpredictable behaviour, and her propensity to ignore the rules of the society, would hurt her son's political career.[23]

Lady Melbourne was right to be concerned; Caroline and her current passion, Byron, rather than try and hide their relationship, flaunted their 'love' in public. Decorum demanded that Caroline and Byron at least try to be discreet, even if everyone knew of the relationship. This was all the more important because of Melbourne's political career. This sort of behaviour did not reflect well on Caroline and may have encouraged others to think poorly of Lord Melbourne or, for the more open-minded and compassionate, to worry about the happiness of their marriage. Given her reckless behaviour, some must have wondered whether Caroline had become so dissatisfied with marriage that she purposely set out to ruin Melbourne's reputation and career. A man willing to challenge and ignore convention when it suited him, Byron, aware of the gossip their relationship had generated, blamed Caroline for their social lapses and lack of discretion and even took to lecturing her about the need for her to maintain a sense of proper decorum.[24] He knew she had become too attached, and he was in way too deep.

While Byron's desire for Caroline had once burnt hot, the mercurial poet just as quickly tired of her and her reckless behaviour and began distancing himself from her. Refusing to take the hint or accept the ending of their relationship, Caroline continued to try and see Byron. When she did gain access to him, she would make a scene by showering him with professions of devotion and eternal love. Byron remained unmoved. Devastated by their break-up, Caroline had little interest in food, lost weight and began to look unwell. Worried about his wife, Melbourne hoped that a trip to Ireland would mend her spirits while preventing further gossip or public embarrassment. The distance did little to cool the relationship as Byron, who must have enjoyed toying with Caroline's emotions, continued to write to her. This gave her false hope, and predictably, when she returned to England, she tried to rekindle their relationship. When she returned, Byron, who, as Lord Broughton put it, was 'very popular with all the ladies …', told Caroline that he had no interest in resuming their physical relationship.[25] Caroline, as she had done before, continued to seek out his company.

Caroline's refusal to accept the ending of the relationship, coupled with her dogged trailing of Byron, had worn the poet's nerves raw. Events came to a head on 6 July 1813 at Lady Heathcote's Ball when Caroline tried, once again, to remind Byron of the love and passion they had once shared. Completely unmoved, Byron refused to admit that he had done anything wrong and made it clear that he wanted nothing more to do with her. His coldness stunned Caroline. In her desperation to elicit an emotional response from Byron, she grabbed a butter knife. Byron told her that if she was going to go Roman, she should aim for her own heart as she had already struck his. Upset with his uncaring language, she reportedly broke a wine glass and tried to slash her wrist.[26] By making a scene, Caroline embarrassed herself, Byron and her husband, who could no longer act as if his wife had not formed an emotional attachment to another man. For married members of the elite, to have an affair was to accept that these relationships were supposed to be fleeting. Forming an emotional attachment to another person challenged the permanency of marriage and the notion that an affair was just a bit of harmless fun.

While Caroline's actions made for good gossip, her behaviour could not be tolerated. After the party, even her friends began to question Caroline's mental state. The famous epitaph she devised for Byron, that he was, 'mad, bad and dangerous to know', could now just as easily be applied to her.[27] By making a scene, Harriet had effectively banished herself from polite company, and the only way back for her was to offer a full apology and to demonstrate how sorry she was for her behaviour.

Caroline refused to act with contrition. Instead of apologising or trying to minimise the scene she had caused at the ball, Caroline used her time in exile to strike back at those she felt had wronged her. She continued to write about Byron and most famously wrote *Glenarvon*. Published in 1816, *Glenarvon* is a thinly veiled attack on certain members of society, including Byron and Lady Jersey. Unhappy victims responded to Caroline's characterisation by further blocking her from polite society. Lady Jersey, for instance, cancelled Caroline's voucher (basically, an admittance ticket) to the famous social club, Almack's.[28] Worse, fearing for her son's political career and tired of Caroline's behaviour, her mother-in-law pushed to have Caroline deemed mentally incompetent and placed within an asylum. Despite the scandal, William wanted no part of his mother's plan.[29] Caroline and William would, in 1825, after twenty years of marriage, agree to a formal separation. After their separation, Caroline's health began to rapidly decline. Although much had passed between the couple, Melbourne, in 1828, braved the fifteen-hour trip to Ireland to be by her side as she passed away.[30]

Well aware of the rules of having an affair, Caroline chose to ignore them. Something within her, whether guilt, petulance, extreme unhappiness, or arrogance, caused her to so brazenly flout society's conventions. In her passion for Byron, Caroline abandoned all discretion. Driven by anger and bitterness over the break-up, she lost her bearings and lashed out at society. While her disappointment in how her life turned out is understandable, her reactions to being marginalised by the fashionable are not. She knew the rules and chose to disregard them.

Even courtesans sometimes struggled emotionally after ending a relationship. Despite being a professional, Sophia Baddeley did not handle the ending of her relationship with John Hanger well. Sophia fell in love with John, who, as a son of an impoverished lord, could not provide for her. Try as the couple might to make it work, John, whom she called Gaby, simply could not afford a kept woman and certainly not one with Sophia's expensive tastes.[31] Not willing to end the relationship, Sophia eschewed the professional ethics of the period and used her own money to fund their life together. While a select number of courtesans managed to have a long career, most had just a small window to acquire enough wealth to support them for the rest of their lives. Sophia could not waste these precious years on the son of a poor Irish peer who had little money and few prospects. If Sophia and her fellow courtesans spent their best years with men who could not afford to set them up in life, they would end up being the one with empty pockets and few prospects. Chasing after love rather than wealth, Sophia lost all perspective. The lovebirds imprudently ran up £700-worth of debt. Worried about upsetting his disapproving father, John once again told Sophia that he could not afford her and advised that they part company.[32] With much reluctance Sophia agreed, and the two separated.

Having made the mistake of falling in love, Sophia suffered from the separation. Upset and unable to sleep, Sophia turned to laudanum. One night, still despairing over John, Sophia overdosed on the drug. According to her long-time companion, Mrs Steele, the near-fatal dose rendered her unable to walk for many weeks and bestowed upon her a lifelong susceptibility to bilious complaints.[33] Luckily for her, young, vibrant and still a desired partner, Sophia had the time, if she was prudent, to fix her financial situation. Courtesans had rules too, including the importance of taking care of yourself, making sure not to let emotions blind your judgment, and earning and saving as much as possible to sustain yourself through what could be a long retirement. From this perspective, ending the relationship with an impoverished patron proved a lucky escape.

As we have seen, it was essential to accept the ending of a relationship with grace. This often proved problematic when another rule of having an affair – do not fall in love – was violated. Since their careers were so short, professional mistresses needed to ensure that they placed financial considerations above emotional ones. Falling in love with the wrong man, especially one incapable of providing for them, could have disastrous repercussions and leave them little money for what could be a long retirement. For members of the ton, developing an emotional attachment challenged the notion that an affair was just a bit of fun and made it much more likely that the relationship would negatively affect their marriage, career and status. Becoming too attached could also allow feelings of jealousy to develop, which could make an affair stressful rather than enjoyable. One only has to look at the correspondence between Horatio Nelson and Emma Hamilton to see the emotional distress caused by bouts of jealousy. Those who became emotionally attached risked a great deal since, as will be covered in the next chapter, the punishments for breaking the rules of having an affair could be harsh (especially for women), and the road to redemption (often only partial) could be long and tortuous.

CHAPTER EIGHT

Must Stay Committed to the Marriage

One of the worst crimes two lovers could commit was to try and form their own exclusive relationship. This often involved leaving the family home by running away with one's lover. Considered one of the greatest violations of having an affair, running away with one's lover struck at the heart of the Georgian state and society. It undermined the accepted norm that an affair was just a bit of harmless fun while highlighting some of the serious repercussions that could occur when lovers did not follow the rules of having an affair. It also challenged the patriarchal attitudes which governed the Georgian state, as by running away with her lover, a wife sent a clear message that she was, and wished to be, outside the control of her husband. Running away with one's lover was an extreme action which, in the Georgian period, often created much gossip and, for women, inevitably led to a loss of reputation and severe punishment, including being barred from society. Men who ran away with another man's wife were often treated less severely socially but did risk financial repercussions for their actions.

This unfortunate situation happened to the Worsleys when Lady Worsley, believing she was above the rules, ran away with her lover, Maurice George Bisset. The trouble began sometime in 1780. By this point, the wealthy heiress, Seymour Worsley (née Fleming), had been married to Sir Richard for five years and had given birth to a son and heir. After a happy start to their lives together, the couple increasingly drifted apart. Sir Richard desired a peerage and spent his time improving his family's reputation and standing, while Seymour wished to have fun and enjoy the wealth and privilege bestowed upon her. Looking for both fun and excitement, Seymour turned her attentions to others, including their neighbour Maurice George Bisset, her husband's friend and political ally. While Sir Richard was busy assuring himself that Bisset would support him in his political ambitions, Seymour had begun an affair with Bisset.[1]

In 1778, Worsley and Bisset's unit was ordered to Coxheath to protect against a potential French invasion. As many leading families descended upon Coxheath, the mood was better suited to a grand ball than a serious military endeavour. National attention was upon the many young aristocrats who had decided to play soldiers, and their misdeeds at camp captured the imagination of the press, cartoonists and the public. The fashion-forward Georgiana, Duchess of Devonshire, had made waves by organising a woman's corps, outfitting all her 'soldiers' in male-inspired military dress.[2] With a name perfect for wordplay, Coxheath allowed commentators to turn Cox into Cocks and to make fun of the merriment and lax attitude of the camp.[3]

At Coxheath, Bisset and Seymour were inseparable. The camp's hardworking rumour mill began to suggest that Bisset and Lady Worsley were having an affair. They certainly were not the only ones: Lady Claremont had a relationship with an apothecary (and subsequently had an abortion); Lady Jersey and the Duke of Devonshire were having an affair, while Lady Melbourne became pregnant after having a tryst with the Earl of Egremont.[4] One popular camp joke suggested that Bisset had become Seymour's aide-de-camp following her wherever she went.[5] The gossiping among his friends and colleagues did not bother Sir Richard.

He ignored any gossip concerning his wife and could even, 'laugh at the scandal'. [6] Sir Richard, as did so many of the officers, had a grand time and must have been disappointed when ordered to break camp. In 1781, Worsley and his unit were ordered back to Coxheath. By this time, however, the fashionable, rather than return to the fields of Coxheath (the fad and excitement had passed), had settled in the more comfortable accommodations provided in nearby Maidstone.[7] Desiring that Bisset would live with them, Worsley tried to think of a way that the three 'friends' could continue to keep such close quarters while in Maidstone without raising suspicions. This concern gets to the heart of having an affair in Georgian England. It was fine for Seymour and Bisset to be lovers. It was even fine that everyone knew. It was also fine that Sir Richard tolerated the affair. However, he and Lady Worsley were to appear happily married, and while a husband could tolerate and act above his wife's indiscretions, he was not supposed to encourage their coupling or to live openly with his wife's lover.

Appearances must be kept up. A husband lived with his wife or must at least appear to. Some couples worked very hard to appear to live together while rarely staying in the same house.[8] What was not, and could not, be permitted, was for your wife's lover to live with you. That challenged the illusion of a happy marriage. And appearances, more so than reality or the truth, is what truly mattered to the Georgian elite. In his desire to have Bisset close, Worsley violated the rules of having an affair. To hide that he wished Bisset to live with him and his wife, Sir Richard leased a large house that allowed him to rent rooms to Bisset. While surely not the norm, this provided adequate cover as long as no one looked too closely.[9]

Aware that his actions and desires violated accepted norms of propriety, Worsley took additional precautions to protect his reputation. Georgian elites believed themselves better and, thus, freer than most but did worry about upsetting the norms of society. In one instance, after witnessing his wife sitting on Bisset's knee while in the company of his fellow officers, Sir Richard reminded Bisset that although, 'Lady Worsley loves you,' that he, 'should not take liberties before company, because it will make idle and censorious people talk'.[10] This quote is revealing. Sir Richard had certainly encouraged Bisset and his wife, and yet he was worried about maintaining a degree of propriety. Again, it was acceptable for people to know of the relationship and even gossip about it, but it was another thing to flaunt it. This went against proper etiquette, especially since Bisset served under Worsley. Bisset's access to his commanding officer's wife could be seen as a direct challenge to Worsley's authority and standing. It is almost certain that the reference to 'idle' people refers to the leaders of society as they were the only ones who could afford not to work. To ensure that any information of their odd living arrangements did not reach the Isle of Wight, Sir Richard, instead of ordering his regular servants to Maidstone, hired a temporary crew that had no connection with his ancestral home. This ensured that whatever the servants may see or suspect would probably stay in Maidstone.[11]

On 4 August 1781, Lady Worsley gave birth to a daughter fathered by Bisset. Sir Richard still seemed to hold no animosity towards Bisset and, in March 1781, granted Bisset, the man who had impregnated his wife, a captain's commission in the South Hampshire Militia. Sir Richard accepted the daughter, named Jane Seymour Worsley, as his own.[12] This was easier to do with a daughter as she would not be entitled to any of the family's property, and Worsley's only real obligation to her would be a dowry when she married. Given Worsley's wealth and income, this was an obligation that he could easily meet. One wonders if he would have done the same if it had been a son? Yes, Worsley had a son and heir, but in the eighteenth-century, mortality rates were high, especially among children, and there was every chance that in this scenario, Bisset's offspring would be the one to inherit not only Worsley's wealth but his title. Given this, it was certainly easier for all involved that Bisset and Seymour produced a daughter.

The birth of Jane unsettled the harmony and delicate balance of the Worsley household. Increasingly, Lady Worsley began contemplating a life with Bisset, free of her husband. The only way to do so would be to obtain a divorce. The problem for the two lovers was that Sir Richard, despite his wife's growing affection for Bisset, had little reason to pursue a divorce. Sir Richard seemed uninterested in other women, already had his male heir, and was more concerned with furthering his political career and winning a peerage than with his wife's affair. He also enjoyed having Bisset as a fixture in their marriage. Sir Richard, a staunch supporter of the king, the man who had the power to give him the peerage that he so desperately wanted, knew that George III disliked divorce, preferring men who stood not only for good government but were doting husbands and fathers as well.

Blurred by passion, on the early morning of 19 November 1781, Bisset and Seymour ran away, hoping to start a new life together. Once he realised Bisset and Seymour had left him, a confused and increasingly angry Sir Richard set upon a plan to first track them down and to subsequently destroy their relationship and reputations. He told the servants that if they wished to remain employed, they would only follow his, and not his wife's, command. Hoping to maximise his wife's discomfort, Sir Richard instructed Seymour's lady's maid, Mary Sotherby, not to give his wife anything without his consent. Sir Richard knew how uncomfortable Lady Worsley would feel without her fine dresses and jewellery.[13] This was just the first step in making Bisset and Lady Worsley suffer for leaving him.

Seymour had committed one of the most egregious violations of the rules of having an affair. She had been allowed (even encouraged) to enjoy Bisset's company, and yet she still tried to replace her husband. By doing so, Seymour opened herself up to criticism and the possibility that Sir Richard would use his wealth, position and power to punish her and the man she tried to replace him with. This decision to run away with her lover shocked society and was an important step on Lady Worsley's road to ruin. As will be covered later, Sir Richard would use the courts in an attempt to destroy the finances and reputations of both his wife and her lover.

Having grown tired of her life and uninspiring husband, Sir Charles Bunbury, Sarah Bunbury (née Lennox) also decided to run away with her lover. Sarah had desperately wanted the so-called perfect life with a loving husband and a brood of children. Lacking in both by 1767, Sarah hoped that an affair might improve her spirits. Sarah enjoyed taking on new personalities and tended to extremes of behaviour. Having decided to play the part of the unfaithful wife, Sarah threw herself into the role.[14] Rumours began to spread of her unhappiness and extra-marital activities, especially her growing affection for her cousin, the dashing Lord Gordon, the second son of Cosmo, Duke of Gordon.[15] In spring 1768, Sarah announced that she was with child. Ignoring the rumours, her family prudently acted as if the child must be legitimate, sending her the warmest of congratulations.[16]

Sarah hoped for a girl. An illegitimate daughter was undoubtedly better than a boy, as a daughter had no claims on family lands and titles. This would allow a permissive husband to look the other way and pretend the child was his own, as Sir Richard Worsley had done. An illegitimate son, especially an heir, could rob an ancient family of its wealth, titles and birthright. Either unwilling or incapable of fathering a child with Sarah (neither of Bunbury's two marriages produced children), Bunbury stated that he would play the part of the father if Sarah would distance herself from Gordon.[17] Although, given the circumstances, a generous offer, tired of her marriage to Bunbury, Sarah decided on a path that flouted the rules of having an affair.

In December 1768, Sarah gave birth to a daughter named Louisa Bunbury. Although Sarah seemed happy and presented the child to her husband's family, Gordon still pulled at her heart, and after giving birth to Gordon's child, Sarah wanted to be with him even more. Sarah wished not only to be with Gordon but to see him recognise their daughter as his own and to make a family with him.[18] Sarah must have known this would not be possible and that seeking to supplant her husband was one of the greatest violations of the rules of having an affair. Nonetheless, blinded by love, passion and a desire for a new life, Sarah took the plunge and ran away with Gordon.

Realising that Sarah had left the family home, the press made much out of her situation. Although they increasingly sought to expose the intimate details of aristocratic life, journals often framed their coverage as a form of public service, one which they believed would allow the public to learn from other people's mistakes and misguided values. In 'An Address to the Public', *Bon Ton Magazine* claimed that it hoped its coverage of aristocratic misdeeds would aid in achieving moral reform:

> We are glad of this; the virtue of society it is our object to maintain; and if that virtue is polluted at the fountain head, 'The Bon Ton' will trace it to its source through all its hidden mazes and wily meanderings, drag the pollutors of the stream from their darkened cave, and hold them up to public scorn, with the statements of truth, the arguments of knowledge, and the moral lessons of genius, aimed at the heart and understanding, and meant to guard the *poor* against the vices, follies, and crimes, which, in our times, have made the terms of *rich* and *contemptible* synonymous.[19]

The Prince of Wales (future George IV) in 1781.

George IV as Prince of Wales, 1781 by Gainsborough Dupont (1754–1797) Andrew W. Mellon Collection, Courtesy National Gallery of Art, Washington, CC0.

Cartoon lampooning George IV.

King George IV and entourage laden with provisions, about to embark from Brighton in the Royal Yacht; representing the extravagant monarch's distressed retreat from England at the time of the Queen's trial. Coloured etching by R. Cruikshank, 1820. Wellcome Collection. Public Domain Mark. Source: Wellcome Collection.

Death of Horatio Nelson at Trafalgar.

The wounding of Lord Nelson on the deck of HMS Victory at the battle of Trafalgar. Engraving by Taylor after R. Corbould. Wellcome Collection. Licence: Public Domain Mark. Source: Wellcome Collection.

The attitudes of Emma Hamilton.

The Attitudes of Lady Hamilton, 1791 by Pietro Antonio Novelli, Ailsa Mellon Bruce Fund, Courtesy National Gallery of Art, Washington, CC0.

Sarah Bunbury. Sarah's decision to run away with her lover would cost her dearly.

Sir Joshua Reynolds (1723–1792), Lady Bunbury Sacrificing to the Graces, 1763–1765. The Art Institute of Chicago (CC0).

Georgiana, Duchess of Cavendish. Georgiana dominated much of the social scene and could set the fashions. Her celebrity status and gambling losses were legendary.

Valentine Green (1739–1813), Georgiana, Duchess of Devonshire, 1780. The Art Institute of Chicago (CC0).

***Above*: George I.**

King George I, head and shoulders, in profile. Engraving by J. Chereau after G. Kneller, 1714. Wellcome Collection. Public Domain Mark. Source: Wellcome Collection.

***Opposite above*: Cartoon depicting Harriette Wilson and her relationship with the Duke of Wellington.**

Henry Heath, active 1824–1835, An Exposé, or Princely Economy in Love: Illustration for Harriette Wilson's "Memoir's", 1825, Etching, hand-colored, Yale Center for British Art, Paul Mellon Collection, B1981.25.1615. – CC0.

***Opposite below*: Cartoon depicting Harriette Wilson and the Duke of Wellington, while also alluding to some of her other prominent patrons.**

Henry Heath, active 1824–1835, British, The Rat Catcher, or Symptoms of Love: Illustration's of Harriette Wilson's Memoir's (Plate I), 1825, Etching, hand-colored, Yale Center for British Art, Paul Mellon Collection, B1981.25.1610. – CC0.

Illustrations of Harriette Wilsons Memoirs— Page 138.
You took up my time for 3 Months and promised me money— but sneaked off without paying me; if you do not fulfill your promise I'll publish the Cranbourn Alley Secrets—
BOND STREET
H Heath Delt
An Exposé, or Princely Economy in Love
Pub. Aug. 27. 1825 by S.W. Fores. Piccadilly

Illustrations of Harriette Wilson's Memoirs. Pl. 1
I have paid 200£! for a kiss, and if you want more you shall have plenty, only don't quiz me
H. H. Delt
The Rat Catcher, or Symptons of Love,
Published Feb. 4. 1825 by S.W. Fores. Piccadilly

Lady Melbourne. Lady Melbourne's relationship with the future George IV likely resulted in her husband being made a Viscount.

John Finlayson, 1730–1776, British, The Right Honorable Elizabeth Lady Melbourne, 1771, Mezzotint on moderately thick, slightly textured, beige laid paper, Yale Center for British Art, Paul Mellon Collection, B1977.14.12925. – CC0.

Lord Byron. Lord Byron's affair with Caroline Lamb was one of the most talked about scandals of the period.

"The Poetical Works of Lord Byron. Complete in one volume. Collected and arranged, with illustrative notes by Thomas Moore, Lord Jeffrey, Sir Walter Scott ... &c. &c. With a portrait, etc". Published by John Murray 1845 – CC0.

Elizabeth Linley, wife of the playwright and politician Richard Brinsley Sheridan. Their extra-marital relationships caused much grief and comment during the period.

Mrs. Richard Brinsley Sheridan, 1785–1787 by Gainsborough Dupont (1754–1797) Andrew W. Mellon Collection, Courtesy National Gallery of Art, Washington, CC0.

Maria Fitzherbert was the long-time companion to the future George IV. Their marriage was not legal under English law. Maria was pushed aside so George could contract a proper and legally binding marriage.

Mrs. Fitzherbert, print, J. Cook, 1786, Harris Brisbane Dick Fund, 1917, Courtesy of the Metropolitan Museum of Art CC0.

Caroline Brunswick married the Prince of Wales (future George IV) in 1795. The two disliked each other and lived separately. Their only daughter died which allowed George's eldest surviving brother William to become King in 1830.

Caroline of Brunswick, Princess of Wales, head and shoulders. Stipple print after Cornelius Höÿer, ca. 1795. Wellcome Collection. Public Domain Mark. Source: Wellcome Collection.

William IV. William before he became King had lived with an Irish actress Dora Jordan. Jordan gave birth to ten of the future King's illegitimate children.

King William IV holding a scroll of the Magna Carta in his right hand. Mezzotint by D. Lucas after R. Bowyer, 1830. Wellcome Collection. Public Domain Mark. Source: Wellcome Collection.

***Above left*: William Hamilton, the husband of Emma (born Amy Lyon). His wife would fall in love with the famous naval hero Horatio Nelson.**

Sir William Hamilton by George Romney (1734–1802) Ailsa Mellon Bruce Collection, Courtesy National Gallery of Art, Washington, CC0.

***Above right*: Charles Francis Greville, the nephew of Sir William Hamilton. It was through Greville that Hamilton met his future wife, Emma.**

Meyer, H. (Henry Hoppner), and George Romney. *The Honourable Charles Francis Greville F.R.S. &c. &c. &c: Second Son of Francis, Earl Brooke, & Earl of Warwick. Obit, 1809*. s.n., London, 1810. Print. By permission of Llyfrgell Genedlaethol Cymru / National Library of Wales. CC – PDM 1.0.

A participant in the Beau Monde, Henrietta Ponsonby's husband threatened her with divorce.

Print made by Joseph Grozer, ca. 1755–1798, British, Viscountess Duncannon, ca. 1785, Mezzotint and etching on moderately thick, moderately textured, cream laid paper, Yale Center for British Art, Paul Mellon Fund, B1970.3.120. – CC0.

An important diplomat, Granville Leveson-Gower, 1st Earl Granville fathered two illegitimate children with Henrietta Ponsonby. He later wed Henrietta's niece Harriet Cavendish.

Sir Thomas Lawrence, 1769–1830, British, Lord Granville Leveson-Gower, later first Earl Granville, between 1804 and 1809, Oil on canvas, Yale Center for British Art, Paul Mellon Collection, B1981.25.736.CC0 – CC0.

Susannah was the unfortunate wife of Theophilus Cibber. Cibber encouraged his wife to have a relationship with the already married William Sloper in the hopes that Sloper would be willing to financially support a complicit husband.

Print made by John Faber the Younger, ca. 1695–1756, Netherlandish, active in Britain, Mrs. Cibber, Mezzotint, Yale Center for British Art, Paul Mellon Collection, B1974.12.425. CC0.

Seymour Fleming married Sir Richard Worsley in 1775. Her relationship with Maurice George Bisset led to one of the most famous criminal conversation trials of the period.

Print made by unknown artist, eighteenth century, Frances, Lady Worsley, undated, Mezzotint on medium, slightly textured, cream laid paper, Yale Center for British Art, Paul Mellon Fund, B1970.3.707. – CC0.

Lady Susan O'Brien (née Fox-Strangways). After marrying William O'Brien, an actor deemed far below her family's dignity; Lady Susan spent several years in exile.

Print made by James Watson, 1740–1790, British, Lady Susan O'Brien, 1772, Mezzotint on moderately thick, moderately textured, cream laid paper, Yale Center for British Art, Paul Mellon Fund, B1970.3.505. – CC0.

Edward, Duke of Kent. Father of Queen Victoria. Edward diligently put money aside to care for his long-time mistress Madame de Saint Laurent.

Print made by unknown artist, nineteenth century, Edward Duke of Kent, Father of Her Majesty Queen Victoria, after 1837, Line engraving with stipple on medium, smooth, white wove paper, Yale Center for British Art, Hohenzollern-Schlaberg-Hughes Collection, Gift Thomas Lowe Hughes, Yale JD 1952, B2011.12.2. – CC0.

Charles James Fox. Prominent politician whose spending and gambling losses were infamous. Fox would marry the former courtesan Elizabeth Armistead in 1795.

Print made by John Jones, ca. 1745–1797, British, The Right Honourable Charles James Fox, 1784, Mezzotint on medium, slightly textured, cream laid paper, Yale Center for British Art, Paul Mellon Fund, B1970.3.129. – CC0.

In this vein, *Town and Country*, one of the leading publishers of aristocratic gossip, asserted that they hoped that Sarah and Bunbury's situation would prevent people 'from choosing their helpmates for life from motives of false ambition or, having chosen them, to pay less attention to their wives than their horses'.[20] Husbands, so far as the *Town and Country* magazine was concerned, should spend time with their wives, for a man who ignored his wife in favour of his hobbies encouraged infidelity, and this neglect could lead to marital breakdown.

Having little control over the situation and tired of having his reputation questioned, Bunbury wanted a divorce. Not wishing to draw further attention to himself, Bunbury only went through the motions of suing the penniless Gordon for damages preferring to focus his attention on his ecclesiastical suit, which could grant him a separation of bed and board.[21] During the case, Bunbury's lawyers focused upon Gordon and Sarah's relationship leaving 'his' daughter out of it. This meant that Louisa Bunbury could be considered a legitimate child as Bunbury never publicly doubted her parentage.[22] Sarah did not contest the charges. Faced with a one-sided case, on 17 June 1769, the court found that, 'Lady Sarah Bunbury, being of a loose and abandoned disposition and being wholly unmindful of her conjugal vow, etc., did carry on a lewd and adulterous conversation with Lord William Gordon.'[23] The formal separation paved the way for Bunbury to seek a parliamentary divorce (which, unlike a separation of board and bed, would allow for remarriage even while their former spouse lived) which was granted in 1776. Six months after the formal separation, Sarah and Gordon had 'broken up', with Sarah returning to her family hoping to salvage her reputation.

Sarah had broken a fundamental rule. Her actions brought negative attention to her family, which an affair was never supposed to do. Bunbury repeatedly demonstrated that he would tolerate his wife's affairs as long as it did not hurt his reputation. His problem with Gordon was not the affair or the child but that the press made him look like a fool. In this context, he had every right to demand that she end her relationship with Gordon. According to her biographer, Stella Tillyard, had Sarah followed the rules of having an affair, she would have, after sufficient time had passed, been allowed to continue her relationship with

Gordon.[24] Although the affair and child conceived out of wedlock were newsworthy on their own, the scorn and uproar came from the fact that by running away with Gordon, Sarah attempted to supplant her husband. This could not be tolerated. At the very heart of aristocratic marriage was the need to protect property and succession; divorce threatened both of these pillars of state and society. Sarah risked all by running away with Gordon. Bunbury and the rules of the period would have let her have her cake (as a wealthy and privileged person) and eat it too (have Gordon for a lover). Sarah's refusal to play by the rules, which were generous in her case, caused unnecessary difficulties for herself and her family. Having violated the rules of having an affair, Sarah would spend years as a social outcast.

Anyone who ignored the rules of having an affair did so at their peril. While women of the beau monde could have affairs, they risked more than men, especially if their actions were judged to have violated the rules for conducting an affair. Julia Johnstone, who wrote a response to the former professional mistress Harriette Wilson's memoirs, complained of this double standard stating that:

> The world is very uncharitable! Man may commit a hundred deviations from the path of rectitude, yet he still can return, every one invites him, in sober truth, he gains an éclat by his failing, that establish him on the Ton, and make him envied, instead of pitied or despised. But woman, when she makes one false step, can retrieve it no more![25]

Because of their transgressions, many Georgians, but especially women since their 'crimes' tended to be judged more severely, had to spend significant parts of their lives in penance, waiting for a chance to return to society.[26] Even those who secluded themselves and endured years of punishment might not fully recover their reputations meaning that some places and people would forever be shut to them.

Just as there were rules for conducting an affair, those caught running afoul of these rules were expected to follow an accepted course of action that would allow for partial re-entrance into society.

After running away with Gordon, Sarah Bunbury knew that if she wished to improve her reputation that she would be expected to follow the dictates of the head of the family, her brother Charles, Duke of Richmond. Charles built a house for her on his Goodwood estate, where Sarah was expected to live out her punishment. In order to repair her reputation, Sarah would also be expected to demonstrate contrition. One of the best ways to do this was to compose letters explaining genuine concern with your previous actions while professing an honest desire to change. Her sister Louisa highlighted this point, stating that it would be prudent for Sarah to ensure to 'use disguise enough to look grave'.[27] In other words, if she were genuinely sorry, that would be most helpful, but if not, she should fake it. The Lennox family hoped that by doing so, Sarah would be forgiven and could once again join society.

Initially, Sarah would be expected to remove herself from society. It was widely believed that a woman who broke the rules of having an affair neither deserved happiness nor the comforts of society and was expected to stay near her family and avoid public places or gatherings. This was not just to punish Sarah but also because her presence, especially around young or unmarried women, could, by association, ruin their reputations. Her only contact with the outside world should be with women who had excellent reputations and were widely known for their decency and moral conduct. By associating with, and being accepted by, women with good reputations, Sarah could improve her own. Her sister Louisa cautioned her to avoid speaking to men in public and to keep away from army officers because of their reputation for seducing women. She also emphasised that Sarah should distance herself from their nephew Charles James Fox, whose 'free notions with respect to religion and women …' may further taint her by association.[28] She must also act as if all of her time was spent in penance and to describe her actions with Gordon as a sudden madness entirely out of step with her character.

Rehabilitating a reputation could be a slow and tortuous process. Having violated the rules of having an affair, it took more than a decade of virtually no social life before Sarah was allowed to partially return to her old life and some of the social circles in which she previously moved.[29] While an evening spent at the theatre or a pleasant stroll through the gardens may have allowed Sarah to feel a bit of her old self, some people and places were forever closed to her. For instance, her notoriety would prevent her from gaining an invitation to court.[30] This was the norm as, after her divorce, Lady Diana Spencer would no longer be welcomed at court.[31]

After partially rehabilitating her reputation, Sarah made a life for herself and even remarried. Remarriage, especially to a man of rank and power, could help to repair a reputation. Not all thought that a divorced woman should be able to remarry. Lady Mary Coke reported that she overheard George III asking whether something might be done to prevent adulterous women from remarrying.[32] This became an important issue, especially after Augustus FitzRoy, 3rd Duke of Grafton, George III's prime minister, had received a parliamentary divorce and his wife, the former duchess, had quickly married her lover. This prompted some to believe that the former duchess had been rewarded rather than punished for her adultery. Nothing came from this, for while the Lords seemed to support attempting to restrict remarriage, such initiatives failed to gain any traction in the Commons.[33] In 1781, Sarah married George Napier, a younger son of Francis Napier, 6th Lord Napier. They would have eight children together. Having children and being seen as motherly helped to further rehabilitate Sarah's image.

Although Sarah's story ends happily, we should not forget that she suffered years of being exiled from society after violating the rules of having an affair. Sarah knew that running away with her lover would almost certainly cause a severe reaction, and yet she still chose to ignore the rules and suffer the consequences. Whether this was rashness on her part or proves her utter dedication to getting out of a loveless marriage depends on perspective.

Running away with one's lover was an extreme action, one that rarely ended well. Although Georgians could and did have flexible marriages, the importance of marriage as a vehicle for passing wealth, titles, and, crucially, for creating legitimate children meant that matrimony needed to be respected and upheld. Central to the rules of having an affair was that the marriage must remain intact and appear happy. No one gained by undermining the institution of marriage, which explained why running away with one's lover could not be tolerated and was often severely punished. The future of England's elite and its governing families rested upon legitimacy (both actual and perceived) to ensure the successful transfer of power and wealth from one generation to the next.

CHAPTER NINE

The Difficulty of Hiding an Affair

While many of the leading men of the period enjoyed showing off their mistress, others decided it was best to keep an affair a secret. The reasons for secrecy varied but could include not wanting to anger or upset their spouse or an established mistress; a desire to be seen as a reliable family man; fears over the financial repercussions of an affair; or possibly the fact that their chosen mistress lacked in prestige and would not improve or might even hurt their reputation. Primarily a personal decision, the desire for secrecy was undoubtedly influenced by whether the relationship transgressed any of the accepted rules of having an affair. For members of the Georgian elite, so long as they conducted a 'proper' affair, they usually did not mind if their friends and certain members of their family knew of their activities, but most wished to keep it out of the newspaper, and this could encourage some people to hide their affair.

As a developing and increasingly popular form of media in Georgian England, newspapers were well aware that English people enjoyed stories about the aristocracy. The equivalent of modern-day celebrities, the press covered numerous aspects of aristocratic life, including their homes, travel, the parties they hosted and attended, and the fashions they wore. Realising that many aristocrats did not like seeing their names in print, specific segments of the press sought to profit from revealing the intimate details of aristocratic life. Magazines such as the *Town and Country Magazine*, especially its Tête-à-Tête series, sought to draw attention to the affairs of leading members of society. Introduced in 1769, the Tête-à-Tête series placed two supposed lovers side-by-side (thus the head-to-head) while speculating and commenting upon their relationship.

A purveyor of gossip, *Town and Country Magazine* privileged telling a good story over accuracy, and this led to the production of tales that could be inaccurate or sometimes completely falsified.[1] At its height, *Town and Country Magazine* had a monthly circulation of 14,000.[2] Based mainly on gossip and rooted in innuendo, there were a total of 312 Tête-à-Têtes before the ending of the series in 1792.[3] This means that numerous Georgian elites had their affairs (real or assumed) printed for all, including their friends, family and spouse, to read.

To increase revenue, newspapers offered aristocrats the chance to suppress a story or, at least, have their name omitted in return for a fee. For some members of the Georgian elite, it was not secrecy per se that they sought, but the idea that commoners may be laughing at them or their marital situation was more than some elites could bear.[4] Others resented any mention of their affairs in the press, for they hoped to keep their liaisons from their more conservative family members. For these reasons, some aristocrats literally paid for privacy. Presses in the early eighteenth century derived much of their income from these fees.[5] While such extortion may have been profitable, around the mid-century, presses moved away from the time-consuming process of extracting money from reluctant or publicity-shy aristocrats to profiting from exposing their intimate personal details to an eager public. A slew of publications began to cover the salacious details of aristocratic lives and culture, publishing stories aimed at titillating their readership with in-depth accounts of aristocratic coupling.

Desperate for any stories concerning aristocratic gossip, some newspapers created private boxes where individuals could submit scandalous stories directly to the press. This allowed jilted, jealous, or mean-spirited members of the beau monde to publicly shame one another without having their identity revealed. Printing such stories, often without actually checking the details, opened presses up to lawsuits, but the increase in circulation made publishing salacious, if sometimes wholly or partially untrue, stories worth the risk.[6]

The demand for salacious materials that contained the intimate details of aristocratic life astounded visitors to England. A traveller to England from Germany during the reign of George III noted the popularity of scandalous stories stating that, 'the most scandalous literature in London consists of the reports of crim. con. and divorce cases which are printed without expurgation. No book is asked for so frequently in the lending library and the editions, reprints and extracts from them prove their popularity.'[7] This was big business, making it worth a publisher's time to try and find and subsequently publish salacious stories.

Asserting that people had a right to privacy, some individuals questioned the morality of publishing detailed accounts of people's personal lives. Others worried that scandalous stories might encourage individuals to try and imitate the loose morality of the aristocracy, which they argued would lead to widespread marital breakdown. Other commentators acknowledged that such stories could have a scandalising effect but still supported publishing tales of aristocratic excess and questionable morality, arguing that it drew attention to the necessity of moral reform of not only the aristocracy but the general public as well.[8] Regardless of a person's perspective on this new form of tell-all journalism, it certainly made keeping an affair private more difficult. For aristocrats who wished to keep their names out of the paper, it meant that they needed to be extra vigilant to ensure that their tryst, which may have been widely known among the ton, did not become tabloid gossip.

Political cartoons were an essential feature of Georgian society. James Gillray and Thomas Rowlandson helped to develop the medium by using their art to challenge the existing order, politicians, the government and the Crown while drawing attention to some of the leading issues and debates of the period. By cleverly, but often cruelly, depicting Georgian life, especially the follies and affairs of its leading members, cartoonists ensured that stories of aristocratic excess and affairs reached a wide audience. Much to his annoyance, George IV was a favoured target for satirists. Sensitive to unflattering characterisations, between 1819–1822 George handed over some £2,600 of taxpayers' money to encourage cartoonists to select other targets for their sharpened pens. For example, the publisher J.L. Marks received more than £500 from a secret fund after agreeing to destroy prints that attacked the king. This provided an important second income stream for Marks.[9] Despite his efforts, numerous graphic, embarrassing and highly critical cartoons of George

IV were published. These images have been preserved for prosperity and remain some of the most enduring images of the former king.

Wealthy Georgians rarely had any privacy, as nearly every hobby or pastime involved other people. Because of their celebrity status, local renown, or just fashionable dress, aristocrats drew attention to themselves, and thus, for those wishing to keep their names out of the press, privacy was not easily achieved. Because they were easily recognisable, aristocrats could not rent rooms in a local inn, and even a mistress tucked away in some cottage in the country produced risks. Because of its size, London provided a degree of anonymity, but for rural peers, the distance to London made installing their mistress in the capital impractical. This encouraged aristocrats who wished for privacy to employ various means to hide their affairs.

Even in their own homes, members of the Georgian elite lacked privacy. Servants would constantly be coming and going, and it would be nearly impossible to engage in an affair without someone noticing. Out of a practical nature and because servants needed access to the whole of the house to carry out their duties, doors were rarely locked, and thus any locked door would likely garner comment and suspicion from staff.[10] This made it extremely difficult to be assured of privacy as any minute a servant could enter the room, which made engaging in a clandestine affair within one's home without someone noticing extremely difficult.

If one did decide to use their own home, Georgian elites knew better than to use their own bed as the location to conduct an affair. Tangled sheets and a disorganised bedroom were tell-tale signs that spouses could easily discover. For instance, the presence of another person in the conservatory might be explained in a way in which their presence in the bedroom could not be. For this reason, and also out of a sense of propriety, couples hoping to keep their liaisons secret often avoided bedrooms.[11] They also had to be careful about how much time they spent alone together. Certainly, it was much easier to explain to one's spouse that an acquaintance had dropped in to inquire about this or that or to borrow a book than to explain why a guest spent hours in the house, raising suspicion that an inappropriate relationship had occurred.

In 1766, Topham Beauclerk and his lover, Lady Diana Spencer, wife to Frederick St John 2nd Viscount Bolingbroke, employed a visit to Spencer's sister, Lady Pembroke, as a way to be together without raising suspicion. They planned to slip away unnoticed and rendezvous in a pre-selected room. They knew they did not have long for their exploits and only risked being away for about ten minutes. Despite slipping away undetected and quickly concluding their tryst, a suspicious servant noticed that the couch looked askew and that window shutters that had been open were now shut.[12] Servants knew exactly how a room should look and any change, however small, might be noticed by the staff. For those wishing to keep their affair secret, many trysts within the home (or, in this case, someone else's home) probably occurred in haste.

The elaborate clothing of the wealthy added another stumbling block to keeping an affair secret. Aristocrats rarely dressed themselves, and much of their clothing, due to the multiple clips, buttons and other fasteners, required the help of a servant to remove and put back on.[13] Trysts were aided by the fact that women did not wear underwear and most sex probably took place fully clothed with their petticoats pushed up. Men lowered their trousers but rarely removed their shirts or other overclothes due to the difficulty of putting them back on. Wrinkled clothing could also be a sign that something untoward had occurred, and this meant that an individual wishing to hide an affair might need to put on a fresh set of clothes before seeing their spouse.[14]

With every affair, an aristocrat risked being exposed by their servants. Since aristocrats relied on servants for the simplest and most intimate tasks, servants often knew of an affair before a spouse had any idea. A lady's maid, better than a husband, would recognise wrinkled clothing, while a valet certainly would have noticed a change in his lordship's behaviour, demeanour and routine and may have even caught the faint whiffs of a woman on his clothing. While keeping an affair hidden from the entire staff was difficult, aristocrats could try and limit knowledge of the affair to only trusted servants or staff whose loyalty they thought they could buy.

There seemed to be no clear rules on how servants should act once they discovered an affair. Should a servant pretend not to see any indiscretions? Was a servant supposed to reveal what they knew to the other spouse? What if they merely suspected something was amiss but had no proof? Should they tell their master or mistress what they suspected? Should servants attempt to find out more or say nothing and hope that the affair never came to light? The lack of defined rules about this matter meant that servants acted in a variety of ways and that the master and mistress of the house could not be exactly sure how servants would respond to learning about an affair.

The discovery of an affair put servants in an awkward position. Once a servant discovered an affair, they had to determine whether they were going to tell their master or mistress what they knew. On the one hand, many servants did not have the same permissive moral code of aristocrats and tended to see affairs as wrong and must have, despite the awkwardness, leaned towards revealing what they knew. On the other hand, servants knew that part of their job included keeping family secrets. Whether to tell could be agonising. Under-butler Robert Malthus, whose story we will cover in a moment, agonised over whether to tell his master of his suspicions. Witnessing his torment, fellow servant Thomas Horner remarked, 'poor Bob is so much affected with the affair that is going on between his mistress and John Rose that he can get no sleep at night, and has drunk at different times great quantities of liquor to obtain sleep, without effect.'[15] At times, servants would be told about an affair out of necessity or a belief that they could be trusted. Some of these servants would become accomplices helping to facilitate and conceal the affair. Helping to hide an affair may have added excitement to a gruelling and often thankless job.[16]

While many servants struggled with whether to reveal an affair, understandably, for many, their primary consideration was their own employment.[17] Servants who had witnessed an affair would also have to consider that if the matter came to light and it surfaced that they knew about it, that they would almost certainly be dismissed for not coming forward. Conversely, servants must have been nervous about revealing what they knew, for it was possible that a husband or wife was already well aware of their spouse's dalliances and would not appreciate discussing such a matter with a servant. Not only could this have created an awkward situation but it may have also illustrated that they did not know how to keep a secret, which might have encouraged their employer to dismiss them. By not revealing what they knew, servants may have hoped that the problem would go away. Exposing their master or mistress may have led to the breaking up of the household, resulting not only in their own dismissal but that of the entire staff. Servants could also go to the offending spouse, and ask them to stop, but this, too, risked making a powerful enemy and could result in immediate dismissal. Servants could also use what they knew as leverage to extract money, gifts and privileges from a master or mistress who did not want their secret to be revealed. This, of course, would be risky and could cost them their jobs, but, as we will see, it offered overworked and underpaid servants a real chance to profit from their situation.

Even couples who did not attempt to hide their affair had to work diligently to achieve a modicum of privacy. This is especially true for their letters which often carried intimate details. Wishing to maintain a degree of privacy, Horatio Nelson worried that someone would intercept or steal his correspondence with Emma. These letters would be valuable, as newspapers were willing to pay handsomely for the personal letters of such famous people. Although Nelson treasured Emma's letters and read them repeatedly, he understood the risk of keeping a record of their relationship, and once he could convince himself to do so, he burned Lady Hamilton's letters. He told her to do the same. Nelson explained that having the letters lying around 'can do no good and will do us both harm if any seizure of them; or the dropping even one of them would fill the mouths of the world …'[18] Emma did not heed his advice and kept the letters, perhaps as a form of protection, to remind Nelson, if need be, of his words and commitments to her; to demonstrate in case of his death that she was his 'true' wife, and because she enjoyed rereading (many of) his letters.

While Nelson and Emma never hid their affair, they did hide the fact that she was pregnant. Knowing that their letters could be intercepted or taken from their possession and read but unwilling to stop writing to one another, Emma and Nelson decided to use code while communicating about Emma's pregnancy and their subsequent child. Nelson would pretend to be a 'Mr Thompson', when talking about the baby. According to their cover story, Nelson, as a favour to an illiterate sailor named 'Thompson', promised to write to his wife, who coincidentally had just given birth to a baby girl. Their attempt to hide their daughter behind the ruse of Mr and Mrs Thompson may have worked except for three problems. Firstly, Nelson could not stick to character. His letters continually confused Mr Thompson's feelings for his wife and baby with his own. Anyone reading the letters would have easily determined that Mr Thompson was, in fact, Nelson and that he and Emma had a daughter. Secondly, Emma and Nelson selected a conspicuous name for their child. No master of subterfuge, Nelson wanted to name their daughter Emma. Thinking that was too obvious and wanting to remind Nelson of his responsibilities, Emma insisted the child be named Horatia.[19] Thirdly, Nelson suggested that the child's parents at the christening should be listed as Johem and Morata Etnorb. Johem and Morata is an anagram formed from Emma and Horatio, and Etnorb is Bronte, the dukedom granted to him in Italy, spelled backwards.[20] It is possible that Emma and Nelson were not actually this bad at subterfuge and keeping secrets but that they wished people to know of their daughter but knew that discretion demanded that they never openly speak of her. If so, the use of code names indicates a willingness to abide by some of the rules of society and having an affair.

After the birth of Horatia, the fiction needed to be expanded. Having hidden her pregnancy, Emma told people that the child had been left to her and that she and Lord Hamilton intended to raise the child as their own. On the conspicuous name of Horatia, Emma told people that they named the adopted child in honour of their childless friend whom they adored. Because Nelson and the Hamiltons were so close, there was an air of truth to the fiction. Indeed, the Hamiltons were accustomed to spending so much time with Nelson that it was not unusual for Horatia to be in Nelson's company. Horatia's visits to Merton, purchased by Nelson as a 'paradise' for him and Emma, often occurred at times when other children, including nieces and nephews, were invited over.[21] These gatherings added cover and allowed Nelson to interact with all the children while paying special attention to Horatia. These efforts largely held, for it was not until 1845 that Horatia, after the publication of some of Nelson's correspondence, knew without a doubt that Nelson had been her biological father.[22]

Georgians had good reason to worry about their letters being read. Similar to today's texts and emails, love letters often gave clear evidence of infidelity, and for those who did not subscribe to the elite's moral codes, the discovery of such letters could spell disaster for their marriage. Merchant Andrew Handyside became aware of his wife's affair after reading a letter from her lover. His wife, Isabella Pender, had been warned by her lover, William Rose Robinson, to destroy the incriminating letter but, similar to Emma, she had neglected to do so. Having read the letter, Handyside asked friends to watch his wife to assist him in gathering conclusive proof of infidelity. According to Isabella, the two lovers were caught alone, 'in a bed room in a house at the head of Canongate'.[23] Realising the letter's role in his undoing, Robinson reminded Isabella that, 'I told you always Isabella that that letter would play damnation with me if you did not burn it.'[24] Robinson, a merchant and not of aristocratic birth, knew that his affair with another man's wife threatened his business and livelihood.[25] Her husband would almost certainly let it be known in Edinburgh that William Rose Robinson was not to be trusted. Keeping an affair secret meant trusting the other person to be careful and to destroy any evidence of the affair.

Unhappily married to Frederick Ponsonby, Viscount Duncannon (1758–1793) and later the Earl of Bessborough (1793–1844), Harriet Spencer and her lover Granville Leveson-Gower (later Viscount and Earl Granville) also used code to protect their privacy. Posted to Russia during the Napoleonic Wars, Granville worried that their letters would be intercepted and read. Harriet also knew that she needed to be careful as Duncannon had already threatened divorce over her previous relationship with Richard Brinsley Sheridan. Before he left, they agreed upon specific code names for the people in their lives, lessening the damage that could be done if one of their letters were intercepted, reached the wrong person, or was made public. This allowed them to share information and gossip about the people in their lives. Although Harriet understood the situation, she did lament having to use code and, understandably, did not like to think about her letters being read.[26] Using code certainly lessened the pleasure of writing, and the feeling that your letters might be read must have taken a lot of the fun and intimacy out of exchanging letters.

Mary Eleanor Bowes went to extraordinary lengths to hide her growing affection for James Graham from her husband. So desperate to keep her attraction to Graham hidden, Mary Eleanor not only used code when writing him but, as an extra precaution, she burned their letters and subsequently swallowed the ashes.[27] Ultimately, the relationship with James never amounted to anything more than a flirtation as Graham enlisted in the army and was posted away in 1775.[28] Despite her precautions, she did not fool her husband who was well aware of her indiscretions. Dying from a chest complaint in 1776, the Earl of Strathmore's last will and testament stated: 'I freely forgive you, all your liberties and follies (however fatal they have been to me) as being thoroughly persuaded they were not the produce of your own mind, but the suggestions of some vile interested monster.'[29] Clearly, hiding an affair or even just a flirtation, even when stringent precautions were used, could be rather difficult.

No matter how many times one partner begged the other to be more discreet, to burn letters, or to ensure that they were not being watched, some people were not very adept at keeping secrets. Ultimately, keeping an affair secret proved rather difficult. One not only had to trust that one's lover would be discreet but that servants would not find out about their affair. Hiding an affair from the staff proved rather difficult. The nature of aristocratic life made a reliance upon servants necessary. Footmen carried letters, coachmen transported the lovers, maids made up beds, lady's maids and valets dressed their employers, and all of these people needed to be trusted to keep their suspicions or knowledge of the affair to themselves. Ultimately, for the elite of England, hiding an affair proved a difficult task.

CHAPTER TEN

Profiting from an Affair: Servants

Since servants played such a crucial and intimate role in aristocratic lives, they often knew more about their master's or mistress's daily life, habits and inclinations than their spouses did. Because servants were so close to their wealthy and privileged employers, they could be the first to notice when something was amiss. While servants were often in a vulnerable position (they could be let go for any reason, at any time, and had little recourse if their wages were unpaid or if they were denied a reference), they could profit and even gain a modicum of power over their employers if they learned, or suspected, that their master or mistress was engaging in an affair that they wished to keep secret.

The story of Lord William Talbot and Frances Scudamore, Duchess of Beaufort, demonstrates the various people who could profit after learning about an affair. Neither Talbot nor Scudamore wished for their respective spouses to know about their coupling. Talbot feared that his wife would learn of his affair and that Henry Somerset-Scudamore, 3rd Duke of Beaufort might sue him for having had relations with the duchess. Both knew that the duke wanted to leave his marriage (he had already been granted a private separation) and would welcome any evidence of his wife's infidelity as the basis for a parliamentary divorce. Trapped in this sexless and loveless marriage, the duchess looked for love and companionship, while it appears that Talbot was primarily interested in a sexual relationship.[1]

Although Talbot and Scudamore tried to hide their affair, keeping it secret from the household staff proved difficult. At first, their coupling occurred primarily at the Beauforts' Grosvenor Street House. The staff noted the frequency of Talbot's visits and that they always seemed to occur when the duke was not at home. This generated much gossip and speculation downstairs. After a servant had walked in on the couple and noticed that the duchess's dress was askew and Lord Talbot had his breeches undone, Talbot and Frances determined that they needed a more private place for their coupling. Eventually, after trying a few other methods, including using dining-room chairs as a bed, they decided to meet in the countryside. The duchess and her groom, John Pember, would ride out of town to meet Lord Talbot, who would drive his own chaise. The two would get into his chaise while the groom stood guard outside.[2] While Pember would have to be trusted not to talk about their coupling, this method ensured that no one would accidentally walk in on them.

Despite these new precautions, servants in the Beaufort household continued to gossip about Talbot and the duchess. The couple did not have the best of luck in keeping their affair secret. For instance, on one occasion, their sexual activities caused the chaise door to fly open, directly exposing them and their activities to Pember.[3] Pember soon informed the duchess that the servants were gossiping about her indiscretions. Unwilling to let go of Talbot, the duchess decided that she needed to buy Pember's silence if she wished to keep her relationship secret. Although the other servants may have suspected her, only Pember had direct knowledge of their affair and could testify to their coupling. To buy his loyalty, the duchess gave Pember 10 guineas. Fearing that the groom might still talk, Talbot took him aside and asked him to help put an end to the gossiping and, as a reward for his services and discretion, gave him another 5½ guineas. The fifteen and a half guineas given to him by the nervous lovers was more than double Pember's annual salary of £7. To ensure his continued loyalty and silence, Pember's salary was soon raised to £15 a year. The duchess would also give him some horses that she no longer wanted, which were worth £40.[4]

Pember clearly had a knack for extracting cash and privileges from his worried employer, allowing him to live above his station. Not only had his salary more than doubled, but the approximately £55 (£40 for the horses and approximately 15½ guineas as the original hush money) he received since becoming a witness to the affair would have, at his initial salary, required him to labour for some eight years to have earned the same amount. It is difficult to believe that either the duchess or Lord Talbot gained as much from their affair as Pember did. Poorly paid and overworked, servants knew, as the case of Pember proves, that catching their employers in a compromising position could lead to a substantial windfall.

Another concern for the couple was what would they do if the duchess became pregnant. Although still legally married, the duchess had agreed to a private separation from her husband. The private separation, and the fact that the duke and duchess hardly ever saw each other, would make it difficult to pass off a child as legitimate. Had she still been with the duke, there would have been a chance that he may have accepted Talbot's child as his own. If a girl, the duke would not have had to worry about passing on a title and property to someone who was not his, and even if it was a boy, he may have accepted the child, for he needed an heir. The price of doing so may have been the ending of her affair with Lord Talbot, which would serve to protect both the duke and 'his' heir's reputation.

Aristocrats might claim a child as their own, knowing that another man had fathered the child. In many cases, husbands may have been unsure. Before the days of paternity testing, one could not always be sure who fathered a child, and prudence probably encouraged accepting the child rather than risk rendering your own son or daughter illegitimate. One of the most notorious examples of men laying claim to a child is the case of Maria-Emilia Fagnani (or Mie-Mie), daughter of the beautiful Marchesa Fagnani. Born in 1771, Mie-Mie's father was most probably the notorious rake William Douglas, 4th Duke of Queensberry. Worried about the cost of supporting a child, Queensberry believed that his wealthy friend George Selwyn might play the part of the supposed lover and enjoy the reputation of having bedded and impregnated such a beautiful and renowned woman. In truth, Selwyn had little romantic interest in women and may have been impotent.[5] Selwyn, as Queensberry had predicted, accepted the position as Mie-Mie's father and developed a close and loving relationship with her.[6] In 1798, Mie-Mie married Lord Yarmouth, who would become the Marquess of Hertford. Both her biological father (Queensberry) and assumed father (Selwyn) left Mie-Mie an inheritance. Selwyn left 'his' daughter some £33,000 in his will. Queensberry left the bulk of his estate, a whopping £150,000, to Mie-Mie.[7]

Given the threat of lawsuit and pregnancy, Scudamore and Talbot did try and end their relationship. Women who entered a private separation were not divorced and were expected, by law, convention and contract, to remain faithful to their husbands. For instance, when Lady Diana Spencer had left her husband Frederick St John, 2nd Viscount Bolingbroke, she knew that she must live a life above reproach or lose access to the £800 settlement.[8] While a private separation granted a wife freedom and control over her finances it could put her in a precarious position as her husband might have her watched hoping to collect evidence of infidelity which would allow him to cut off any support and, if he wanted, to seek a divorce. Despite being fully aware of the risks and knowing the duke had much to gain from any evidence of her infidelity, the duchess and Talbot's passion for one another won out over prudence, and the affair continued.

By the end of 1741, Frances had become pregnant with Talbot's child. Determined to keep the pregnancy secret, Lord Talbot rented a house in Chipping Warden, Northamptonshire, where Frances could be placed away from prying eyes. He also rented another house in London. Talbot planned to secretly move the duchess to London just before she gave birth and to use the London house afterwards for her recovery. The thinking must have been that Frances could only be away from society for so long and that they needed to get her back to London as quickly as possible. The practicalities of the birth may have also influenced Talbot to prefer London. In the capital, finding a respectable physician accustomed to handling illegitimate births and keeping secrets would be much easier. Enjoying the peace and quiet provided by Chipping Warden and after delaying the move to London several times, the duchess eventually waited too long as she went into labour while still residing in the country.[9]

Having not stuck to the plan, the duchess needed to improvise. She ordered the gardener to go fetch a midwife. Having delivered the midwife, the gardener was sent out again, this time to get Dr Adams, a physician, and man midwife, who lived some 15 miles away. Pember embarked on an even longer ride, some 30 miles, to inform Lord Talbot about the impending birth. The duchess gave birth to a daughter before the arrival of Dr Adams, or Lord Talbot. A fortunate escape, as the doctor would have been one more witness to the birth, and the duchess had no way of knowing whether he would keep their secret. Despite having just given birth, Frances had the presence of mind to send a servant to tell the doctor that his services were no longer needed. As directed, the servant gave Dr Adams 10 guineas for his troubles.[10]

Although, in this case, the duchess gave birth before the doctor arrived, patients who desired privacy did worry that the attending physician would gossip about the birth of an illegitimate child. Although the notion of doctor–patient confidentiality was still in its infancy, most physicians held their tongues. Their job was to aid in delivery, not to worry about who fathered the child. William Hunter, older brother to the famous anatomist and surgeon John Hunter, attended numerous aristocrats and became widely known for his discretion. Popular among the ton, Hunter had supervised more than a dozen healthy royal births.[11] When, in 1767, Lady Diana Spencer found herself pregnant with a child not fathered by her estranged husband, it was Hunter to whom she turned. Hunter not only had a reputation for secrecy but would, if necessary, arrange for further care, including depositing the newborns he delivered in the Foundling Hospital. Fearing discovery or that someone might see him entering the house, Lady Diana asked Hunter to visit her after dark. After the birth, Hunter suggested that Lady Diana keep him informed about her recovery. He advised that when writing to him, that she adopt the name of one of the nurses he worked with to ensure that she was not identified.[12] Rather than charge worried aristocrats exorbitant fees, Hunter's reward for his discretion came from invitations to dinners, parties, and the prestige associated with serving aristocratic customers. And, of course, rubbing elbows with the aristocracy ultimately improved his business. By 1765, Dr Hunter had acquired some £20,000 from his practice.[13]

Frances also gave the midwife, Mrs Stiles, 20 guineas for her role in the delivery and to buy her silence. The couple jointly pledged to give

Mrs Stiles an additional 20 guineas a year for as long as she kept their secret. Mrs Stiles reassured the couple by telling them that in her line of work, she had become accustomed to keeping other people's secrets. The duchess advised Mrs Stiles to give her husband only a small portion of her reward, for she believed that if she gave him the whole amount, he would become suspicious and demand to know exactly where the money had come from.[14]

Still worried about discovery, Talbot wanted to win over Mrs Duffell, the gardener's wife and makeshift nurse, to their cause. He told her he could not have sexual relations with his wife, for they had been told that another pregnancy would endanger her health. While such an explanation would probably have sufficed, he further stated that given the situation, he had considered going abroad (clearly celibacy was not worthy of consideration) but had, 'heard that the duchess of Beaufort had a passion for me, and I thought it better to make use of her in that way than common women'.[15] Having fathered a child with the duchess, Talbot must have felt that his casual fling had become much more serious.

The plan had been to deposit the child with the already sourced wet nurse in London. Having given birth at Chipping Warden rather than in London had complicated this plan and meant that key components of childcare, including the wet nurse, remained in the capital, leaving the duchess with the difficult task of caring for a child in secret. For the first two days, the duchess took it upon herself to breastfeed Fanny.[16] After two days, it was agreed that the duchess should no longer feed the child, and Talbot helped drain her breast milk by sucking on her breasts and spitting the milk into a basin. We do not know who subsequently fed the child, but their daughter Fanny was eventually taken to London and placed with another family responsible for raising her. Sadly, Fanny died shortly after the move to London.[17]

The birth of a child may have acted like a wake-up call to Talbot, who, from the beginning of their relationship, worried about discovery. Talbot was right to be concerned. Having long suspected that his wife was sexually involved with Talbot, Somerset-Scudamore had been gathering evidence against the couple in preparation for launching a suit. After collecting what he believed to be sufficient evidence, the duke sued Talbot for criminal conversation. Somerset-Scudamore hoped to not only punish his wife and her lover but wanted to use the case as the basis for a parliamentary divorce, which would allow him to remarry and hopefully father a legitimate heir.[18] Incensed by the publicity brought on by Somerset-Scudamore's suit, Talbot's wife demanded that he agree to a private separation. In no position to negotiate, Talbot agreed to a private separation which provided his wife £3,000 a year. Seeing the humour in the situation and well aware that his suit had caused so much strife and discomfort, the duke remarked, 'I pity Lord Talbot to have met with two such tempers as our two wives.'[19] Somerset-Scudamore received a parliamentary divorce in March 1744, granting him the right to remarry, although it did him little good as he died in February of the following year and his titles passed to his brother. Shortly after the divorce, Frances married Charles Fitzroy, an illegitimate son of the 2nd Duke of Grafton. She died in 1750 while giving birth to a daughter.

Although John Pember received life-changing wealth for his role in suppressing the Duchess of Beaufort's affair with Lord Talbot, it was no match for the money that Mary Eleanor, the Dowager Countess of Strathmore, gave to Elizabeth Planta to encourage her to keep Mary Eleanor's relationship with George Gray, an entrepreneur and man about town, secret. Worried that she could not trust her children's governess, Mary Eleanor judged it best to buy Planta off and get her out of the picture. Mary Eleanor offered Planta £2,000 in return for Elizabeth leaving the home and promising to keep all the family secrets to herself. Although it must have been difficult to leave the children and a family for which she had served more than twenty years, £2,000 was life-changing money.[20] To put this money in perspective, Elizabeth's sister Frederica worked at the royal court as a tutor for a salary of a £100 a year.[21]

While servants could receive life-changing money from anxious aristocrats hoping to buy their silence, it could also cause them to lose their position. William Flockton, who worked for Lady Diana and her husband Frederick St John, 2nd Viscount Bolingbroke, knew that Lady Diana was having an affair with Topham Beauclerk. At first, Flockton's knowledge of the affair proved a financial boon. For instance, on one occasion, Lady Diana gave Flockton a guinea as a reward for his silence. For Flockton, a guinea represented two months' salary.[22] The bribe backfired; knowing that there was money to be made and having become frustrated by Topham's propensity to order him around, Flockton began to spy on the couple.[23]

Lady Diana soon carried Topham's child. This made her even more sensitive about their relationship. She reacted by firing any staff, including Flockton, who knew of her affair.[24] The decision to get rid of staff who knew intimate and uncomfortable details not only came from a desire to silence staff and get them away from the house but may also have stemmed from the discomfort that came from the levelling of roles, as servants who knew their master's secrets had some power over their employers. This power challenged the natural order of Georgian society and may have encouraged those who wished to keep their dalliance a secret to remove staff who knew of their affair. However, by firing their staff, employers, including Lady Diana, lost all control over their former employees, and given the right situation, their intimate knowledge could harm them. Having lost their jobs, former servants might wish to spread what they knew far and wide and could even profit by selling what they knew to the press.[25] Angry with the way Lady Diana treated him, Flockton exacted his revenge by testifying on behalf of Lord Bolingbroke at their divorce hearing.[26]

Masters and the servants they bribed in return for their discretion and silence had to be careful that the servant's newfound wealth did not create unwanted attention. During the Georgian era, few servants had the time or means to markedly increase their incomes, and thus other servants were naturally suspicious when one of their own began spending much more than their measly salaries would allow. While some may have believed that a servant's newfound wealth or expensive possessions came from an inheritance or some other tale, many would have suspected that they had been bought off, were stealing, or engaged in some other nefarious activity. While Georgians may not have been the best at noticing or caring for their servants, they did have an eye for prestige goods, and these items in the hands of a poorly paid servant may have encouraged employers to ask questions of the servant. Further inquiries, especially by the unknowing husband or wife, may have led them to discover their spouse's affair, resulting in the servant losing access to their hush money and, most likely, their position as well.

Servants could also profit by becoming the object of their employer's affection or entering into a relationship with their master or mistress. This event occurred when Clara Louisa, wife of William Middleton, fell in love with the newly arrived servant John Rose. Having given birth to eight children within ten years, Clara Louisa had grown bored of her life.[27] Hired in July 1791 to serve as groom and occasionally at table, John Rose, an attractive young man, had caught the eye of Clara Louisa. Infatuated with Rose, Clara Louisa began supplying Stockeld Park's newest servant with fine clothes. Visitors to Stockeld could tell something was not quite right, having witnessed the excessive attention that Clara Louisa paid to the new groom. Her husband, William, did not notice his wife's attraction or growing attachment to Rose.

More perceptive than William, Rose's fellow servants observed that the groom, who had arrived wearing shabby clothing and, having had to borrow money just to make his way to Stockeld, began dressing more like a man of means than as a member of the servant class. Knowing how difficult it was for a member of their class to acquire money and fine goods, the servants suspected that something was amiss. This encouraged the staff at Stockeld to monitor Clara Louisa, who had been spending significant time alone at the stables with Rose.[28]

The upper crust of Georgian society was not supposed to mix socially with their servants. A physical relationship between a mistress and a male servant was considered one of the most heinous forms of betrayal and an absolute breach of the rules of having an affair. Such a relationship not only challenged the bonds of fidelity but questioned the patriarchal order by upsetting the balance between a master and his servants.[29] For a servant to have a sexual relationship with his master's wife meant that he had access to, and possessed his employer's most sacred possession. Worse, the servant could impregnate his master's wife, and, if he was none-the-wiser, a man's whole lineage could be 'tainted' by the servant. Although approaches to a wife's infidelity varied, few husbands who cared about their lineage or reputation would tolerate their wives having affairs with, or even affection for, those whose only purpose, in their minds, was to serve them.

Servants began to speculate and gossip about the extent of Rose and Clara Louisa's relationship. To prevent the staff from talking, Clara Louisa began speaking to members of the staff individually, telling them that they were mistaken and that she had done nothing wrong with the groom. She also made sure to provide sceptical staff members with gifts or other benefits to remind them of their place, her power over them, and as a reward for their expected silence. For instance, Clara Louisa encouraged Hodgson, a man who claimed to have witnessed her and Rose alone in a dressing room beside the family's bathing well, to change his story by arranging for his sick daughter to receive medical treatment at Leeds infirmary. In return for her assistance with his daughter, Hodgson told both the butler and the under-butler that he made the story up.[30]

Trusting that she had suppressed all the gossip, Clara Louisa continued to pay special attention to Rose. This ensured that, despite her efforts, the staff continued to speculate about what might be happening between their mistress and the groom. Unable to stop the servants from talking and unwilling to stay away from Rose, Clara Louisa thought it best to tell her husband of the accusations being levelled at her and to assure him that she had done nothing wrong. William believed his wife and, given that he was already contemplating travelling abroad in the spring, suggested this would be a convenient time to rid themselves of their staff.[31] William, as did many members of his class, saw his servants as disposable and had no qualms about letting them go when he no longer needed their services. For Clara Louisa, this would mean that she would lose Rose.

Just before Christmas in 1792, William's older brother came to stay with the family. In his room, Marmaduke Maxwell found a letter from Clara Louisa's lady's maid Hannah Canridge telling Maxwell of the feelings that Clara Louisa had developed for Rose. Before deciding what to do, Maxwell summoned Hannah and the under-butler, Robert Malthus, and questioned them. These inquiries convinced Maxwell that his brother's wife had developed an inappropriate attachment to the groom and may have even committed adultery.[32]

Maxwell believed that he was responsible for protecting his family and its reputation and that he must intervene in what may be seen as a private issue between William and his wife. He instructed Hannah and Robert to inform Rose that his services were no longer required.[33] Maxwell did not think it necessary to consult with his brother before dismissing one of his employees. As we have seen with Lady Susan Fox-Strangways and what society deemed her inappropriate marriage, Maxwell would have known that he could be blamed for ignoring or not properly dealing with a problem that might negatively impact his family and its reputation.

Looking to further profit from the situation, Rose complained that he was being let go without warning, money, or cause. Hoping to avoid further scandal, Maxwell gave Rose £10 to speed up his removal. Rose accepted the money and readied himself to leave. As he packed his bags, Rose had a change of heart and sent the money back to Maxwell.[34] Rose may have figured that he could extract more than he had been paid to leave or that there was still profit to be made by remaining. Rose had a comfortable job, and he may have been unwilling to give that up. He may have also genuinely cared for Clara Louisa or at least enjoyed her company and did not wish to be separated from her. In the early hours of the morning, having changed his mind once again, a conflicted Rose collected the £10 and left.[35]

The following morning, Clara Louisa learned that after consulting with Hannah Canridge and Robert Malthus, Maxwell had ordered Rose from the house. Visibly shaken by the news, Clara Louisa fired Hannah on the spot, telling her that no one would keep her from Rose. Enraged by the sending away of Rose, she cruelly told her maid that 'he [Rose] should live there [Stockeld] when this respondent [Hannah Canridge] was starving for a morsel of bread'.[36] This not only spoke to how deeply Clara Louisa felt towards Rose but also to the little care or responsibility that some members of the gentry felt towards their staff. It also demonstrates employers' power over their staff and the vulnerable position of servants within Georgian England.

Was Clara Louisa right to fire Hannah? Was there an unspoken bond of trust between a lady's maid and a mistress that had been violated when Hannah wrote to Maxwell? Most mistresses expected their maids to keep their secrets, and maids, for their part, understood that this was a part of their responsibilities. Much of this may rest on the intention of Hannah's letter. If Hannah wrote the letter to protect her mistress and her reputation, Hannah's dismissal appears unfair. While there is some evidence that Hannah enjoyed the drama of the situation, she did seem to be acting in what she believed to be her mistress's best interest. At one point, after witnessing Rose embrace Clara Louisa, Hannah not only yelled at Rose but also struck him, which suggests an emotional attachment to her mistress and a desire to protect her.[37] At no point did she attempt to profit from the affair by trying to trade her silence for a financial reward. Also, we should remember that had Rose left that night in December, Hannah would have succeeded in protecting her mistress, her job, and the tranquillity of Stockeld. And, of course, unbeknown to the staff, William planned on letting them go in the spring anyhow. Had William forewarned the staff instead of seeing his servants as disposable, Hannah surely would have held her tongue, and much drama may have been avoided. Before she left, Hannah demanded both a month's salary and a reference. She received neither.[38]

Desperate to hold on to Rose, Clara Louisa told her husband that his brother had received unreliable information from a disgruntled Hannah and her accomplice Robert Malthus. Accepting his wife's version of events, William summoned Malthus and released him from his duties, telling him that he had to be out of the house in two hours. Just like Hannah, Robert found himself unemployed and with no chance of getting a reference. William insisted that Rose be reinstated. By showing faith in Rose, William hoped to demonstrate to all that the rumours were baseless.[39]

William's faith in his wife would not last. A new butler, William Davis, told his master that he had seen Rose enter Clara Louisa's bedchamber in the middle of the night. William had reached his breaking point. He ordered his wife from the house, informing her that all their children, including their 9-month-old baby, would remain with him.[40] Enraged by his wife's actions, William brutally attacked all that Clara Louisa loved and ordered that her beloved horse and dog be killed. Bent on revenge,

William did all he could to upset his wife and ruin her reputation. A friend of William's mother wrote a scandalising and inaccurate piece published by *Bon Ton* magazine claiming that witnesses could testify to having seen Rose and Clara Louisa committing adultery. William also tried to trick her into admitting guilt by offering to forgive her after she admitted to the affair. Clara Louisa did not bend to her husband or fall for his tricks, and having the support of much of the wider community, many of their friends, and her family, denied having done anything inappropriate or improper.[41]

William sued Rose for criminal conversation. His lawyers asked for £10,000 in damages. William did not do this for money – he knew Rose had none – but to punish him. William would have been well aware that even if he won a tenth of that amount, Rose would be unable to pay and would likely be sent to debtors' prison.[42] William must have been confident of his ability to win the case, or he would not have risked further embarrassment by airing his family's dysfunction in a public forum.[43] What William knew of the law and criminal conversation suits is unknown, but he almost certainly would have been advised that a husband who failed to protect his wife from falling into folly was not well looked upon by the courts or juries.[44] One way of understanding what occurred is that William was negligent in his duty as a husband and missed obvious clues caught by nearly everyone else associated with Stockeld. William risked not only losing the case but being seen as a blind fool who could not see what everyone else had already realised. Represented by Clara Louisa's lawyer, Rose's defence argued that no evidence of adultery existed but conceded that given the 'circumstances and situation … a small measure of damages will suffice'.[45] The court eventually sided with William and assessed a judgment of £500 in punitive damages plus legal costs amounting to an additional £154. At the salary he received when he first arrived at Stockeld Park, it would have taken Rose more than ninety years to pay. Whatever profit Rose had extracted from his relationship with Clara Louisa had been erased by this judgment.

Not much is known about Clara Louisa's life after the judgment except that she lived until 1833, probably relying on her family for support. It is also presumed that she paid the judgment against John Rose, possibly as part of a settlement with William.[46] Until the judgment against Rose, Clara Louisa had received a court-ordered alimony of some £600, which after having been found guilty of committing adultery, was reduced to a £100.[47] After the judgment. Rose severed ties with Clara Louisa. William had lost his wife and much of his happiness; servants had lost their jobs over what may have been, as no concrete evidence was ever presented, nothing more than an infatuation, albeit a very inappropriate one for the period.[48] Rose had profited only a short while. He received money, gifts, and an easier workload, but ultimately his relationship with his master's wife not only broke up a family but resulted in he and many of his fellow servants losing their jobs.

Servants could profit from their employers' desire to keep extra-marital affairs secret. In return for their silence and sometimes their help, servants could receive gifts, hush money, and a reduced workload. However, such rewards were often temporary. In most of the above examples, servants ultimately lost their jobs because of what they knew. Employers did not like having a servant hold power over them and rewarded servants only so long as they felt they needed to and, when it suited them, they would relieve their servants of their position. Those who best profited from hiding an affair or illegitimate birth were not actual employees but doctors, wet nurses and midwives who were paid for their silence, and because they did not work directly for these people, they did not have to worry about a subsequent loss of position. Although the temporary intrigue of an affair and the chance at some fast money must have been appealing, when set against the long-term consequences of unemployment or leaving without a reference, most servants were probably better off not knowing about their employers' extra-marital affairs.

CHAPTER ELEVEN

Profiting from an Affair: Gentry, Aristocracy and the Middling Sort

Men could gain power, position, and receive financial rewards as a result of their wives' extra-marital affairs. Knowing that his wife's affair with a rich and powerful man could bring financial rewards, employment opportunities, or political power, a husband might encourage his wife to take on a lover. She would be expected to work diligently to ensure that her extra-marital affair brought tangible benefits to her husband. Other family members, including fathers, brothers and sons, could also be rewarded directly or indirectly because a female member of their family had become a mistress to a powerful and wealthy man.

Although he did not actively promote the affair, Peniston Lamb benefited handsomely from his wife's involvement with the Prince of Wales (future George IV). Shortly after his wife began a relationship with the prince, Peniston, in 1782, was rewarded with the position of Gentleman of the Bedchamber at George's primary residence, Carlton House. Probably a payment in kind for tolerating the affair, and almost certainly due to Lady Melbourne's encouragement, the promotion provided convenient cover for Lady Melbourne's close proximity to the prince.[1] After his wife gave birth to a son whom the prince almost certainly fathered, Melbourne received further honours including being made a viscount.[2] The Prince of Wales would develop a reputation for rewarding complicit husbands, as both the Marquis of Hertford and the Earl of Jersey received valuable royal appointments after their wives became involved with the prince.[3]

George Augustus also rewarded John McMahon for allowing him access to his wife. After an initial introduction, Mrs McMahon invited the prince to drop by any time. Enchanted by this woman, the prince did so often. Each time he did, John McMahon made himself scarce. The prince rewarded McMahon with two military promotions and eventually offered him the prestigious and important position as his royal secretary. After having been complicit in the conquest of his wife, McMahon continued to serve George by arranging for the prince to meet other women as well. McMahon's responsibilities may have included more than arranging women for the prince – he may have even had relations with them before presenting them.[4] McMahon's willingness to allow the prince access to his wife allowed him to become a trusted confidant and was the beginning of his long and profitable relationship with the future George IV.

Georgian parents could also profit if their daughter formed a relationship with a rich and powerful man. John Delaval, 1st Baron Delaval, actively looked for ways his already married daughter Sarah could help increase her family's power and prestige. An alluring, confident and flirtatious beauty, not afraid to challenge convention, Sarah, once, on a hot day, came to the dinner table naked from the waist up.[5] Having noticed that his daughter had caught the eye of Frederick, Duke of York and Albany, Lord Delaval did all he could to encourage their coupling. Her husband, George Carpenter, 2nd Earl of Tyrconnel, seeing the value of such a close connection to the royal family, also did all he could to encourage a relationship between his wife and Frederick. To make matters easier for the Duke of York and to ensure that he and his family were always at hand, Lord Delaval bought his daughter a beautiful home near the prince's place at Weybridge.[6] The press, as it did with all royal affairs, covered their coming and goings in quite some detail. Because of the rewards that such a relationship could bring, when the affair ended, it appeared that her father and husband were more upset than Sarah.

Famous actress and talented singer Susannah Cibber had also been encouraged by her husband to have an affair. Her husband, actor, playwright and theatre promoter Theophilus Cibber, had noticed that

William Sloper, the son of a wealthy country gentleman, had become besotted with his wife. Married and with two sons, William spent any moment he could spare gazing up at Susannah as she plied her trade. Always looking for profit, Theo befriended the wealthy young man and asked him for a loan. No stranger to debt, Theo soon owed William £400. Realising that £400 was more than Theo could repay, Sloper suggested that Theo allow him to visit his wife, telling him that he would enjoy teaching Susannah backgammon. Theo agreed and explained to Susannah that she must be warm and friendly to Sloper as Theo owed him a sum of money beyond his capacity to repay.[7]

Susannah did not wish to meet with William, for doing so risked her own carefully guarded and cultivated reputation. Realising that most of the public saw actresses as no different than mistresses or even prostitutes, Susannah did all she could to ensure that, as a woman of the stage, she defied such classification by presenting herself as an educated and respectable woman.[8] Nonetheless, at her husband's insistence, Susannah met with Sloper.[9] To her surprise, Susannah enjoyed William's company. A country gentleman at heart, William's conversation was respectful rather than sexual. He talked of his life, mentioning how much he missed his home in Berkshire.[10]

As William and Susannah grew closer, Theo's creditors began to circle. The Cibbers needed to leave London, fearing that if they remained, much of what they owned would be repossessed to pay Theo's extensive debts. Unwilling to be separated from Susannah, Sloper decided that they should head for the country as a group. Having already become accustomed to supporting the Cibber household, Sloper rented a home for the three of them in Kingston. Behind his back, Theo began to refer to William as 'Mr Benefit'.[11] Theo, Susannah and William found themselves in a relationship of mutual convenience. Sloper needed the care and comfort he received from Susannah; Theo required Sloper's money to stay ahead of his creditors and avoid the dreaded debtor's prison; and Susannah needed Theo's presence to protect her reputation.

The Georgian state supported the absolute authority of the husband, and any relationship that challenged this authority was frowned upon.

Knowing this, Theo used his position as husband to his advantage and let William know, in no uncertain terms, that William's access to his wife would only last for as long as he benefited. To ensure that both William and Susannah understood that the triad only existed as long as he wished and that as the husband, he reigned supreme, Theo would walk his wife to William's bedroom each night to personally hand her over.[12] The message was clear: Susannah was his property, and only he decided how and what she did and if William wanted access to his wife he would have to ensure that he made it worth Theo's while. Theo was not the only husband to insist on this sort of ritual. In the criminal conversation trial of Mr Hacket, accused of having an affair with the wife of George Mansergh, Mr Moor, a witness for the defence, testified to also being an 'intimate acquaintance' of Mrs Mansergh. He claimed 'That the husband was accustomed to bring her to him at night.' According to Moor, on one occasion, after bringing his wife to his door he 'bade' Moor to 'take care of her'.[13]

Despite William's financial assistance, Theo's uncontrolled spending led him to fall deeper into debt. Theo's creditors, both old and new, began vigorously pursuing him for payment. To avoid his creditors and after considering his options, Theo decided to flee to France.[14] Although outside the jurisdiction of his creditors, Theo could no longer closely monitor and control Susannah and William. They were, however, not free of him entirely and continued to send money to France to pay for his maintenance. William and Susannah used Theo's weakened position to push for a separation. Susannah wrote to Theo in France to inform him that if he let her go, they would help him with his creditors, paving the way for his return to England. To demonstrate that they would not forget about him financially, Susannah's letter was accompanied by an even larger than usual amount of money.[15] Even as his hold over his wife and her lover weakened, Theo, as husband, could and did, profit from his wife's affair with another man. Although he wanted to return to England, and the prospect of having his debts cleared must have been enticing, Theo would not let Susannah go, for he knew that if he did, he would no longer be able to rely upon either of them for money or support. Theo's plans involved continuing to profit from his wife's affair.

Worried about losing control and unwilling to let his wife gain any independence, Theo, despite the risk of being seized by his creditors, made his way back to England. Although he had no money and few prospects, as the husband, Theo still held much power over both his wife and her lover. He could, for instance, sue William for committing adultery and taking his wife from him.[16] Suing William would provide another way for Theo to profit from his wife's affair, and the threat of ruining William and Susannah's reputations ensured that Theo could still dictate the terms of their relationship.

A month after Theo's return from France, Susannah announced that she was pregnant. This changed Susannah and William's position, for they did not want to give Theo a chance to claim the child as his own. If able to do so, Theo would, as husband and father, have complete control over William, Susannah and the child. This would have increased Theo's ability to profit from the affair. William and Susannah responded by distancing themselves from Theo. Although this meant risking that Theo might opt to find satisfaction, revenge, and a further way to profit by suing William for criminal conversation, they saw this as a better option than allowing him to claim the child as his own, which would have allowed Theo to fully exercise his rights as the child's father.[17]

Theo responded to Susannah's unwillingness to go along with his plans by suing Sloper for criminal conversation. He asked the court for £5,000 in damages. Although a tremendous sum, juries had awarded as much as £10,000.[18] A judgment in his favour would provide Theo with yet another method of profiting from his wife's affair. On the surface, Theo had a good case. William had manipulated a friendship (or at least it might look that way) to gain access to a friend's wife. This was considered a particularly heinous act as it challenged the bonds of male friendship and civility.[19] William not only had an affair with Susannah but could be shown to have turned her against him, for he had never hidden his intention to take Susannah from Theo. Also unwilling to let Theo have any rights as a father, William would have to admit to impregnating Susannah.

The court met on 5 December 1738. The meeting of the court provided Theo the opportunity to seek revenge against William for cutting him off while further profiting from his wife's affair. Not burdened with having to establish that an affair had occurred, the prosecution went to great lengths to establish the role that the Cibber family had in making Susannah a star. Theo's father, the famous actor, theatre manager, playwright and long-serving Poet Laureate, Colley Cibber, testified that, 'I believe I was the person who chiefly instructed her …' and that, 'When they married, she was a singer, but there were better voices.'[20] The idea was to show that Theo had lost not only the comfort of his wife but also her income. The prosecution claimed that Theo was doubly entitled to her money, for he was not only her husband but also because of the crucial role that he and his family had played in training Susannah.

William's lawyers argued that Theo had encouraged the affair. In its opening statement, the defence was clear that it 'hoped that nothing criminal had passed between them, but if there had, the Plaintiff had certainly encouraged it, and had no pretence to come to a Jury, for damages'.[21] Juries were less likely to grant 'wronged' husbands significant financial rewards if they believed that the husband had encouraged the affair or, after learning of the affair, allowed it to continue.[22] Not convinced by Theo or his version of events, but cognisant that William did have an affair with Susannah, the jury ordered Sloper to pay £10 in damages. At the time, £10 was the smallest banknote in circulation.[23] Although such a meagre amount could be seen as nothing more than a slap on the wrist, the fact that he had been found guilty meant that if Sloper continued to live with Susannah, he risked another lawsuit and could be sure that the court, on a second occasion, would not be so lenient.[24]

Still looking for ways to profit and worried that Susannah and William would abandon him, Theo continued to monitor the couple. After gathering new evidence, Theo brought a second suit against Sloper, doubling the amount he sought in damages to £10,000. The court met on 4 December 1739. Still not convinced by Theo's argument but cognisant that William had once again broken the law, a second jury awarded Theo £500 in damages. This judgment was more than Theo had ever earned in a single year. Realising that they may never be free of Theo, William and Susannah retired from society and Susannah from the stage, hoping that this would stop Theo's suits and limit his ability to profit from the affair.[25]

After two years of laying low, Susannah and William eventually emerged in Ireland with a determination not to let the past decide their future. Crucially, in 1741 Susannah accepted an offer that allowed her to return to the stage in Dublin. Susannah was still a large draw and was offered £300 for the season.[26] Both William, who first fell in love with Susannah while she performed on the stage, and Susannah desired, despite the risks of another lawsuit, that she continue her career. This is different from many other men of the period, who, once they became an actress's patron, tried to convince her to leave the stage. Their reasons for doing so varied but some did not like the idea of other men ogling their mistress, while others disliked having to accommodate their acting schedule, preferring that their mistress always be available to them.

Susannah was not alone in her decision to stay up on the stage. Dora Jordan, mistress to the Duke of Clarence, continued her theatre career while giving birth to ten of the future king's children. Despite her responsibilities to the duke and her children, Dora remained a consummate professional and for twenty-five years held the position as England's most famous actress.[27] But even the self-confident Dora wavered and at the insistence of the duke, who wished her to act more like a 'proper wife', left the stage in 1805 to live as his mistress with their children at his home Bushy Park. Missing her life as an actress and with the duke always short of money, after a year and a half away from the stage, Dora returned to acting.[28]

After success in Ireland, William and Susannah moved back to England in 1742. The transition was made easier by the death of William's father. William stepped into the breach winning his father's old parliamentary seat, moving into his house, and ably managing his family's business and financial interests. This changed how some people viewed Susannah, perceiving her no longer as an actress that might lead a young heir into disrepute but instead as a woman of substance that confirmed his position and status.[29] Important men, especially those who had already produced heirs, were expected to have a mistress. As a famous actress, Susannah could even be an asset to a country gentleman, helping him navigate London's complex social and political life.

Although Theo had profited from suing Sloper after his two successful criminal conversation suits, the courts lost patience with him and his claims that he deserved compensation as a wronged husband. Although he profited immensely from his wife's affair, without the assistance of the courts, Theo could no longer extract money from Sloper.

Having lost the ability to sue Sloper, Theo finally agreed to a private agreement that legally separated him from Susannah.[30] William and Susannah were finally free of Theo and had no fear of being sued. They lived as virtual man and wife until Susannah's death in January 1766. Although their daughter had been born illegitimate, because of her mother's wealth, she was able to find a suitable husband. In 1767, she married Reverend James Burton, a landholder in Wiltshire and Hampshire.[31] When William Sloper died in 1789, he left his estate to his two legitimate sons.[32] These sons had shielded William and Susannah from much potential criticism, as William did not impoverish his sons or his wife in his pursuit of Susannah nor was any of his property transferred to her. William did not neglect his business or political duties, and when his father died, he quickly and efficiently took over all his father's responsibilities. While often absent from his sons, this was the norm for many father–son relationships during the eighteenth century. William did not settle money on their illegitimate daughter; Susannah earned enough from her stage career to leave their daughter a comfortable living.[33] While the two violated many of the principles of the period, their relationship never challenged two of the most important pillars of the upper crust of Georgian society: property and inheritance.

The preceding chapter has shown the numerous ways an affair could prove profitable. Husbands could gain in purse and position by promoting or turning a blind eye to their wives' affairs. For the Earl of Tyrconnel, Lord Melbourne and John McMahon, their wives' extra-marital affairs with members of the royal family increased their political power and position. In the case of Theo Cibber, he got temporary relief from creditors, a place to live, and his living expenses covered because another man coveted his wife. When they tried to free themselves from him, Theo used the courts as a means of further profiting. But there were limits to how much profit could be made. Royal dukes and, indeed, the Prince of Wales may have tired and moved on, or in the case of Theo, after being awarded £510 in criminal damages, no one wished to see him further profit from his wife or believed his claims of being a wronged husband. Once again, we are reminded of the centrality of marriage and that since marriage was expected to be for life, society largely tolerated affairs and that much flexibility could be found regarding how a married couple chose to live.

CHAPTER TWELVE

Profiting from An Affair: Professional Mistresses

Professional mistresses needed to consider how they would manage their careers. Certainly, they must never forget that they worked for money and to improve their lot in life. Careful money management was essential for professionals who wished to have a comfortable retirement. While their expensive tastes were the leading culprit in draining their bank accounts, giving money to friends and family could also upset efforts to save for their future. Since living costs were so high and their careers so short, good economy and saving for the future were paramount. This escaped many of the leading women of the period who struggled to keep their spending in check. For those who did not save their money and were without an annuity to rely upon, there were really only two outcomes as they reached the twilight of their careers: marry a man capable of providing for them (possibly their current patron) or spend the rest of their days in poverty.

Since there was often a significant age difference between a man and his mistress, many mistresses worried about what would happen if, or for most probably when, they outlived their long-standing patron. Such concerns were particularly acute for a mistress who had served her patron for numerous years and had given him 'her best years' and no longer had many other suitors or prospects. What would she do for money and support? What if she simply could not find another patron? Would he leave her money in his will? Did her former patron even believe it was his responsibility to provide for her after his death? These concerns and unanswered questions about their future contributed to the worry that many professional mistresses must have felt.

Some men chose to do nothing and did not provide for their mistress after death. Even if everyone knew about the affair, many men did not want to state publicly in their will for all interested parties to see that they had a mistress. Somehow, the process of writing it down legitimised it and made the relationship seem more enduring than either of them expected it to be. This is why it was important for a mistress to secure an annuity upfront (which, of course, was preferable and when she had the most bargaining power), but if not possible, at least during the relationship. Of course, it worked the other way too. A will was one way to recognise a relationship or even a child without having to face any of the consequences. In his will, George IV left £10,000 to George Seymour Crole, which confirmed that he believed Crole to be his natural son.[1] In another example, Lord Robert Spencer, son of Charles Spencer, 3rd Duke of Marlborough, willed Woolbeding House to Diana, daughter of his mistress Henrietta Bouverie, confirming the rumours that Diana was his natural daughter.[2] Rather than wait and see if she had been included in his will, George IV's last mistress, Lady Conyngham, took matters into her own hands and as the king lay dying she stole away in a coach filled with a host of valuable items taken from Windsor Castle.[3] A man who did not care what others thought of him, Francis Seymour, 3rd Marquess of Hertford's will let his friends and family know exactly what he thought of them while stating that he wished that 15,000 francs be given to his mistress Angélique Borel.[4]

Despite the difficulties, many men found a way to provide for a former mistress even after their death. When Edward was made the Duke of Kent and, crucially for the in-debt Edward, had his income increased to £12,000 a year, the duke immediately began putting money aside for his mistress, Madam de Saint Laurent, in case something should happen to him.[5] Even as his debts grew, Edward continued to contribute money towards an investment fund for Saint Laurent.[6] That the duke placed his mistress's financial future above his other financial obligations demonstrates how deeply he cared about her and that whatever the future might bring, he wanted to ensure that she was taken care of.

Leading Georgians might rely upon a trusted friend or family member to help care for a former mistress after they died. This might involve financially supporting her or ensuring that she found another patron. When his brother Maurice, a commissioner of the Customs and Excise, died, Horatio Nelson insisted that his agent find a way to care for his brother's former lover. Whether his brother had asked him to do so, or whether Nelson did so on his own accord, is unknown. Whatever the case, his concern and willingness to pay for his dead brother's mistress's maintenance demonstrates an understanding of how deeply his brother might have felt for this woman while reinforcing Nelson's generosity of spirit. Nelson understood that his brother's former mistress, who had poor sight and was now middle-aged, would probably have had difficulty securing another patron.[7] Nelson clearly believed that the living had some obligation to take care of a fallen friend or family member's mistress if they had the capacity to do so.

Although Nelson expected others to help take care of Emma, he still made sure to include her in his will. Nelson's will left Merton Place to Emma as well as a £500 annuity derived from his estate tied to his Italian dukedom.[8] Knowing Emma's propensity for excess, and, in an effort to further protect her, Nelson requested that as a 'legacy to my king and country, that they will give her an ample provision to maintain her rank in life'.[9] He also asked king and country to care for his adopted daughter, Horatia Thompson, but stated that in the future, he wished her to be known only as Horatia Nelson.[10]

Emma certainly needed financial support. In two short years, Emma lost the support of her husband, Sir William (d. 1803), and her lover Horatio Nelson (d. 1805). Knowing first-hand the frustration that came from being a poor gentleman, Hamilton, who had no natural children, had sympathy for his nephew Charles Greville and this encouraged him to leave most of his estate to Charles rather than his wife Emma.[11] By leaving most of his estate to his nephew, Hamilton ensured that most the money and estates stayed within the family. He may have also presumed that Nelson would, and maybe should, be the one who chiefly provided the funds necessary to take care of Emma. Whatever his views or feelings on the matter, Hamilton did not leave Emma a pauper as his will granted her a behest of £300 and an annuity of £800 a year.[12] This should have been enough to take care of Emma, her mother and her children.[13] When you consider that Nelson also left her an annuity and a house Emma should have been able to manage but her grief, coupled with an inability to rein in her expenditure, led to her financial ruin.

While numerous parliamentarians had mistresses of their own, they did not believe that parliament, the public purse, or the nation, regardless of Nelson's heroics and sacrifice, should provide for a dead man's mistress. This was not out of penny-pinching as, after the death of her estranged husband, Fanny received both money and honours, including a £2,000 pension for the remainder of her life.[14] The biggest benefactor, one which demonstrated that it was still very much a man's world, was Nelson's brother who not only inherited Nelson's viscountcy but was elevated to Earl Nelson in honour of his brother. Never one to turn down the chance to enlarge his purse, Reverend William Nelson, now Earl Nelson of Trafalgar, saw an opportunity to extract more out of the occasion and began soliciting funds to build a house that suited his dignity as a peer of the realm. While it ignored Nelson's request and left Emma to fend for herself, the thankful nation acceded to the wishes of the newly minted Earl Nelson. William received approximately £100,000 to buy and furnish a house and a pension of £500 a year for himself and all future earls.[15] In 1814, Earl Nelson purchased Standlynch Park, which would be renamed Trafalgar Park.

By ignoring the rules of having an affair, Emma and Nelson hurt their reputations and, ultimately, Emma's financial future. It suited both Emma and Nelson to behave as if they were married. Nelson considered Emma his 'true' wife and ignored Fanny, while they increasingly treated Sir William as a close family friend.[16] Despite her love for Nelson and desire to someday be his wife, Emma was clear: she would never divorce Sir William. Hamilton was by far the eldest of the group, and unless Fanny should die unexpectedly, there was no way that Nelson could remarry. Nelson and Emma had to be content with pretending to be man and wife.

Content to play wife to two men, Emma forgot some of the cardinal rules of being a mistress. She did not siphon off any of Nelson's money for herself, nor did she demand some of the regular financial compensations that a mistress could rightly expect. For instance, long-serving mistresses often insisted that their patrons not only provide them with an annuity but settle money on any children that they might produce.[17] This protected both mother and child, for it would ensure that the child would have enough money to make it in England despite the 'abnormal' circumstances of their birth. Emma had not done this because she genuinely believed that she and Nelson would be together forever and that the man who so desperately wanted a child would never desert her. This was a huge mistake. When Nelson fell at Trafalgar, his will had left Horatia an annuity of only £200 a year. This was on top of the bequest to her mother, but since Emma could not control her spending, it would bring many hardships to the lives of them both. Emma would eventually be pursued for unpaid debt and took 12-year-old Horatia to the 'sponging house' (a place of temporary confinement) rather than face it alone. She could have saved Horatia this misery by sending her to live with a relative or family friend, but Emma selfishly took her daughter with her.[18] Had they followed the conventions of having an affair, Emma would have had a large estate from her many years as Nelson's mistress and Horatia a legacy which could have helped pay for her maintenance and ultimately be used as a dowry.

Unfortunately for Emma, she learned that despite what she and Nelson thought and all their language of love, what parliament and the law respected was the traditional family. It would not be Horatia, Nelson's beloved daughter, who would gain a comfortable life after her father's death but his legitimate wife, Fanny, and his grasping brother. The rules were in place to protect all parties; convinced that they were above such things, Nelson and Emma hurt not only themselves but their child, Nelson's reputation, Emma's financial future, and Fanny, who was simply shunted aside. By awarding Fanny and not Emma numerous honours and financial benefits, parliament demonstrated that no one believed that a mistress should ever supplant a wife.

Despite earning a tremendous amount of money during her career, Sophia Baddeley's careless attitude towards money, her generosity and her expensive tastes meant that Sophia spent way more money than she could ever hope to repay. While many people took advantage of Sophia's generosity, some of her closest friends and admirers begged her to be more careful and to consider her future. As her biographer, Elizabeth Steele, puts it, Lord Pigot 'gave her the best advice', advising Sophia that her 'beauty would not last forever; and recommended it to her, to pursue her pleasures with prudence, and save for a rainy day'.[19] This seemed to have little impression on Sophia, who responded, 'I will have my frolics and pleasures, convinced I shall not live to be old.'[20] Diamonds were her biggest weakness; in a three-year period, she had spent the equivalent, in today's money, of approximately £250,000 on jewellery.[21] While outrageous spending and gambling debts would have been the norm with the people she often rubbed shoulders with, Sophia forgot an important rule: no matter how much respect one was given, or how fashionable, or how accepted one was by members of the aristocracy, she was not one of them. Sophia's inability to save money forced her to flee England, first to Dublin and then to Edinburgh, to avoid her creditors. She died destitute in Scotland at the age of only 41.[22]

Since the costs associated with being a kept mistress were so high, losing her patron could cause an almost immediate financial crisis. This crisis was exacerbated by the fact that many mistresses lived on credit. During their relationship, tradesmen, bankers and shopkeepers all happily extended credit, but once word got out that they were no longer under the protection of a wealthy patron, a professional mistress could find it very difficult to purchase the necessities of life and their trade. Worse still, suddenly, tradesmen who never seemed to worry about getting paid would show up demanding that their accounts be settled.[23] Even professionals who had been bought off with an annuity faced economic hardship, for while such money helped, it did little to solve their short-term problems and meant that they would have to use all their skills to keep their creditors at bay and avoid the dreaded debtors' prison.

Relying on former patrons and friends was risky and unlikely to have a positive outcome. Few former lovers, having obtained what they wanted, could be counted upon, and we saw in the previous chapter how leading men could neglect to live up to their promises. There were exceptions. William Hickey, a kind and generous man, upon hearing that the professional mistress Lucy Cooper had been thrown in debtors' prison, placed 10 guineas aside for her and encouraged others to do so as well. Due to his efforts, £50 was raised to help with her release.[24] John Spencer, son of Jack Spencer, a notorious seducer and man about town, also generously provided money to aid one of the women that his father had wronged. Indeed, upon hearing and verifying his deceased father's role in the downfall of the famous courtesan Fanny Murray, who was in desperate need of money as she was being held for debt, John cleared her debts and provided her with a yearly annuity of £200. He also convinced the actor David Ross to take her as his wife.[25] In another example, some of Harriette Wilson's former lovers raised enough money to cover her dowry, enabling her to marry Colonel William Henry Rochfort, which ensured that she, unlike many of her peers, was able to retire in comfort.[26]

Courtesans had no landed estate to lease, and much of what they owned was a gift, rented, or had little resale value; thus, while courtesans looked the part, their balance sheets often told another story. If things ever got tight, there were few assets a professional mistress could count upon. Jewellery and fine dresses had little resale value and were the tools of her trade. Since a courtesan needed to look the part, selling such items was not really a viable option. After losing the protection of Melbourne, a desperate Sophia sold her jewels and only received about a third of their actual value.[27] She also returned to the stage to increase her income and in the hopes of attracting a new patron. Time was not on her side, and Sophia quickly learned that the demand for her company and her earning power had significantly decreased. Having made many desperate and poor choices, Sophia, who had lived like, and had relationships with, the aristocracy, would eventually attach herself to a servant. Having broken with Sophia over her poor decisions, Mrs Steele remarked, 'To think that she should thus far fall …'[28] Sophia no longer could attract the best and struggled to appease, delay and dodge her creditors before eventually dying in debt, addicted to laudanum. Due to the high costs associated with her profession and lifestyle, if a professional mistress was to find herself without a patron, she must quickly find another before debt collectors came calling, especially if she, like Sophia, lacked an annuity.

Blackmailing former lovers could provide desperate or spurned courtesans another way to profit from their careers. Possessing some incriminating letters written by a young George, Prince of Wales, Mary

Robinson, a seasoned professional, threatened to have them published unless paid to suppress them. Knowing the prince's flair for the dramatic, one can imagine that these were rather damaging. In 1781, his father, the king, informed the prime minister that, 'My Eldest son got last year into an Improper relationship with an actress, a Woman of indifferent Character and he sent her Letters and made foolish Promises. Colonel Hotham has settled to pay the enormous sum of Five Thousand Pounds for their return.'[29] That his disapproving and relatively frugal father paid £5,000 in return for the letters, all but confirmed their sensitive nature. The prince did, however, learn his lesson and, later on in life, instructed Sir William Knighton and the Duke of Wellington that once they heard of his death to immediately search his room and make sure that they destroyed all his letters. Sadly, these are now lost to history, but we know from the duke that such letters were of a sexual nature and that the duke, rather liberal in his thoughts and attitudes about sexual relationships, claimed to have been astonished by the subject matter.[30]

A tell-all biography offered another method for a professional mistress to profit from her career. One of the first to try to use print as a way of blackmailing former lovers, Theresa Constantia Phillips had been offered £1,000 for a tell-all account of her life. Before its release, she offered her former lovers the opportunity to remove their stories in return for an annuity.[31] The Earl of Chesterfield offered her £200 to remove him from her account; Theresa demanded £500. He refused to pay, and thus, the earl features prominently in her *An Apologia for the Conduct of Mrs Theresa Constantia*.[32] The aforementioned Harriette Wilson, having suffered numerous broken promises from the leading men of the period, decided to publish her memoirs, in part to exact revenge on those who had broken their word. In February 1825, on the eve of what would become the first edition, Wilson promised that she would remove a person from her biography in return for a significant payoff. George IV cut a deal to ensure that his role in her life was largely kept from the public.[33] The king was not the only one to pay, as it was rumoured that Wilson had secured around £10,000 in payoffs.[34] One of Wilson's chief targets, the Duke of Wellington, refused to pay, uttering the delectable response of, 'publish and be damned'.[35] She responded by publishing a scathing portrait of the duke, including mocking his appearance, saying that his dress resembled that of a rat-catcher.[36]

One way for a professional mistress to secure her future and ensure she did not end up in poverty was to marry her patron. Although rare, there were enough examples of a commoner marrying a nobleman or a mistress becoming an aristocrat's wife to fuel literature, theatre, and the dreams of many women hoping that a marriage to a dashing gentleman or aristocrat would improve their lot in life. Having made her name as Polly Peachum in John Gay's *Beggar's Opera*, Lavinia Fenton won the attentions of Charles Powlett, 3rd Duke of Bolton. As his mistress, she gave him three illegitimate children. When his wife died, she married the duke, a man twenty-three years her senior, becoming a duchess. The beautiful Gunning sisters, Mary and Elizabeth, also married into the aristocracy. The former wed the Earl of Coventry, while Elizabeth became the wife of the Duke of Hamilton. Harriette Wilson's sister Sophia, who had also been a professional mistress, married Baron Berwick.[37] This marriage, or rather what Harriette perceived to be Sophia's haughty attitude after becoming a lady, drove a wedge between the two sisters. Harriette responded by getting a box at the theatre directly above Sophia and using the height advantage to spit on her sister.[38] Other examples include Kitty Fisher, who married Lord Maynard, and Elizabeth Farren, who became the wife of the Earl of Derby, while Harriet Powell married the Earl of Seaforth.[39] Although certainly not the norm, these examples remind us that, for a limited few, it was possible to gain admittance into the aristocracy.

Not all courtesans proved incapable of saving money. Elizabeth Armistead managed her money well. Her reign as the chief lady of the town lasted some ten years, and because of self-control and good money management, she was able to save enough to have a comfortable retirement.[40] Her shrewd business sense, coupled with her long reign at the top allowed her to secure two annuities. With this money, Elizabeth could afford to purchase two homes, both located in fashionable neighbourhoods.[41] That Elizabeth bought two homes with the money she earned is impressive, especially considering that this was a period when few women could claim to have freehold over a single property.

Women who did have exclusive rights to a property most probably received them as an inheritance or as a widow; they rarely purchased them with their own money as Elizabeth had done.

Elizabeth fell in love with and married one of the leading men of the period. After nearly a decade of living as virtual man and wife, in 1795 Elizabeth married the famous and skilled politician Charles James Fox. A man of fine pedigree and royal blood, Fox loved her deeply. Elizabeth had admired Fox for a long time and, upon becoming his mistress, worked hard to lessen his love of late nights, gambling and large amounts of food and wine.[42] Since Fox had spent and gambled away several fortunes (it has been estimated that by his twenty-fifth birthday Fox had already lost some £140,000), it was her wealth that ultimately sustained and supported their marriage.[43] When Fox died in 1806, George, Prince of Wales, who had a history with both Fox and Elizabeth, kindly awarded Elizabeth a pension worth £500 a year.[44] Combined with the money that she had saved from her days as a professional, the pension helped to ensure that Elizabeth had a comfortable retirement.

Unfortunately, the example set by Elizabeth was not a model followed by most professional mistresses. Sophia Baddeley, with her out-of-control spending and little thought for the future, seemed to be the norm. It is sad to think that women like Sophia, who had once had access to great riches, had so little in the end. To ensure a good retirement required the discipline to set money aside for the future. Failing that, an annuity could make all the difference. While many former professionals who had an annuity lived, in modern parlance, pay-check to pay-check, successful and shrewd mistresses could acquire multiple annuities during their careers. Mary Robinson, for instance, received annuities from both the Prince of Wales and Lord Malden and, although less certain, Grace Elliott may have received annuities from the Prince of Wales and Lord Cholmondeley.[45] Despite their large incomes, many of the leading women who failed to save their money or secure sufficient annuities needed to marry a man of means to avoid having to endure a meagre and often impoverished retirement.

CHAPTER THIRTEEN

Illegitimate Children: What to do?

A direct consequence of the affairs conducted by England's ruling elite, illegitimate children challenged the centrality of marriage and inheritance as they could impact on the passing of wealth and property to legitimate heirs. They also served as reminders of past relationships and threatened an affair's transient and light nature by tying two people together for life. Given the importance of presenting a happy and healthy marriage, those faced with the prospect of bringing an illegitimate child into the world might opt to do so in secret. Leading Georgians disliked scandal, and the birth of an illegitimate child would create much gossip and could even lead, especially for women, to being punished by being excluded from society or even exiled by their spouse or family.

While affairs could be enjoyed by men and women (with men still given more license and less likely to be punished if their extra-marital relationships violated the rules of having an affair), there was a clear double standard when it came to illegitimate children. Although a husband could acknowledge his illegitimate children and even raise them among his legitimate children, women were often expected to give birth in secret and to place the child in the hands of another person to raise. The clearest and oft-used example is that of the Duke and Duchess of Devonshire. Although Georgiana raised the duke's two illegitimate children alongside their legitimate children, when she became impregnated by Charles Grey in 1791, the duchess had to go to the continent to give birth in secret. Unlike the illegitimate children fathered by the duke, this child was not raised among her legitimate half-siblings but instead raised by Grey's parents. The duchess had to remain abroad for some two years before being welcomed back by the duke. Georgiana also had to promise never to see Grey again but had no say over who her husband spent his time with.[1] Although the duke would forgive her, the lesson was clear: only he could produce children outside of their marriage without facing a stiff punishment.[2]

Lawyer and sexual biographer James Boswell believed that, given his privileged station in life, it was a positive outcome if he impregnated one of his many sexual partners. Explaining his logic to his friend Jean-Jacques Rousseau, Boswell stated that as a rich man he could 'take a number of girls. [If] I get them with child, … I give them dowries and marry them off to good peasants who are very happy to have them … I, on my side, have had the benefit of enjoying a great variety of women …'[3] While Boswell's assertion that a generous dowry encourages 'good peasants' to marry a woman who is carrying another man's child is informative, one should remember that Boswell had contracted gonorrhoea some seventeen times and that his former lovers may also have contracted the disease and, if infected, might pass it to her new husband or child.[4]

Boswell's sexual escapades and attitude demonstrate that wealthy and unmarried Georgian men could father illegitimate children with near impunity. The Duke of Clarence, who had ten children with his mistress Dora Jordan, still travelled in the highest social circles and eventually became king. Although often financially dependent upon his actress/mistress for love and comfort, to say nothing of her money, as their children grew they could accompany their father when he visited other leading lights of Georgian society; their mother, Dora Jordan, because of her background, would often be left at home.[5] Dora understood that William, because of his privileged position, offered her children much more than she ever could. Indeed, five of her daughters married into the aristocracy.[6] Some mothers made the heart-wrenching decision to give away their children to former lovers. For instance, Clair Clairmont ultimately chose to leave her child with the much better-placed Lord Byron.[7] This must have been very difficult to do, but mothers understood the advantages that men of high (or for William the highest) birth could offer to their children. Such knowledge probably did little to aid the emotional distress that would have accompanied such separation.

Going abroad remained a popular option for hiding a pregnancy. Travelling abroad while pregnant must have been a difficult and nerve-wracking experience. Given the hardships of eighteenth-century travel, bumpy roads, carriages that were utterly unforgiving, and bad roadside hotels with uncomfortable and small quarters, it is amazing that the English elite were so enthused with foreign travel.[8] While the glimpses of antiquity offered by Greece or the warm weather, food and culture of the south of France coupled with a lifetime of fond memories and the status attributed to those who had travelled abroad made travel an exciting and important component of aristocratic life, this was of little comfort if one's reason for travelling was to conceal a pregnancy. Not only would these women have to endure a long and uncomfortable trip it meant that they would give birth in a place with which they had little or no familiarity. Afterwards, their children would most likely be deposited with a family on the continent or back in England. Many parents would follow the lives of these children from afar, and it was not unusual for aristocrats to contribute financially to their unrecognised illegitimate children's futures.[9] Having to give away a child must have been very difficult and should be set against the frivolity and ease with which many men and women entered an affair.

Some women were able to give birth to illegitimate children without leaving England. This involved either a husband who looked the other way, was complicit, or one that could be deceived. Harriet's husband, Lord Duncannon, probably did not know about either of his wife's two children fathered by Granville Leveson-Gower. Harriet and Granville's first child, named Harriet, was born in 1800. The most significant challenge was not hiding Harriet's pregnancy from her husband but from her often disapproving and demanding mother.[10] The interfering and ever-vigilant Lady Spencer chided her children when their letters failed to live up to her exacting standards or provide sufficient insights into their day-to-day living.[11] Luckily for Harriet, her mother assumed she had poor health and knowing that things were rocky between Harriet and Duncannon, Lady Spencer did not think it was a good time for a visit and decided to stay away.[12]

Despite the difficulties of hiding a pregnancy, the birth and a new child, only a small group of trusted friends ever knew about little Harriet.

Granville and Harriet's second child, George Arundel Stewart, was also born in England and kept hidden from Duncannon. Although foster parents raised Harriet and George, Harriet and Granville monitored them closely. Around the age of 12, Harriet came to live with Granville, viewing him as her guardian.[13] After her marriage to George Osborne, the future Duke of Leeds, Granville continued to be present in her life and even helped the couple out financially. George Stewart never married and, during his youth, travelled extensively. Later in life, he became Granville's private secretary.[14] Despite Harriet and Granville's involvement in their children's lives, they never told them that they were their actual parents.[15] Whether the children suspected a more familial connection with either Harriet or Granville is unknown.

A husband could shield a wife from claims that she had given birth to an illegitimate child. Presumably, as in the example above, if Harriet and her husband still shared a bed, she may have tried to pass off the two children fathered by Granville as her husband's legitimate offspring. Even if Duncannon suspected that Harriet and George were not his, he might have accepted them, since the two children fathered by Granville proved little threat to the inheritance or family line of Duncannon as Harriet had already given Duncannon three legitimate sons and one legitimate daughter. While some men may have had no idea about their wives' affairs, others knew and were willing to say nothing and raise another man's child to avoid scandal. When Elizabeth Sheridan's relationship with the dashing radical politician Lord Edward Fitzgerald resulted in a child, her husband, Richard Brinsley Sheridan, accepted his wife's daughter as his own to protect her reputation and avoid any scandal.[16] The reasons for accepting another man's child as one's own varied, but leading Georgians may have done so to protect a spouse's reputation, because they may have needed an heir, or since they already had an heir did not worry that a third or fourth child would affect their lineage. In an era before paternity tests, some men may have been unsure whether a child was actually theirs or had been fathered by another man. Given that illegitimacy could cut one off from inheritance and would make their life much more difficult, such doubts were usually best kept to oneself.

In 1776, Mary Eleanor Bowes, the Dowager Countess of Strathmore, found herself in the unfortunate position of being pregnant with another man's child only a few months after her husband's death. George Gray, her lover, had much to gain from impregnating Mary Eleanor and must have hoped that now that she was carrying his child, Mary Eleanor would agree to marry him. Mary Eleanor had tried to avoid getting pregnant, stating that, 'All the time of my connection with Mr Gray, precautions were taken.'[17] As Wendy Moore points out, given Mary Eleanor's comment that, 'an instant's neglect always destroyed', they probably practised the pull-out method.[18] Mary Eleanor must have considered trying to pass the child off as her husband's but possibly guessed that, given his declining health and subsequent death, few would have believed that he had been able to father a child.

After considering her options, Mary Eleanor informed Gray that she wanted to attempt an abortion rather than give birth to an illegitimate child. Not wanting to risk being identified, she asked Gray to 'bring me the quack medicine he had heard of for miscarriage'.[19] Described by Mary Eleanor as 'a black inky kind of medicine',[20] the 'quack medicine' may have been a compound that included the bark from the poplar tree, although other herbal mixtures were also used.[21] Although Gray did purchase the medicine, he warned her that the concoction could be poisonous and might cause long-term health effects. Despite these warnings, Mary Eleanor decided to consume the abortive and subsequently miscarried.[22]

The unwanted pregnancy and subsequent abortion did not change Gray and Mary Eleanor's behaviour, as Gray continued to visit her bedchamber every other night. The couple had agreed upon such a system to ensure that their passion for one another did not wane and that every other night they could be assured of a good night's sleep rather than a late-night romp.[23] Such frequent coupling increased the chances of pregnancy. Despite the 'precautions', Mary Eleanor became pregnant four times in 1776. Four unwanted pregnancies in a year suggests that either contraceptive was not used or, if it was employed, it had been implemented improperly or haphazardly. If, as Wendy Moore suggests, they practised the pull-out method, they appear to have been pretty poor at it.

When the dowager countess found herself pregnant a second time, she once again turned to the abortive 'quack medicine', and another miscarriage ensued. The third time, however, the medicine failed to work. Mary Eleanor turned to another method involving an emetic that induced vomiting while consuming a large quantity of brandy infused with pepper. Mary Eleanor had another miscarriage.[24] A fourth pregnancy followed, and after the usual methods failed to produce an abortion, she turned to John Hunter for help. The medicine he supplied did not work, and Mary Eleanor would deliver her sixth child the following year.[25] That a rich dowager countess went to such great lengths and risked her health to try and prevent giving birth to an illegitimate child demonstrates the degrees to which Georgian society looked down upon women for bringing an illegitimate child into the world.

A married woman could attempt to pass off an illegitimate child as legitimate by, once becoming aware of her state, immediately having relations with her husband, hoping that he would believe that he had fathered the child. Mary Eleanor's second husband, Andrew Robinson Stoney, used a version of this manoeuvre to pass off one of his illegitimate children on his lover's husband. A man who had sex with numerous women, Stoney had impregnated his son's wet nurse. Although he did not care that his wife knew about the situation, Stoney preferred to keep Mrs Houghton's husband from learning the truth. This proved problematic as her husband lived in London while she worked at Gibside in Yorkshire. A master manipulator, Stoney, sent the husband a letter instructing him to immediately head north, stating that his wife was very ill. Shortly after the wet nurse's husband arrived, Mrs Houghton made a quick 'recovery' so much so that she could have intercourse with her husband. The husband, satisfied with his wife's health, returned to London. Stoney and Mrs Houghton could now pass the child off as legitimate.[26] The husband had his doubts, especially since the child, a daughter, was born only six months after their coupling. Jesse Foot, a surgeon, and friend of Stoney told the doubtful husband that it was possible to give birth to a healthy child after only six months. Whether the husband actually believed this or not is unknown. Georgian men could be relatively ignorant of the pregnancy process, and this lack of knowledge could be used to trick unsuspecting husbands. For this lie and his services to Stoney, Foot pocketed an extra fee.[27] This example shows the extent to which Georgians would go to hide an illegitimate child. That the doubtful husband accepted the story also demonstrates that some husbands realised that even if they had their misgivings, it was often easier to recognise a child as their own than to doubt its parentage.

For those members of the Georgian elite who engaged in extra-marital affairs, bringing an illegitimate child into the world was not only a concern but often a reality. Some, like Mary Eleanor Bowes, Dowager Countess of Strathmore, had multiple abortions rather than giving birth to an illegitimate child. Rather than face society's disapproval, other leading Georgians decided to hide their situation by giving birth in secret and giving the child to others to raise. Giving away a child must have been very difficult. That so many parents monitored their children's development and found ways to help them signifies a real and enduring attachment. That many parents never revealed their true identities to protect themselves and their children's image tells us much about how Georgian elites viewed and treated those of illegitimate birth. The significance, stress and emotional strife of bringing an illegitimate child into the world must be set alongside the frivolity and lightness at which many affairs were entered into.

CHAPTER FOURTEEN

Criminal Conversation: Be Prepared to Defend Yourself

One of the biggest risks of having an affair was the possibility of being sued for criminal conversation. An evocative term, criminal conversation suits were an eighteenth-century development that allowed a husband to sue his wife's sexual partner. During the eighteenth and first half of the nineteenth centuries, criminal conversation suits replaced duelling as one of the primary methods of restoring honour and dignity for a cuckolded husband.[1] Large judgments for the plaintiffs allowed wronged husbands to financially gain from their wives' affairs while punishing the offending parties by contributing to the defendants' financial ruin. Criminal conversation suits upheld the patriarchal nature of Georgian society as only men could sue other men; women were viewed as their husbands' property. Criminal conversation suits were often necessary to secure a parliamentary divorce. There were approximately 500 criminal conversation cases up until 1857, when a new marriage act, which simplified the process of divorce, made suing for damages largely unnecessary.[2]

A criminal conversation suit could be levelled at any time, meaning that a husband who had once tolerated an affair but later soured on the idea could suddenly bring forth a lawsuit. As we have already covered, after promoting and profiting from his wife's infidelity, Theo Cibber, once the money and his control over the couple ended, brought two criminal conversation suits against his wife's lover. Similarly, although he tolerated and even encouraged their coupling, upon learning that his neighbour and political ally George Bisset had run away with his wife, Sir Richard Worsley sued Bisset for criminal conversation.

The trial of Worsley vs. Worsley began on 21 February 1782. At first glance, Sir Richard had an excellent case, for no one disputed that Bisset and Lady Worsley had engaged in a sexual relationship. Nor could it be denied that as a friend, comrade and subordinate, Bisset had committed a heinous betrayal by running away with Lady Worsley. The fact that Bisset benefited from Sir Richard's kindness, and had even been promoted by Worsley, would almost certainly be held against him and might prove decisive in convincing a jury to award Sir Richard a large settlement.

The awarding of money at a criminal conversation trial was based on two distinct factors, both of which reflect assumptions made by Georgian law and people. The first assumption was that Lady Worsley was Sir Richard's property. The prosecution would argue that Bisset had damaged Sir Richard's property by denying him the exclusive company of his own wife.[3] The second assumption was that any insult done to a gentleman was infinitely worse than one suffered by a member of the lower orders. The great majority of English people were accustomed to insults to their character and dignity, so, as the law reasoned and juries tended to reinforce, what was one more injustice/indignity for a commoner to have to endure? For a gentleman like Sir Richard, accustomed to having his way and whose pride and dignity were important to him, having to deal with such an indignity entitled this already entitled man to much more. Furthermore, gentlemen were believed to feel more deeply as their education and foreign experience sharpened and increased their sensitivity. According to the thinking of the day, this made what Bisset did to the supposedly tender heart of Sir Richard much worse. Edward Bearcroft, a lawyer for the prosecution, had argued this point before. In the case of Edward Dodwell vs. The Rev. Henry Bate Dudley, Bearcroft asserted, 'it was essential for them to remember that the Plaintiff was a man of fortune, and therefore the action in point of trespass was greater on that account.'[4]

Bent on seeking revenge, Worsley sought the astronomical sum of £20,000 in restitution.[5] This amount would have bankrupted almost any man in the country. Certainly, it was beyond what Bisset could pay. Aiming to ruin Bisset, Worsley, who had previously considered buying

Bisset's land, knew that his neighbour received approximately £1,500 a year from leasing his property.[6] Sir Richard thus sought around thirteen years of rent in damages. Worsley desired to punish Bisset and to see him lose all he held dear. He may have hoped that Bisset would be unable to pay the judgment and would be forced to live out his days in exile or debtors' prison.[7]

Criminal conversation cases nearly always began with the prosecution explaining that the marriage had once been happy and that the couple would have continued to enjoy marital bliss if it had not been for the defendant. In another case where he served as the prosecution, Bisset's lawyer, Edward Bearcroft, employed this strategy, stating that his client, Edward Dodwell:

> and his wife had, for the space of twelve years, lived together in the utmost harmony and love, and might have continued in that happy state, had not the defendant [The Rev. Henry Bate Dudley] interrupted the enjoyment of their bliss by seducing, and afterwards criminally conversing with the plaintiff's wife, which, being done, produced, what such conduct is always sure to produce, unhappiness and discord.[8]

Sir Richard's legal team used a similar tactic, stressing how happy the Worsleys had been before Bisset had interfered in their lives.

Worsley's legal team advised him that the surest way to ensure victory over Bisset would be to have someone directly witness their coupling. Given their odd living arrangements and Sir Richard's reputation as a voyeur, Worsley almost certainly witnessed Bisset and Seymour together. Sir Richard could not testify to knowing about his wife and Bisset, for it would have prompted the jury to wonder why he did not immediately confront Bisset. To be granted the damages he sought, Sir Richard needed to present himself as the wronged husband rather than the man who turned a blind eye to Bisset and Seymour, only to sue Bisset after they fled.

To gain direct evidence of Bisset and Seymour's coupling, James Farrar, who had the pre-trial task of gathering evidence for Worsley, turned to the hotel's manager, Mr Weston, for help. He met with Weston and told him that his establishment was harbouring two runaway lovers and that his client, the husband, desperately needed the hotel's help in bringing his wife and her lover to justice. Mr Weston agreed to help. He instructed his staff to follow Farrar's instructions and do all they could to help him secure evidence.

The first task was to have Lady Worsley, who had refused to identify herself, reveal her identity to a hotel staff member. To encourage her to do so, the staff informed her that someone left a riding habit for a lady but as far as they could tell, they did not know a lady was staying at the hotel hoping that the promise of fresh clothes, something Lady Worsley desperately lacked, would prompt Seymour into revealing her identity. Desperate and tired of the maids, Seymour relented, telling them that she was indeed Lady Worsley and that the riding habit must be for her.

The next part of the plan involved giving Mary Sotherby, Lady Worsley's lady's maid, a few items to deliver to Seymour. It was her job to enter the room so that she could later testify that she saw her mistress and Bisset living together in the hotel. To ensure that he had enough witnesses, Farrar also sent the groom, Philip Deishta, to identify the couple.[9] During the case, these witnesses could definitively state that Bisset and Lady Worsley were living together in the hotel. For instance, a member of the hotel's staff, waiter Thomas Bourne, later testified that he 'took them to be man and wife' while clarifying that the room had only one bed.[10]

Given the mounting evidence against him, Bisset needed a strong defence. Bisset's defence team believed that the best way to avoid having to pay the ruinous damages sought by Sir Richard was to demonstrate that Bisset, rather than being a seducer of Lady Worsley, was just one of many men who, over the course of her marriage, had sexual relations with Sir Richard's wife. The argument would be that Bisset did not ruin Worsley's property; it had already been damaged by a long list of men before Bisset ever took Seymour as a lover. Bisset's defence team would strive to demonstrate that Sir Richard had been aware of Lady Worsley's indiscretions and had even gone so far as to encourage them. Bisset's defence would be that Sir Richard liked to share his wife and that his only grievance occurred after Bisset had run away with Lady Worsley. The defence would further claim that Bisset's motivation for running away with Lady Worsley stemmed from a desire to protect her from Sir Richard's perversion. Bisset would play the tortured man, caught between the woman he loved and the flawed friend to whom he wished to be loyal. This would be a compelling defence.

Bisset's defence rested upon his willingness to ruin Lady Worsley's reputation. He needed to show her to be little better than a common whore, a woman who, with her husband's knowledge, had freely granted her favours to a host of men. But how to prove this? The most effective and compelling method would be to have former lovers testify to having had a sexual relationship with Seymour. This defence would only work if sanctioned by Lady Worsley, for the only way a gentleman would ever reveal such details in open court was if they had Seymour's permission to do so. Confronted with either ruining her reputation and potentially saving Bisset from ruin or saying nothing and seeing her lover likely thrown into debtors' prison or being forced to flee into exile, Lady Worsley had a difficult decision to make.

As a woman who had frequently flaunted conventions, Seymour decided to stick with Bisset. Not only did she promise to help in Bisset's defence she also agreed to write to her previous lovers imploring them to testify. This could not have been easy. Although she could not have been happy with the prospect of having her extra-marital affairs aired in court, Lady Worsley probably had few other options. It was unlikely that Sir Richard would have welcomed her back at this point. If she refused to aid Bisset, Lady Worsley would have lost not only Sir Richard's protection but also Bisset, the man she loved. The cost would be extremely high, for, in an effort to save Bisset, Seymour would have to endure having her sexual history revealed in court. This would almost certainly ruin her reputation.

With Lady Worsley's help, the defence produced a cadre of witnesses willing to discuss their previous involvement with Seymour. Bisset's defence team believed that this would conclusively prove to the court and members of the jury that Sir Richard had long ago lost the exclusive rights to Seymour's body. The defence's first witness was Lady

Worsley's long-time friend and former lover, George William Coventry, Viscount Deerhurst. Deerhurst, despite his reputation as a rake, seemed quite vexed at the prospect of testifying in open court, with the *Morning Herald* reporting that his lordship seemed 'particularly distressed at his situation'.[11]

Aristocrats could make for difficult witnesses. Neither the law nor the etiquette of society could force Deerhurst, within the confines of a civil trial, to disclose any information he wished to keep private. Understanding his position and privilege on various occasions, Deerhurst reminded the court that he should not be pressed for details. He made it clear to the court that he had come to defend a friend and tell his story and that he would not, under any circumstances, answer impertinent questions or reveal confidences. For instance, when pressed for more details, Deerhurst turned to the judge and asked, 'I hope I am not called to betray any private conversation?'[12] The judge assured Deerhurst, his social superior, that he would not be asked to betray any confidences and encouraged the defence to move on.[13]

After dancing around the issue, Deerhurst informed the court that Sir Richard had encouraged him to pursue Lady Worsley. According to Deerhurst, Sir Richard commented that, 'many young men had tried her to no effect; and that I had permission to try my chance with her'.[14] Deerhurst explained that at first, he did not take this expression at face value and assumed that it stemmed from Sir Richard's odd humour.[15] While still a guest of the Worsleys, he determined that Sir Richard was serious and, unsurprisingly, given his reputation, Deerhurst pursued Lady Worsley. Late one night, Deerhurst sneaked into Lady Seymour's dressing room, a private room adjacent to her bedchamber. While Deerhurst did not say precisely why he did so, the jury would have understood that there could only be one reason why a man, especially a man with Deerhurst's reputation, would be in a woman's dressing room. Deerhurst stated that upon leaving the dressing room, sometime around 4 a.m., he encountered Sir Richard. While the jury would have known why Deerhurst was there, it was less obvious why her husband was loitering around her dressing room at that time and, more importantly, why Sir Richard, having seen Deerhurst, did not do anything about it.

Deerhurst claimed that Sir Richard did not seem upset, never spoke of the matter, did not demand that he leave their home, and, afterwards, made no attempt to keep the two apart. Deerhurst testified that he stayed another few days and left on his own accord, not because an enraged or jealous husband chased him off.[16] This was damning testimony.

Bisset's defence team emphasised that Worsley had known about Lady Worsley's behaviour and even participated in the 'ruining' of his wife. Edward Bearcroft told the court the infamous bathing-house story, which, if believed, demonstrated to the court the depths of Sir Richard's involvement in his wife's indiscretions. It is alleged that Sir Richard, knowing that his wife was naked in the bathing house, encouraged Bisset to stand on his shoulders so Bisset could watch Seymour as she emerged from the bath, while they were at Maidstone.[17] Reliving the events of the bathing-house story, Bearcroft stated that Sir Richard shouted, 'Seymour! Seymour! Bisset is looking at you; and they all went off together in a hearty laugh at the transaction which had passed.'[18] Hoisting another man onto your shoulders so that he might look at your naked wife is not the behaviour of a man concerned with protecting his wife or of a supposedly wronged husband. This tale caught the public's imagination, featuring in numerous satirical cartoons.[19]

Bisset's defence team attacked the image of Worsley as a devoted and loving husband, explaining that he derived pleasure from his wife's affairs. Sir Richard, according to Bearcroft, 'not only acquiesced …' to his wife's affairs 'but even excited and encouraged it'.[20] Bearcroft explained that he had ignored the advice of 'many Ladies of Distinction …' who 'had frequently remonstrated with Sir Richard on that subject, and told him that, if he did not attempt to restrain her conduct, her character would be ruined and destroyed …'[21] In short, Worsley had been well aware of his wife's behaviour and not only did he allow it to occur but encouraged her to take on lovers.

In a criminal conversation case, defence attorneys routinely attack the plaintiff's character arguing that it was the husband's actions or character deficiencies that had led to a separation of affections. In the Dodwell vs. Dudley case, Mr Mingay, the lead lawyer for the defence (Bearcroft led the prosecution in this case), emphasised the many character faults of the plaintiff, asserting that he had not only 'been inattentive, negligent and careless, but rude, barbarous, and brutal …'[22] Furthermore, the defence accused the husband of having odd, inappropriate and disgusting interests including being a long-time follower of 'a science [dissection], for which the delicacy, the taste, and the feelings of a beautiful female, were ill adapted …'[23] Continuing with his opening statements, Mingay stated that despite his wife asking him not to, 'he approached her with his hands covered with all the nauseous filthiness of such pursuits,' concluding that 'this might have furnished a delicate lady with an apology for abandoning her husband'.[24] After detailing a few other character flaws and questionable hobbies for a gentleman to pursue, Mingay returned to dissection, stating that:

> If a man of this description expected a young beautiful female, delicately and politely educated, to shew towards him much conjugal affection, it was not wonderful that he was disappointed; for, who could expect that action of such repulsive practices, appearing with his hands covered with the blood of bodies, while his hungry hounds were quarrelling over the flesh he had been slicing, could ever be an engaging companion to a lady.[25]

Defence lawyers knew that by attacking the plaintiff's character, even if they ultimately lost the case, they might succeed in reducing the fines their clients would be ordered to pay.

Bisset's lawyers argued that Sir Richard was too preoccupied with his political career and general social climbing to give his wife the attention, protection and direction she so clearly needed. Witness after witness gave the impression that Worsley had neglected his duties, failed to protect his wife, and had a habit of leaving his wife alone in male company. Lord Peterborough, a good friend of Deerhurst and an acquaintance of Lady Worsley, testified that in all the occasions on which he had seen Lady Worsley socially, he had never once met her husband.[26] Bouchier Smith, who had married Lord Deerhurst's illegitimate half-sister, testified that on one occasion he witnessed Lady Worsley asking her husband to join their party but that Sir Richard declined the invitation encouraging his wife to travel without him or even a chaperone.[27] James Graham, the Marquess of Graham and later Duke of Montrose, told the court that while he had known Lady Worsley for some three or four years, he had never once met Sir Richard.[28] These witnesses brought home the point that the 'property' to which Sir Richard had claimed to have deeply cared for and highly valued, had been neglected and, if ruined, had been damaged long before Lady Worsley had even met Bisset.

While many of the witnesses who knew Seymour socially hinted at having had a sexual relationship with her, few admitted to it. Worried that the jury might miss the allusions to sexual intercourse or be confused by their often-vague answers, the defence called Lady Worsley's physician to the stand. Under normal circumstances, Dr William Osborne would not have been required to provide the court with private medical information. However, like other witnesses, Lady Worsley wrote to Osborne asking him to set aside medical confidentiality and tell the court what he knew about her medical history. When called to the stand, the doctor made it clear that he understood and respected the necessity and inviolability of medical confidentiality and that he was only testifying at the explicit request of his patient Lady Worsley.[29] Dr Osborne proceeded to tell the court that he had attended Seymour in August 1780 for a complaint caused by venereal disease.[30] The timing of this treatment suggests that she contracted venereal disease from the Marquess of Graham.[31] Lady Worsley asked a lot of Dr Osborne. By talking in open court, especially in a case covered by the press, Dr Osborne risked his reputation, and this probably cost him business, as elites were almost certain to avoid a doctor who could be compelled to reveal their secrets. Well aware of this fact, Osborne wanted to leave the stand as quickly as possible and, after answering six questions, stated that he no longer wished to talk about the matter, and Lord Mansfield promptly excused him.[32] Seymour's willingness to have it revealed in court that she not only engaged in numerous extra-marital affairs but that she had contracted a venereal disease speaks of a woman willing to sacrifice what remained of her reputation for a man she loved.

Sir Richard's lawyers were caught off guard by Bisset's defence. They never imagined that Seymour would be so willing to ruin her reputation in an effort to protect Bisset. As the case developed, it increasingly concerned itself with the character and culpability of Sir Richard rather than, as he intended, the actions of Bisset. Before deliberation, Lord Mansfield instructed the jury that if Sir Richard 'had been privy to the prostitution of his wife', then he was entitled to nothing as he had played a hand in her ruin.[33] It is interesting that while Bisset and Lady Worsley's relationship was on trial, the case came down to the actions of Sir Richard. Was he a man who had been wronged, or had he taken some pleasure and played a role in the ruin of his wife?

The jury took nearly an hour to decide. This was longer than most juries of the period, as they usually only needed a few minutes to determine guilt or innocence and, if appropriate, to settle on damages.[34] Ultimately, the jury decided that Bisset had wronged Sir Richard. There was no denying that Bisset and Seymour had a physical relationship and had tried to run away together. However, given that Sir Richard had been negligent, had not protected his wife, and may have even encouraged her affairs, the jury awarded him the derisory and humiliating amount of a shilling in damages.

Neither Sir Richard nor Lady Worsley recovered their reputation after the trial. Sir Richard had been mocked as a voyeur, and Lady Worsley's reputation was ruined beyond repair. The case received tremendous publicity, with the best-selling court transcript going through an astounding seven printings in the first year.[35] Lady Worsley knew that as a disgraced woman, she would be barred from most female company. One of the double standards of the day was that while disgraced women were shunned by respectable females, they were not excluded from male company. Since men were not judged by the company they kept, her former male friends would continue to socialise with Seymour, meaning that while she lost many of her female friends, she kept the same male company as she had before the trial.[36] Although Sir Richard continued to collect art and ancient sculptures, he increasingly withdrew from society, ultimately failing to receive the peerage that he so desperately desired. Shortly after the death of Sir Richard in 1805, Seymour, now 47 years old, married her 26-year-old lover John Lewis Cuchet. She died in 1818.

Although Bisset's defence had won the day, the trial and the £20,000 in damages sought by Sir Richard demonstrated how risky having an affair during the Georgian period could be. One could be humiliated in court, and the damages, if awarded, could prove ruinous. Because of such risks, criminal conversation lawsuits were at odds with the easy-going nature that was supposed to define aristocratic affairs and acted as a counterweight to the generally free-spirited nature of Georgian society. It also highlights that a lover must ensure to play by the husband's rules and not provoke them into seeking satisfaction via the courts. Like the threat of pregnancy and illegitimacy, criminal conversation suits reminded leading Georgians that affairs could have real and lasting repercussions.

Conclusion

The preceding work has employed extra-marital affairs to gain insight into the Georgian state and society. It has sought to explore the rules of having an extra-marital affair during the period and the punishments meted out to those who broke the rules. Although extra-marital affairs were accepted and even expected, there were proper ways of conducting an affair. The violation of these rules could lead to dire social and financial consequences. This investigation has highlighted the complexities of Georgian social relations and the impact that class and gender had in shaping attitudes towards marriage, extra-marital affairs and fidelity.

Family was believed to be the bedrock of the Georgian state and society and, because of this, ending a marriage was especially difficult. Until 1857, a divorce could only be accomplished with a parliamentary bill. Because ending a marriage proved so difficult, leading Georgians often had flexible marriages that could accommodate other sexual partners. While this flexibility made marriage (especially for those thrown together in a political or economic match) more tolerable, appearances mattered. Regardless of what spouses thought of each other, both spouses were expected to appear happy in public and never put a lover before their spouse.

Marriage served as the best vehicle for cementing family alliances and passing wealth, status and power to the next generation. During the Georgian period, elite Georgians were expected to prioritise having children, and especially a male heir, above all else. While affairs were often tolerated, no relationship should impede the creation of legitimate heirs. To maintain their social and political dominance, Georgian elites needed to ensure that their wealth and property passed from one legitimate and recognised generation to the next.

Class, as it did for all aspects of Georgian life, affected how affairs were viewed. Monarchs and their princely sons were expected to have mistresses. George I and George II helped make such relations acceptable by building upon the established practices of the restoration court. Thanks to Charles II and his court, by the Georgian period it would have seemed odd for a king not to be sexually aggressive, to have numerous mistresses, and to father illegitimate children. Part of the power and mystic of being a king was expressed by sexual prowess, real or imagined. While George III thought differently, he could not get his sons or many of the aristocracy to adopt his belief in fidelity and family life.

George III's desire for the English ruling elite to demonstrate good moral character and to take the task of being a loving father and husband seriously found a more ready audience within the homes of the middling sort. For members of the middling sort, an affair could negatively impact one's career, standing and reputation. For the lower orders, an affair might produce an illegitimate child that they may not have the money to support. While there was much worry that the lower classes would adopt the lax morality of the upper class, ultimately, the working class lacked the social and financial power that granted the aristocracy their relative sexual freedom.

Gender was an important factor in how affairs were understood. While upper-class women, for the most part, could and did engage in extra-marital affairs, they had to adhere to additional rules. Firstly, it was expected that any married woman would remain faithful until she produced a legitimate male heir. Secondly, unlike their husbands, they were never to form a relationship or engage in sex with a servant or someone from the lower classes. Such an action challenged the accepted order of things and pitted two pillars of the Georgian state, patriarchy and class, against each other. Thirdly, while men were not judged by the company they kept and could surround themselves with women of questionable morality and standing without it impacting on their reputation, women were judged by the company they kept, which severely restricted their freedom, mobility and social world.

Women who broke the rules of having an affair also suffered harsher and more enduring punishments than their male counterparts. While a man who had an unsanctioned affair with another man's wife might find himself hauled into court and fined for his actions, women who violated the rules could be exiled from polite company. These women were cast adrift, never able to regain their place or access the exclusive world of the fashionable. Some, such as Georgiana, Duchess of Devonshire, were exiled and forced to live abroad after giving birth to another man's child and only regained their place after promising never to see their former lover again. After marrying William O'Brien, an actor deemed far below her family's dignity, Lady Susan Fox-Strangways spent several years in exile. Even after enduring this punishment, she was not forgiven nor welcomed back. After running away with her lover, Sarah Lennox, wife to Charles Bunbury, was placed under the control of her family and spent years trying to recover her reputation and place within elite society. This rarely happened to leading men. For leading men, social exile was most often the result of accumulating more debt than they could pay, forcing them to flee England to ensure that they remained beyond the reach of their creditors.

Infidelity and the rules that governed extra-marital affairs were (and are) socially constructed and, for elite Georgians, these rules attempted to obviate the problems associated with socio-political marriages coupled with the difficulty of obtaining a divorce. These rules were in place to protect bloodlines, property and reputations. This led to flexible marriages, which were governed by a widely accepted and understood code of rules. These rules, like those today, coupled with the punishments (or lack thereof) for their violation, provide important insights into the ways in which class, gender and power intersected during an important period in England's social and political development.

This study has shown that we need to recalibrate our understanding and framing of Georgians and the Georgian period. While their money and status gave Georgian elites tremendous power and freedom, it did not trump everything, for they had to adhere to a set of social rules. To violate such rules could lead to harsh punishments, especially for aristocratic women. Interestingly, the 'rules' that applied to leading

Georgians were primarily constructed by themselves. So, one wonders why, since Georgian elites made the rules of having an affair, the punishments for violating them are so harsh? One way of approaching the question is to employ a gendered lens. That women suffered harsher and longer-lasting punishments reinforced and preserved male dominance and power. That men were not judged by the company they kept, but women were, ultimately provided elite men much more freedom while serving to severely restrict the movement and freedom of their wives and daughters. Although leading Georgians were expected to take care of their mistresses and live up to their promises, they suffered very little if they did not keep their word. One could be sued, lose face among friends, or find oneself mentioned in a tell-all book, but ultimately men like the Duke of York or Lord Melbourne who did not pay the allowance they promised, or neglected to set up an agreed upon annuity, faced minimal backlash for their actions. Ultimately, the rules of having an affair buttressed the power and dominance of elite males – highlighting the patriarchal and class attitudes which defined the Georgian era.

Endnotes

Introduction

1. For this work, the Georgian period will encapsulate the rule of George I–George IV while also including William IV.
2. While most Britons married, there were exceptions, especially among the younger sons and daughters of the elite. Douglas Hay and Nicholas Rogers, *Eighteenth-Century English Society* (Oxford: Oxford University Press, 1997), 39.
3. Jane Austen, *Emma: A Novel* (London: John Murray, 1816).
4. A notable exception would be Hannah Grieg's *The Beau Monde.* Interested in the culture of the fashionable in Georgian England, Grieg provides an analysis of the punishments meted out to some of the leading women of the period for their sexual indiscretions. Hannah Grieg, *The Beau Monde: Fashionable Society in Georgian London* (Oxford: Oxford University Press, 2013).
5. Concerned with cultural rather than political developments, the Restoration Era in this work is broadly conceived and encompasses the entire period of later Stuart monarchs.
6. Charles II's sons would inherit some nine dukedoms. Antonia Fraser, *King Charles II* (London: Phoenix, 2002), 538.
7. John Van der Kiste, *William and Mary: Heroes of the Glorious Revolution* (Stroud: The History Press, 2008), 31.
8. David Starkey, *Crown and Country: The Kings and Queens of England: A History* (London: Harper Press, 2010), 370.
9. David Starkey asserts that James had converted in 1668. Starkey, *Crown and Country,* 366.

Antonia Fraser believes James's conversion occurred early in 1669. Antonia Fraser, *King Charles II,* 332.

10. Antonia Fraser, *King Charles II*, 452.
11. Van der Kiste, *William and Mary*, ix.
12. Starkey, *Crown and Country,* 369.
13. Van der Kiste, *William and Mary*, 35.
14. John Miller, *James II* (New Haven and London: Yale University Press, 2000), 75.
15. Charles II as quoted in Michael Farquhar, *Behind the Palace Doors: Five Centuries of Sex, Adventure, Vice, Treachery, and Folly from Royal Britain* (New York: Random House Trade Paperbacks, 2011), 138.
16. Catherine Sedley as quoted in Farquhar, *Behind the Palace Doors*, 138*n.*
17. Princess (later Queen) Anne as quoted in Starkey, *Crown and Country*, 389.
18. Van der Kiste, *William and Mary*, 91.
19. Starkey, *Crown and Country,* 390.
20. Ibid.*,* 369.
21. Although Mary's letters are rather sexually charged, it is probably best to view her feelings towards Frances as what we would today call an innocent crush. Maureen Waller, *Sovereign Ladies: The Six Reigning Queens of England* (New York: St Martin's Press, 2007), 254.
22. For an evaluation of why it is referred to as the Glorious Revolution, see: James R. Hertzler, 'Who Dubbed It "The Glorious Revolution?"', in *Albion: A Quarterly Journal Concerned with British Studies* vol. 19, no. 4 (Winter, 1987): 579–585.
23. Van der Kiste, *William and Mary*, 34.
24. William Ferguson, *Scotland's Relations with England: A Survey to 1707* (Edinburgh: Saltire Society, 1994), 246–247. Neil Oliver, *A History of Scotland* (London: Weidenfeld & Nicolson, 2010), 293.
25. Monica Hall, *A Visitor's Guide to Georgian England* (Barnsley: Pen & Sword History, 2017), 47.
26. Andrew C. Thompson, *Britain, Hanover, and the Protestant Interest, 1688–1756* (Woodbridge: Boydell Press, 2006), 46.

27. Rebecca Fraser, *Story of Britain; From the Romans to the Present: A Narrative History* (New York: W.W. Norton & Company, 2006), 412–413.
28. Robert Folkestone Williams, *Memoirs of Sophia Dorothea, Consort of George I: Chiefly from the Secret Archives of Hanover, Brunswick, Berlin, and Vienna; Including a Diary of the Conversations of Illustrious Personages of those Courts, Illustrative of Her History, with Letters and other Documents. In Two Volumes,* vol. I (London: Henry Colburn, 1845), 217–223.
29. Hall, *A Visitor's Guide to Georgian England*, 4.
30. The *Morning Chronicle* explained 'that there are two codes of morality in sexual matters in this country – one for common life and another for fashionable life'. The *Morning Chronicle* as quoted in Donna T. Andrew, *Aristocratic Vice: The Attack on Duelling, Suicide, Adultery, and Gambling in Eighteenth-Century England* (New Haven & London, 2013), 234.
31. Andrew, *Aristocratic Vice,* 4.
32. Ibid., 230.
33. Christopher Hibbert, *Queen Victoria: A Personal History* (London: Harper Collins, 2000), 3.
34. Joanne Bailey, *Unquiet Lives: Marriage and Marriage Breakdown in England, 1660–1800* (Cambridge: Cambridge University Press, 2003), 165.
35. Douglas James, 'Parliamentary Divorce, 1700–1857', in *Parliamentary History* vol. 31, no. 2 (2012), 170.
36. Sybil Wolfram, 'Divorce in England 1700–1857', in *Oxford Journal of Legal Studies* vol. 5, no. 2 (Summer, 1985), 162.
37. Old English Proverb as quoted in A. Roger Ekirch, *Birthright: The True Story that Inspired Kidnapped* (New York and London: W.W. Norton & Company, 2010), 26.
38. Lady Holland to the Marchioness of Kildare as reproduced in *Correspondence of Emily, Duchess of Leinster* vol. I edited by Brian FitzGerald (Dublin: Stationery Office, 1949), 326.
39. Duchess of Brunswick as quoted in Wendy Moore, *Wedlock: The True Story of the Disastrous Marriage and Remarkable Divorce of*

Mary Eleanor Bowes, Countess of Strathmore (New York: Three Rivers Press, 2009), 263.

40. For the ways in which the 1753 Act strengthened the hands of the traditional male elite, see: David Lemmings, 'Marriage and the Law in the Eighteenth Century: Hardwicke's Marriage Act of 1753', in *The Historical Journal* vol. 39, no. 2 (June, 1996): 339–360.
41. Hay and Rogers, *Eighteenth-Century English Society*, 37.
42. Sir William Temple as quoted in Mary Poovey, *The Proper Lady and the Woman Writer: Ideology as Style in the Works of Mary Wollstonecraft, Mary Shelley, and Jane Austen* (Chicago: University of Chicago Press, 1985), 13.
43. We should not take this as a complete democratisation of society. Grieg, *The Beau Monde*, 3–4.
44. Kate Williams, *England's Mistress: The Infamous Life of Emma Hamilton* (New York: Ballantine Books, 2006), 47.
45. John Wade, *Women, Past and Present: Exhibiting Their Social Vicissitudes; Single and Matrimonial Relations; Rights, Privileges, and Wrongs* (London: Charles J. Skreet, 1859), 371.
46. Some scholars argue it is best to view prostitution as part of the local economy see: Tim Hitchcock, *English Sexualities, 1700–1800* (New York: St Martin's Press, 1997), 94.
47. On the fees charged by streetwalkers, A.D. Harvey states that a shilling was the going rate. A.D. Harvey, *Sex in Georgian England: Attitudes and Prejudices from the 1720s to the 1820s* (London: Phoenix Press, 2001), 89. Jo Manning asserts that the going rate was even less, around 9d (it took 12d to make a shilling). Jo Manning, *My Lady Scandalous: The Amazing Life and Outrageous Times of Grace Dalrymple Elliott, Royal Courtesan* (New York: Simon & Schuster, 2005), 4.
48. Williams, *England's Mistress*, 50–51.
49. For a good overview of these manuals, see: E.J. Burford, *Wits, Wenchers and Wantons: London's Low Life: Covent Garden in the Eighteenth Century* (London: Robert Hale, 1986), 102.

50. Lisa Hilton, *Mistress Peachum's Pleasure: The Life of Lavinia, Duchess of Bolton* (London: Phoenix Press, 2006), 19.
51. David M. Turner, *Fashioning Adultery: Gender, Sex and Civility in England, 1660–1740* (Cambridge: Cambridge University Press, 2002), 49.

Chapter One

1. Hay and Rogers, *Eighteenth-Century English Society*, 39
2. E.S. Turner, *Amazing Grace: The Great Days of Dukes* (Stroud: Sutton Publishing, 2003), 18.
3. Carola Hicks, *Improper Pursuits: The Scandalous Life of an Earlier Lady Diana Spencer* (New York: St Martin's Press, 2001), 157.
4. Topham Beauclerk as quoted in Lady Mary Coke, *The Letters and Journals of Lady Mary Coke, Volume 2, 1767–1768*, edited by J.A. Home (Bath: Kingsmead, 1970), 212.
5. Turner, *Amazing Grace*, 174–175.
6. Lawrence Stone, *The Family, Sex and Marriage in England 1500–1800* Abridged Edition (New York: Harper, 1979), 304.
7. John Shebbeare as quoted in Katherine Ashenburg, *The Dirt on Clean: An Unsanitized History* (Toronto: A.A. Knopf, 2007), 126.
8. Mary Wollstonecraft, *A Vindication of the Rights of Woman: Abridged, with Related Texts*, edited by Phillip Barnard and Stephen Shapiro (Indianapolis: Hackett, 2013), 54.
9. Although never really happy, the marriage between Topham and Diana got worse as Topham aged. As Mrs Steuart Erskine remarked, 'In the latter part of Mr Beauclerk's life the man of pleasure grew morose and savage, and Lady Di had much to suffer from his temper; so had his children, to whom he was a selfish tyrant, without indulgence or affection.' Beatrice Caroline Erskine, *Lady Diana Beauclerk: Her Life and Her Work* (London: T.F. Unwin, 1903), 116.
10. Viscount Bolingbroke as quoted in John Canon, *Aristocratic Century: The Peerage of Eighteenth-Century England* (Cambridge: Cambridge University Press, 1984), 71.

11. Canon, *Aristocratic Century*, 71.
12. Barbara White, *Queen of the Courtesans: Fanny Murray* (Stroud: The History Press, 2014), 158–159.
13. Norman S. Poser, *The Birth of Modern Theatre: Rivalry, Riots, and Romance in the Age of Garrick* (London: Routledge, 2018), 136–137.
14. Canon, *Aristocratic Century*, 71.
15. Roy Porter, *English Society in the 18th Century* (London: Penguin Books, 1990), 56.
16. As Edward Boucher James remarked, 'Secure in their own high position, the Worsleys were not always hurrying up to London to dance in the ante-chambers of the Ministerial dispensers of patronage.' Edward Boucher James, *Letters, Archaeological and Historical: Relating to the Isle of Wight,* vol. I (London: Henry Frowde, 1896), 489.
17. Hallie Rubenhold, *Lady Worsley's Whim: An Eighteenth-Century Tale of Sex, Scandal and Divorce* (London: Chatto & Windus, 2008), 32.
18. Christopher Hibbert, *The Grand Tour*, (London: Thomas Methuen, 1987), 15. See also: George Brauer, *The Education of a Gentleman: Theories of Gentlemanly Education in England* (New Haven: College & University Press, 1959), 156.
19. E.P. Thompson, *Making the English-Working Class* (New York: Vintage Books, 1966), 43.
20. This was not Worsley's first trip to the continent. Those responsible for his education believed that young Worsley still had much to learn and that a second trip would help remove some of the rough edges acquired from rural life allowing him to appear more like a proper gentleman. Rubenhold, *Lady Worsley's Whim*, 11–12. Hibbert states that during the Georgian period the method of travel had become more standardised with tourist heading to Naples via France and Switzerland and returning to England by travelling though Germany and the Low Countries. Hibbert, *The Grand Tour*, 25.
21. Rubenhold, *Lady Worsley's Whim*, 22.
22. Ibid, 18–19.

23. Ibid., 23–24.
24. Ibid., 25.
25. Ibid., 26.
26. Brides were largely free to wear any colour except for black. See: Manning, *My Lady Scandalous*, 54.
27. Horace Walpole as quoted in Edward Charles Ponsonby Lascelles, *The Life of Charles James Fox* (London: Oxford University Press, 1936), 19.
28. Grieg, *The Beau Monde,* 213.
29. Burford, *Wits, Wenchers and Wantons*, 215.
30. Harriette Wilson, *Memoirs of Harriette Wilson,* (London: W. Dugdale, 1825), vol. III, 189–190.
31. Grieg, *The Beau Monde,* 213. See also: Sarah Lennox, Henry Fox, Baron Holland, Mary Eleanor Anne Dawson, Countess of Ilchester, Giles Stephen Holland Fox-Strangways, Earl of Ilchester, Henry Edward Napier, *The Life and Letters of Lady Sarah Lennox, 1745–1826: Daughter of Charles, 2nd Duke of Richmond, and Successively the Wife of Sir Thomas Charles Bunbury, Bart., and of the Hon. George Napier; Also a Short Political Sketch of the Years 1760 to 1763 by Henry Fox, 1st Lord Holland,* vol. I (London: John Murray, 1901)*,* 224.
32. Stella Tillyard, *Aristocrats: Caroline, Emily, Louisa and Sarah Lennox, 1740–1832* (London: Chatto & Windus, 1994), 301.
33. Some people believed that Emily and Ogilvie had already married. See: Brian FitzGerald, *Emily Duchess of Leinster, 1731–1814: A Study of Her Life and Times* (London: Staples Press, 1949), 144–145.
34. Tillyard, *Aristocrats*, 302.
35. Lennox, et al., *The Life and Letters of Lady Sarah Lennox,* vol. I, 240.
36. Ibid., 240–241.
37. Ibid., 241.
38. Ibid.
39. Tillyard, *Aristocrats*, 319–322.
40. Ibid., 319–321.
41. Venetia Murray, *An Elegant Madness: High Society in Regency England* (London: Viking, 1999), 150.

42. Lady Melbourne as quoted in David Cecil, *The Young Melbourne & Lord M* (London: Bello 2017), 16.
43. Murray, *An Elegant Madness*, 150–151.
44. Paul Douglass, *Lady Caroline Lamb: A Biography* (New York: Palgrave Macmillan, 2004), 36.
45. Ethel Colburn Mayne, *A Regency Chapter: Lady Bessborough and her Friendships* (London: Macmillan, 1939), 125.
46. Douglass, *Lady Caroline Lamb*, 43. Susan Normington places Peniston's annual allowance at £3,000. Susan Normington, *Lady Caroline Lamb: This Infernal Woman* (London: House of Stratus, 2001), 29.

Chapter Two

1. Tillyard, *Aristocrats*, 72–73.
2. Nicola Phillips provides an excellent example of a gentleman who struggled and ultimately failed to control his son's desire to live like an aristocrat. Nicola Phillips, *The Profligate Son; Or A True Story of Family Conflict, Fashionable Vice, and Financial Ruin in Regency Britain* (New York: Basic Books, 2013). Julia Johnstone's biography provides numerous examples of families trying to control the spending of younger family members. Julia Johnstone, *Confessions of Julia Johnstone: Written by Herself in Contradiction of the Fables of Harriette Wilson* (London: Benbow, 1825).
3. Julia Johnstone tells the fascinating tale of Harriette Wilson trying to get an annuity from both the Marquis of Worcester and his father, the Duke of Beaufort. Johnstone, *Confessions of Julia Johnstone.*
4. Harriette Wilson, *Memoirs of Harriette Wilson,* (London: W. Dugdale, 1825), vol. I.
5. Margaret Stuart as quoted in Roy Porter and Lesley Hall, *The Facts of Life: The Creation of Sexual Knowledge in Britain, 1650–1950* (New Haven: Yale University Press, 1995), 24.
6. Tillyard, *Aristocrats*, 73.
7. FitzGerald, *Emily, Duchess of Leinster, 1731–1814*, 13.

8. Tillyard, *Aristocrats*, 99.
9. Roy Porter and Lesley Hall's, *The Facts of Life* contains much useful information about sex and pregnancy, including when various authorities and historical figures believed that pregnant women should abstain from having intercourse.
10. Emily FitzGerald as quoted in Tillyard, *Aristocrats*, 99–100.
11. Tillyard, *Aristocrats*, 319–321.
12. Moore, *Wedlock,* 322–323.

Chapter Three

1. Lord Carlisle, for instance, worried that he may become stricken with gout after having abstained from intercourse for some time. Porter, *English Society in the 18th Century*, 260.
2. Phillips, *The Profligate Son,* 49–50.
3. Tom Ambrose, *Prinny and His Pals: George IV and His Remarkable Gift of Friendship* (London and Chester Springs: Peter Owen Publishers, 2009), 22.
4. Porter, *English Society in the 18th Century*, 261.
5. Henry Fox, Baron Holland as quoted in Anthony Fletcher, *Gender, Sex, and Subordination in England 1500–1800* (New Haven and London: Yale University Press, 1995), 343.
6. Henry Fox as quoted in Phillips, *The Profligate Son*, 49–50.
7. Phillips, *The Profligate Son*, 72.
8. Katie Hickman, *Courtesans: Money, Sex and Fame in the Nineteenth Century* (New York: William Morrow, 2003), 4.
9. Lucy Worsley, *The Courtiers: Splendor and Intrigue in the Georgian Court at Kensington Palace* (New York: Walker & Co., 2010), 5.
10. George II as quoted in Andrew C. Thompson, *George II: King and Elector* (New Haven and London: Yale University Press, 2011), 124.
11. Thompson, *George II,* 92.
12. Queen Caroline as quoted in Fraser, *The Story of Britain,* 422.
13. Worsley, *The Courtiers*, 14–15.
14. Hickman, *Courtesans*, 37.

15. Murray, *An Elegant Madness*, 20.
16. Saul David, *Prince of Pleasure: The Prince of Wales and the Making of the Regency* (London: Abacus, 1999), 62–63.
17. T.H. White, *The Age of Scandal: An Excursion through a Minor Period* (Harmondsworth: Penguin Books, 1962), 191.
18. Creevey noted that the prince remained a frequent crier stating that he cried just as much with his new mistress Lady Hertford as he had done when with Fitzherbert. Thomas Creevey, *Thomas Creevey's Papers, 1793–1838,* edited by John Gore (Harmondsworth: Penguin Books, 1985), 90–91.
19. This was a common tactic used by the prince. Fergus Linnane, *The Lives of the English Rakes* (London: Piatkus, 2010), 223.
20. Murray, *An Elegant Madness*, 20.
21. Beau Brummell as quoted in Murray, *An Elegant Madness*, 20.
22. Ian Kelly, *Beau Brummell: The Ultimate Man of Style* (New York: Free Press, 2006), 98.
23. Ibid., 73.
24. Robert Morrison, *The Regency Years: During Which Jane Austen Writes, Napoleon Fights, Byron Makes Love, and Britain Becomes Modern* (New York: W.W. Norton & Company, 2019), 254.
25. Murray, *An Elegant Madness,* 30.
26. I.M. Davis, *The Harlot and the Statesman: The Story of Elizabeth Armistead & Charles James Fox* (Bourne End: The Kensal Press, 1986), vii.
27. Ann Catley states that a mercer who was short of credit and arrested for debt (only to be rescued by an inheritance) had, in six months, spent around £500 buying her gifts. Ann Catley, *A Brief Narrative of the Life of the Celebrated Miss Catley. Containing the Adventures of that Lady in her Public Character as a Singer, and Private one of a Courtezan.* London, 1780.
28. Wilson, *Memoirs of Harriette Wilson,* vol. I, 67.
29. Elizabeth Steele, *The Memoirs of Mrs Sophia Baddeley: Late of Drury-Lane.* 3 vols. (Dublin: Printers for Messrs. Colles, Moncrieffe, Gilbert, Exshaw, Wogan [and 9 others], 1787) vol. 1, 79.

30. Fergus Linnane, *Madams: Bawds & Brothel Keepers of London* (Stroud: The History Press, 2009), 140.
31. John Brewer, *Sentimental Murder: Love and Madness in the Eighteenth Century* (London: Harper Collins, 2004), 98.
32. C.G. as quoted in Julie Peakman, *Lascivious Bodies: A Sexual History of the Eighteenth-Century* (London: Atlantic Books, 2005), 9–10. For the original newspaper advertisement, see: *The Midnight Ramble, Or, The Adventures of Two Noble Females: Being a True and Impartial Account of their Late Excursion through the Streets of London and Westminster* [With Plates and Newspaper Cuttings Interleaved]. London: B. Dickinson, 1754. This particular clipping was found affixed between pages 18 and 19.
33. Steele, *The Memoirs of Mrs Sophia Baddeley,* vol. I, 68.
34. Hickman, *Courtesans*, 50–51.
35. Porter, *English Society in the 18th Century*, Np.
36. Hickman, *Courtesans*, 51.
37. For a fascinating discussion of the costs of entertainment and aristocratic culture, see: Robert D. Hume, 'The Value of Money in Eighteenth-Century England: Incomes, Prices, Buying Power – and Some Problems in Cultural Economics', in *Huntington Library Quarterly* vol. 77, no. 4 (Winter, 2014): 373–416.
38. Steele, *The Memoirs of Mrs Sophia Baddeley,* vol. I, 198.
39. Linnane, *Madams*, 142.
40. Hickman, *Courtesans*, 53.
41. Steele, *The Memoirs of Mrs Sophia Baddeley,* vol. I, 27.
42. Hickman, *Courtesans*, 51.
43. Phillips, *A Profligate Son*, 253. William Jackson died in 1828.

Chapter Four

1. Claire Tomalin, *Mrs Jordan's Profession: The Story of a Great Actress and a Future King* (London: Penguin Books, 1995), 45.
2. Hickman, *Courtesans*, xviii.

3. Steele, *The Memoirs of Mrs Sophia Baddeley,* vol. I, 198.
4. Wilson, *Memoirs of Harriette Wilson,* vol. I, 205–206.
5. Linnane, *Madams*, 66–67.
6. Sally Pridden as quoted in Capt. Charles Walker, *Authentic Memoirs of the Life, Intrigues and Adventures of the Celebrated Sally Salisbury* (London, 1723), 126.
7. Steele, *The Memoirs of Mrs Sophia Baddeley*, vol. I, 188–189.
8. Hickman, *Courtesans*, xviii.
9. *The Life of Miss Anne Catley, Celebrated Singing Performer of the Last Century: Including an Account of Her Introduction to Public Life, Her Professional Engagements in London and Dublin, and Her Various Adventures and Intrigues with Well-Known Men of Quality and Wealth* (London, 1888), 63.
10. Frances Murray, *Memoirs of the Celebrated Miss Fanny Murray. The Second Edition* (London: J. Scott, 1759), 63.
11. After Brummell's fall from grace, Harriette Wilson reportedly set the fashion among the young men at Oxford. See: Harriette Wilson, *Memoirs of Harriette Wilson,* (London: W. Dugdale, 1825), vol. II, 69.
12. Edward, Duke of Kent as quoted in Mollie Gillen, *The Prince and His Lady: The Love Story of the Duke of Kent and Madam de St Laurent* (New York: St Martin's Press, 1970), 19.
13. Gillen, *The Prince and his Mistress*, 254.
14. Steele, *The Memoirs of Mrs Sophia Baddeley* vol. I, 184.
15. Ibid.
16. Hickman, *Courtesans,* 47.
17. Steele, *The Memoirs of Mrs Sophia Baddeley* vol. I, 229.
18. White, *Queen of the Courtesans,* 111.
19. *The Life of Anne Catley*, 13.
20. Hickman, *Courtesans*, 66.
21. The Georgian period would see a transition from husbands demanding satisfaction for illicit and unsanctioned affairs with their wives by means of duelling to suing individuals for criminal conversation. Lawrence Stone, *Road to Divorce: England 1530–1987* (Oxford: Oxford University Press, 1990), 239–240. For the

relationship between gambling and honour see: John Smail, 'Credit, Risk, and Honor in Eighteenth-Century Commerce' *Journal of British Studies* vol. 44, no. 3 (July 2005): 455.

22. W. Clarke, *The Authentic and Impartial Life of Mrs Mary Anne Clarke: Including Numerous Original Letters and Anecdotes of Persons Deeply Interested, Never Before Published. With a Compendious View of the Whole Proceedings, Both Public and Private, Illustrative of the Late Important Investigation of the Conduct of His Royal Highness, the Duke of York, &C., &C.* (London: T. Kelly, 1809), 19.
23. For more on breach of promise, see: Sally Holloway, *The Game of Love in Georgian England: Courtship, Emotions, and Material Culture* (Oxford: Oxford University Press, 2019), 143–165.
24. Maria Foote and Joseph Hayne, *Fairburn's Edition of the Trial Between Maria Foote, the Celebrated Actress, Plaintiff and Joseph Hayne, Esq. Defendant, for a Breach of Promise of Marriage; including the Evidence at the Full length, Speeches of Counsel, &c. And the Whole of the Lover Letters* (London: John Fairburn, 1825), 4.
25. Some courtesans such as Elizabeth Armistead did have patrons on both sides of the aisle. Although she had spent much of her career with members of the Whig party, Armistead had once served as the mistress to the ardent Tory the Duke of Dorset. Davis, *The Harlot and the Statesman*, 28.
26. Lord Melbourne as quoted in Steele, *The Memoirs of Mrs Sophia Baddeley,* vol. I, 191.
27. Steele, *The Memoirs of Mrs Sophia Baddeley,* vol. I, 191.
28. Ibid., 123.

Chapter Five

1. Thomas Day's life, relationships and views on women have been explored by a variety of scholars. Some notable studies include: James Keir, *An Account of the Life and Writings of Thomas Day, Esq.* (London: John Stockdale, 1791); Peter Rowland, *The Life and Times of Thomas Day, 1748–1789, English Philanthropist and*

Author, Virtue Almost Personified (New York: Lampeter, 1996); Sir Samuel Haslam, *The Exemplary Mr Day, 1748–1789, Author of Sandford and Merton* (London, Faber & Faber, 1935); Wendy Moore, *How to Create the Perfect Wife: Britain's Most Ineligible Bachelor and His Quest to Train the Ideal Mate* (New York: Basic Books, 2013).

2. Moore, *How to Create the Perfect Wife*, 203.
3. Ibid., 121–122.
4. Day stuck to his word. When he found Lucretia poorly suited to his purposes, he set her up as an apprentice with a milliner and left her £400 to help her attract a suitable husband. Moore, *How to Create the Perfect Wife*, 101.
5. Williams, *England's Mistress*, 86.
6. Ibid., 18–19.
7. Peakman, *Lascivious Bodies*, 2.
8. Ibid., 11.
9. In reference to her early years in London, Emma wrote to the celebrated painter George Romney in 1791 reminding him of their former days: 'you have known me in my poverty … I own through distress my virtue was vanquished, but my sense of virtue not overcome.' Emma Hamilton to George Romney as reproduced in Hugh Tours, *The Life and Letters of Emma Hamilton: The Story of Admiral Nelson and the Most Famous Woman of the Georgian Age* (Havertown: Pen & Sword, 2020), 87–88.
10. Flora Fraser, *Beloved Emma: The Life of Emma Hamilton* (London: Weidenfeld and Nicolson, 1986), 8.
11. This point is not certain. Many biographers acknowledged it as a possibility and some sources suggest it was so but there is no direct proof. Williams argues that Emma probably did work at the Temple of Health stating that it best explains how she went from scratching out a living in London to working as a mistress for leading Georgians. Williams, *England's Mistress*, 55.
12. Joan Druett, *She Captains: Heroines and Hellions of the Sea* (London: Simon & Schuster, 2001), 182; Fraser, *Beloved Emma,* 12.

13. The child was most likely fathered by Sir Harry. Hibbert offers that Willet Payne could have also been the father. Christopher Hibbert, *Nelson: A Personal History* (Reading: Mass: Addison-Wesley, 1994), 83. According to Fraser, Emma believed that the child was fathered by Sir Harry. Fraser, *Beloved Emma*, 13.
14. Fraser, *Beloved Emma,* 17. The child's full name was Emma Carew.
15. Williams, *England's Mistress*, 83.
16. Fraser, *Beloved Emma,* 67.
17. Williams, *England's Mistress*, 88–89.
18. Charles Greville to Sir William Hamilton as reproduced in Tours, *Letters of Emma Hamilton*, 36.
19. Williams, *England's Mistress*, 87.
20. Charles Greville as quoted in David Constantine, *Fields of Fire: A Life of Sir William Hamilton* (London: Weidenfeld & Nicolson, 2001), 136.
21. Alternatively, after getting his heiress, Greville may have planned to sell the house as a means of paying back what he owed. Hibbert, *Nelson,* 83.
22. Williams, *England's Mistress*, 85.
23. Hibbert, *Nelson,* 83.
24. Edgar Vincent, *Nelson: Love & Fame* (New Haven & London: Yale University Press, 2003), 288.
25. Charles Greville to Sir William Hamilton as reproduced in Tours, *Letters of Emma Hamilton*, 39.
26. Fraser, *Beloved Emma,* 66–67.
27. Struck by her beauty, Hamilton paid Reynolds to paint Emma so that he would have an image of her to take back with him to Naples. Fraser, *Beloved Emma,* 38.
28. Sir William Hamilton as quoted in Constantine, *Fields of Fire*, 139.
29. Charles Greville to Sir William Hamilton as reproduced in Tours, *Letters of Emma Hamilton*, 43.
30. Hibbert, *Nelson,* 86.
31. Fraser, *Beloved Emma,* 64.
32. Emma Hamilton as quoted in Walter Sichel, *Memoirs of Emma, Lady Hamilton, the Friend of Lord Nelson and the Court of Naples:*

With a Special Introduction and Illustrations (New York: P.F. Collier, 1910), 76. Emma spelt 'friend' as 'freind' on this occasion
33. Williams, *England's Mistress*, 113.
34. Emma Hart to Charles Greville as reproduced in O.A. Sherrard, *The Life of Emma Hamilton* (London: Sidgwick & Jackson, 1927), 95–96.
35. Greville's mineral collection was especially impressive and, at the time of his death, valued at some £13,000. Fraser, *Beloved Emma,* 346.
36. Emma Hart as quoted in Colin Simpson, *Emma: The Life of Lady Hamilton.* London: The Bodley Head, 1983), 51.
37. Hibbert, *Nelson,* 88–89.
38. Constantine, *Fields of Fire*, 170–171.
39. Williams, *England's Mistress*, 128.

Chapter Six

1. Commonly known as Drury Lane, its official name is The Theatre Royal, Drury Lane.
2. Mayne, *Lady Bessborough and her Friendships,* 163.
3. Janet Gleeson, *Privilege and Scandal: The Remarkable Life of Harriet Spencer, Sister of Georgiana* (New York: Crown Publishers, 2006), 105.
4. Tomalin, *Mrs Jordan's Profession*, 98.
5. Elizabeth Sheridan as quoted in Tomalin, *Mrs Jordan's Profession*, 98.
6. Both Eliza and Frances had been noted beauties. Fintan O'Toole, *A Traitor's Kiss: The Life of Richard Brinsley Sheridan* (New York: Farrar, Straus and Giroux, 1998), 141.
7. Elizabeth Sheridan as quoted in Margot Bor and Lamond Clelland, *Still the Lark: A Biography of Elizabeth Linley* (London: Merlin Press, 1962), 151.
8. Elizabeth Sheridan as quoted in O'Toole, *A Traitor's Kiss*, 255.
9. Tillyard, *Aristocrats,* 105–107.

10. Bailey, *Unquiet Lives,* 149.
11. Most famously, James Gillray, *A Cognocenti Contemplating ye Beauties of ye Antique* (1801).
12. William Young as quoted in Terry Coleman, *The Nelson Touch: The Life and Legend of Horatio Nelson* (Oxford: Oxford University Press, 2002), 230.
13. Charles Lock as quoted in Hibbert, *Nelson,* 175.
14. Horatio Nelson as quoted in Alfred Morrison ed., *The Collection of Autograph Letters and Historical Documents: The Hamilton and Nelson Papers,* (United Kingdom: Private Circulation, 1894), 8.
15. Nisbet Hamilton Grant, *The Letters of Mary Nisbet of Dirleton, Countess of Elgin* (London: John Murray, 1926), 24.
16. Hibbert, *Nelson,*199–200.
17. Thomas Troubridge as quoted in Tom Pocock, *Horatio Nelson* (New York: Alfred A. Knopf, 1988)*,* 208–209.
18. Horatio Nelson as quoted in Hibbert, *Nelson,* 175.
19. Terry Coleman, *Nelson: The Man and the Legend* (London: Bloomsbury, 2002), 249.
20. Hibbert, *Nelson,* 131.
21. Ibid.*,* 226.
22. Williams, *England's Mistress*, 262–263.
23. Pocock, *Horatio Nelson,* 265.

Chapter Seven

1. Gleeson, *Privilege and Scandal*, 261.
2. Harriet Duncannon as quoted in Gleeson, *Privilege and Scandal*, 263.
3. Ibid.
4. Gleeson, *Privilege and Scandal*, 263.
5. Richard Brinsley Sheridan as quoted in John Cam Hobhouse, Lord Broughton, *Recollections of a Long Life*, Vol. 2, 1816–1822, edited by Charlotte Hobhouse Carleton (Cambridge: Cambridge University Press, 2011), 102.
6. Hobhouse, *Recollections*, 102.

7. Horatio Nelson to Emma Hamilton as reproduced in Morrison, *Hamilton & Nelson Papers,* 118.
8. Horatio Nelson as quoted in Esther Meynell, *Nelson's Lady Hamilton* (London: Methuen & Company, 1907), 297–298.
9. Horatio Nelson to Emma Hamilton as reproduced in Morrison, *Hamilton & Nelson Papers*, 118.
10. Nelson's letter to Emma in February 1801 states: 'I have a letter from Sir William; he speaks of the Regency as certain, and then he thinks you will sell better – horrid thought.' Horatio Nelson to Emma Hamilton as reproduced in quoted in Morrison, *Hamilton & Nelson Papers,* 113.
11. Horatio Nelson as quoted in Morrison, *Hamilton & Nelson Papers*, 116.
12. Ibid.
13. Vincent, *Nelson,* 400.
14. Horatio Nelson to Emma Hamilton as reproduced in Horatio Nelson, *Nelson: The New Letters* edited by Colin White (Woodbridge, The Boydell Press, 2005), 46.
15. Sir William Hamilton as quoted in Dudley Pope, *The Great Gamble* (London: Weidenfeld and Nicolson, 1972), 167.
16. Horatio Nelson as quoted in Hibbert, *Nelson,* 292.
17. Hibbert, *Nelson,* 117.
18. Tom Pocock. Nelson's Women (London: André Deutsch Limited, 1999), 84–85.
19. Richard Bulkeley to Horatio Nelson as reproduced in Morrison, *Hamilton & Nelson Papers*, 91.
20. Nelson's search for love is detailed in Pocock's *Nelson's Women*.
21. Horatio Nelson as quoted in Morrison, *Hamilton & Nelson Papers*, 113.
22. Horatio Nelson as quoted in Coleman, *Nelson,* 248.
23. Murray, *An Elegant Madness*, 151.
24. Morrison, *The Regency Years,* 141.
25. John Cam Hobhouse, Lord Broughton, *Recollections of a Long Life: With Additional Extracts from His Private Diaries*, edited by Lady Dorchester (London, John Murray, 1910) vol. 1, 14.

26. For a lively retelling of this incident, see: Alexander Larman, *Byron's Women* (London: Head of Zeus, 2016), 113–115.
27. Caroline composed this famous epitaph after first meeting Byron. Vere Foster, *The Two Duchesses: Georgiana, Duchess of Devonshire, Elizabeth, Duchess of Devonshire* (London: Blackie & Son, 1898), 284.
28. She would later be readmitted. Douglass, *Lady Caroline Lamb*, 214.
29. Gleeson, *Privilege and Scandal*, 347.
30. Douglass, *Lady Caroline Lamb*, 285.
31. Steele, *The Memoirs of Mrs Sophia Baddeley,* vol. I, 15.
32. Ibid.
33. Ibid.

Chapter Eight

1. Bisset was seen as an important ally in securing the parliamentary seat of Newport which Worsley won in 1780. Rubenhold, *Lady Worsley's Whim*, 44.
2. Amanda Foreman, *Georgiana: Duchess of Devonshire* (New York: The Modern Library, 1998), 63–64.
3. James Gillray's, *A Trip to Cocks Heath* (1778) being an obvious example.
4. Foreman, *Georgiana*, 64–66.
5. Rubenhold, *Lady Worsley's Whim*, 50.
6. Sir Richard Worsley as quoted in Rubenhold, *Lady Worsley's Whim,* 38.
7. Robert Pye Donkin, *The Trial with the Whole of the Evidence between the Right Hon. Sir Richard Worsley, Bart, and George Maurice Bissett, Esq. Defendant for Criminal Conversation with the Plaintiff's Wife,* 5th edition (London: G. Kearsley, 1782), 3–4.
8. Hicks, *Improper Pursuits,* 144.
9. Rubenhold, *Lady Worsley's Whim,* 51.
10. Sir Richard Worsley as quoted in Rubenhold, *Lady Worsley's Whim,* 52.
11. Rubenhold, *Lady Worsley's Whim,* 51.

12. Ibid., 52.
13. Ibid., 73–74.
14. Tillyard, *Aristocrats*, 260.
15. In response to the rumours, the Countess Ilchester stated: 'Lady Sarah had many admirers, but her cousin, Lord William Gordon, son of the third Duke of Gordon, was the only one whose feeling she at all reciprocated.' Lennox, et al., *The Life and Letters of Lady Sarah Lennox,* vol. I, xi.
16. Tillyard, *Aristocrats*, 264.
17. Ibid., 265–267.
18. Lennox, et al., *The Life and Letters of Lady Sarah Lennox,* vol. I, 223.
19. *The New Bon Ton; Magazine; or, Telescope of the Times,* vol. I (May to October 1818), iv.
20. Tillyard, *Aristocrats*, 272.
21. Ibid., 282.
22. Maureen Waller, *The English Marriage: Tales of Love, Money and Adultery* (London: John Murray, 2009), 195–196.
23. *Trials for Adultery: or, the History of Divorces. Being Select Trials at Doctors Commons, For Adultery, Cruelty Fornication, Impotence,* &c. *From the year 1760, to the present time. Including the Whole of the Evidence on Each Cause*, vol. 3 (London: S. Bladdon, 1779), 2.
24. Tillyard, *Aristocrats*, 285.
25. Johnstone, *Confessions of Julia Johnstone,* 52.
26. Grieg, *The Beau Monde,* 215.
27. Louisa Conolly as quoted in Brian Dolan, *Ladies of the Grand Tour: British Women in Pursuit of Enlightenment and Adventure in Eighteenth-Century Europe* (New York: Harper Collins, 2001), 122.
28. Louisa Conolly as quoted in Tillyard, *Aristocrats*, 292.
29. Grieg, *The Beau Monde,* 202.
30. Tillyard, *Aristocrats*, 293.
31. Hicks, *Improper Pursuits*, 190.
32. Mary Coke, *The Letters and Journals of Lady Mary Coke*, edited by J.A. Home, vol. 3 (Edinburgh: David Douglas, 1889–1896), 52.
33. F.P. Lock *Edmund Burke. Volume 1, 1730–1784* (Oxford: Oxford University Press, 2007), 307.

Chapter Nine

1. Cindy McCreery, 'Keeping up with the *Bon Ton*: the Tête-à-Tête series in the Town and Country Magazine', in *Gender in Eighteenth-Century England: Roles, Representations and Responsibilities* edited by Hannah Barker and Elaine Chalus (London & New York: Longman, 1997), 213.
2. Turner, *Amazing Grace*, 156–157.
3. McCreery, 'Keeping up with the *Bon Ton*', 208.
4. Some journals, such as the *Cuckold's Chronicle*, specifically sought to expose and mock those whose partners participated in affairs.
5. Andrew, *Aristocratic Vice,* 10.
6. Moore, *Wedlock*, 8.
7. An unnamed German visitor as quoted in Hitchcock, *English Sexualities*, 16. A similar claim was made in the pamphlet, *The Evils of Adultery and Prostitution with an Inquiry into the Causes of their Present Alarming Increase* (London, T. Vernon, 1792), 48–49.
8. Andrew, *Aristocratic Vice,* 10.
9. Ambrose, *Prinny and His Pals*, 119–120.
10. Maria Nicolaou, *Divorced, Beheaded, Sold: Ending an English Marriage, 1500–1847* (Barnsley: Pen & Sword, 2014), 113–114.
11. Lawrence Stone, *Broken Lives: Separation and Divorce in England 1660–1857* (Oxford: Oxford University Press, 1993), 119; Stone, *Road to Divorce*, 269.
12. Hicks, *Improper Pursuits*, 162–163.
13. Ibid., 162.
14. Edward Dodwell, *Adultery Trial in the Court of King's Bench Before Lord Kenyon, And a Special Jury, Between Edward Dodwell, Esq. Plaintiff, And The Rev. Henry Bate Dudley, Defendant, For Crim Con* Second Edition, (London: H.D. Symonds, 1789), 7.
15. Lambeth Palace Court Archives (LPCA), 4523.
16. Leah Leneman, *Alienated Affections: The Scottish Experiences of Divorce and Separation, 1684–1830* (Edinburgh: Edinburgh University Press, 1998), 136.
17. Turner, *Fashioning Adultery*, 77.

18. Horatio Nelson to Emma Hamilton as reproduced in Walter Runciman, *Drake, Nelson, and Napoleon* (New York and London: G.P. Putnam's, 1920), 76.
19. Coleman, *Nelson,* 246. Hibbert suggests another reason for not naming the child Emma pointing out that Nelson did not know that Emma already had a child named Emma. Hibbert, *Nelson,* 243.
20. Coleman, *Nelson,* 246.
21. Ibid., 293.
22. Winifred Gérin, *Horatia Nelson* (Oxford: Clarendon Press, 1970), 297.
23. Isabella Pender as quoted in Leneman, *Alienated Affections*, 59.
24. William Rose Robinson as quoted in Leneman, *Alienated Affections*, 59.
25. Leneman, *Alienated Affections*, 59.
26. Gleeson, *Privilege and Scandal*, 252–253.
27. Mary Eleanor Bowes, The Countess of Strathmore, *The Confessions of the Countess of Strathmore; Written by Herself. Carefully Copied from the Original Lodged in Doctor's Common* (London: W. Locke, 1793), 9.
28. Moore, *Wedlock,* 89.
29. Earl of Strathmore as quoted in Moore, *Wedlock,* 93.

Chapter Ten

1. Stone, *Broken Lives*, 119.
2. Nicolaou, *Divorced, Beheaded, Sold,* 114.
3. Ibid.
4. Stone, *Broken Lives*, 120–121.
5. Brian Fothergill, *The Strawberry Hill Set: Horace Walpole and His Circle* (London: Faber and Faber, 1983), 88.
6. Turner, *Amazing Grace*, 181–182.
7. Manning, *My Lady Scandalous*, 201–202.
8. Hicks, *Improper Pursuits*, 158.
9. LPCA, 377–379.
10. Stone, *Broken Lives*, 124–125.

11. Moore, *Wedlock*, 137.
12. Hicks, *Improper Pursuits*, 174.
13. Ibid.
14. LPCA, 122.
15. LPCA, 268.
16. Most aristocratic women did not breastfeed their children. Moore, *Wedlock*, 81.
17. LPCA, 111–112.
18. Criminal Conversation cases increasingly became an important step in seeking a parliamentary divorce. Wolfram, 'Divorce in England 1700–1857', 160.
19. Duke of Somerset-Scudamore as quoted in Stone, *Broken Lives*, 131.
20. Moore, *Wedlock*, 103–104.
21. Ibid., 84.
22. Hicks, *Improper Pursuits*, 164.
23. Ibid., 171.
24. Ibid., 180.
25. Manning, *My Lady Scandalous*, 73.
26. Hicks, *Improper Pursuits*, 193.
27. Kate Felus, *The Secret Life of the Georgian Garden: Beautiful Objects and Agreeable Retreats* (London: I.B. Tauris & Co., 2016), 135.
28. Stone, *Broken Lives*, 183–184.
29. Ibid., 243.
30. Ibid., 185–186, 188.
31. LPCA, 4149.
32. Ibid., 1572–1573.
33. Ibid., 1573.
34. Ibid., 935–936.
35. Ibid., 1574.
36. Ibid., 746.
37. Ibid., 294.
38. Stone, *Broken Lives*, 194. See also: LPCA, 761.
39. Lawrence Stone states that Clara Louisa, seeing the errors of her ways but fearing that she would be unable to resist him, asked for Rose not to return, but William insisted. Stone, *Broken Lives*, 194–195.

40. Felus, *The Secret Life of the Georgian Garden*, 136.
41. Nicolaou, *Divorced, Beheaded, Sold*, 75.
42. Stone, *Broken Lives*, 233.
43. For more on the ways in which an adultery trial negatively impacted a reputation, see: Junko Akamatsu, 'Revisiting Ecclesiastical Adultery Cases in Eighteenth-Century England', in *Journal of Women's History*, vol. 28, no., 1: Spring 2016, 20.
44. Andrew, *Aristocratic Vice,* 158.
45. Mr Allen as quoted in Stone, *Broken Lives*, 233.
46. Stone, *Broken Lives*, 246.
47. Nicolaou, *Divorced, Beheaded, Sold*, 75–76.
48. Stone, *Broken Lives*, 245.

Chapter Eleven

1. Jonathan David Gross, *Byron's 'Corbeau Blanc' Life and Letters of Lady Melbourne* (Texas A&M University Press, 1998), 27.
2. Douglass, *Lady Caroline Lamb*, 36.
3. Ambrose, *Prinny and His Friends*, 116–117.
4. Ibid., 116–118.
5. Moore, *Wedlock*, 310.
6. Ibid.
7. Mary Nash, *The Provoked Wife: The Life and Times of Susannah Cibber* (Boston and Toronto: Little, Brown and Company, 1977), 108–109.
8. O'Toole, *A Traitor's Kiss*, 391.
9. Nash, *The Provoked Wife*, 109.
10. Ibid.
11. *Tryal of a Case for Criminal Conversation, between Theophilus Cibber, Gent., Plaintiff, and William Sloper, Esq., Defendant* (London: T. Trott, 1739), 26.
12. Nash, *The Provoked Wife*, 113.
13. *Trial of J. Hacket, Esquire for Adultery with Mrs Mansergh in the Irish Court of Exchequer on December 10th 1807* (London: J. Day, 1807), 11–12.

14. Nash, *The Provoked Wife*, 116–117.
15. Ibid., 118.
16. Ibid., 123.
17. Ibid.
18. See for instance, *The Trial of R. Fergusson, Esq. For Crim. Con. with the RT. Hon. Lady Elgin, Before R. Birchall, Esq. Under-Sheriff, In the Sheriffs Court, Tuesday, Dec. 22, 1807* (London: J.B. Bell and J. De Camp, 1807).
19. Turner, *Fashioning Adultery*, 187.
20. *An Account of the Life of that Celebrated Actress, Mrs Susannah Maria Cibber with Interesting and Amusing Anecdotes. Also the Two Remarkable and Romantic Trials Between Theophilus Cibber and William Sloper* (London: Reader, 1887), 29.
21. *The Life of that Celebrated Actress*, 40.
22. Turner, *Fashioning Adultery,* 91.
23. *The Life of that Celebrated Actress*, 7; Poser, *The Birth of Modern Theatre*, 116.
24. Nash, *The Provoked Wife*, 147–148.
25. John Fyvie, *Tragedy Queens of the Georgian Era* (London: Methuen, 1909), 70.
26. *The Life of that Celebrated Actress*, 9.
27. Tomalin, *Mrs Jordan's Profession*, 6.
28. Ibid., 192.
29. Nash, *The Provoked Wife*, 184–185.
30. *The Life of that Celebrated Actress*, 10–11.
31. Nash, *The Provoked Wife*, 319.
32. Ibid., 322.
33. Ibid., 319, 322.

Chapter Twelve

1. Manning, *My Lady Scandalous*, 301.
2. Davis, *The Harlot and the Stateman*, 154.
3. Linnane, *English Rakes,* 219.
4. Ibid., 212–213.

5. Gillen, *The Prince and His Lady,* 123.
6. Ibid., 136.
7. Hibbert, *Nelson,* 275.
8. Coleman, *Nelson,* 336.
9. Horatio Nelson as quoted in George Lathom Browne. *Nelson; the Public and Private Life of Horatio, Viscount Nelson: As Told by Himself, His Comrades, and His Friends* (London: T. Fisher Unwin, 1891), 325.
10. Coleman, *Nelson,* 324.
11. Constantine, *Fields of Fire*, 2.
12. Ibid., 264.
13. Ibid., 284.
14. Vincent, *Nelson*, 585.
15. Coleman, *Nelson,* 336.
16. Although Nelson did not like to be reminded of Fanny, he never forgot his wife. In his will, he ordered that an annuity of £1,000 be settled upon Fanny. She had to sue her brother-in-law William to force the estate to pay. Coleman, *Nelson,* 336–337.
17. Brewer, *Sentimental Murder,* 147.
18. We know that the Matchams were keen to have her. Vincent, *Nelson,* 585.
19. Steele, *The Memoirs of Mrs Sophia Baddeley* vol. I, 192.
20. Ibid.
21. Allan Chilvers, *The Berties of Grimsthorpe Castle* (Bloomington: AuthorHouse, 2010), 204.
22. Manning, *My Lady Scandalous,* 45.
23. Hickman, *Courtesans*, 71–72.
24. Peakman, *Lascivious Bodies*, 55.
25. Burford, *Wits, Wenchers and Wantons,* 79; 83.
26. Peakman, *Lascivious Bodies*, 95.
27. Linnane, *Madams*, 143.
28. Elizabeth Steele as quoted in Linnane, *Madams*, 144.
29. George III as quoted in Burford, *Wits, Wenchers and Wantons,* 220.
30. Ambrose, *Prinny and His Pals*, 201–202.
31. White, *Queen of the Courtesans,* 19.

32. Linnane, *Madams*, 68.
33. Ambrose, *Prinny and His Pals*, 199–200.
34. Linnane, *Madams*, 157.
35. Duke of Wellington as quoted in White, *Queen of the Courtesans*, 19.
36. Wilson, *Memoirs of Harriette Wilson,* vol. I, 147. Julia Johnstone, a former friend of Harriette Wilson, published her own narrative to try and clear her name and that of some of her friends for what she saw as Wilson's inaccurate characterisations and telling of events. Johnstone, *Confessions of Julia Johnstone*.
37. Peakman, *Lascivious Bodies*, 91. Harriette had eight sisters. Of the nine Wilson sisters, six had careers as courtesans. Linnane, *The Lives of the English Rakes,* 209.
38. Linnane, *The Lives of the English Rakes,* 209.
39. Manning, *My Lady Scandalous*, 9.
40. Hickman, *Courtesans*, 100.
41. Ibid., 101. Hickman asserts that one of the annuities came from General Richard Smith and that the other may have been from George Cavendish.
42. Davis, *The Harlot and the Statesman,* 81.
43. Porter, *English Society in the 18th Century,* 238.
44. Ambrose, *Prinny and His Pals*, 42.
45. Manning, *My Lady Scandalous*, 297–298.

Chapter Thirteen

1. Charles Spencer, Earl Spencer, *The Spencers: A Personal History of an English Family* (New York: St Martin's Press, 2000), 148–149.
2. Hay and Rogers, *Eighteenth-Century English Society*, 43.
3. James Boswell as quoted in James Boswell, *The Journals of James Boswell, 1762–1795* edited by John Wain (New Haven: Yale University Press, 1991), 112.
4. Harvey, *Sex in Georgian England,* 2.
5. An exception was when he visited with his brothers, many of whom had lived as virtual man and wife with their mistresses.
6. Tomalin, *Mrs Jordan's Profession*, 7; 232–233.

7. Ibid., 263.
8. For the importance and some of the difficulties associated with embarking on a grand tour, see: Christopher Hibbert, *The Grand Tour* and Brian Fothergill, *The Strawberry Set*, 49. For a study of leading women who travelled abroad, see: Katharine Glover, *Elite Women and Polite Society in Eighteenth-Century Scotland* (Woodbridge: Boydell & Brewer, 2011): 139–164.
9. Gleeson, *Privilege and Scandal*, 368–369.
10. Janet Gleeson states that Harriet's eldest son John was in Germany during this time. Caroline had been sent to visit her mother at St Albans, and Willy was at sea with the navy. Gleeson does not know the exact whereabouts of Duncannon during this time but asserts it was clear that he was not with his wife and did not know about her pregnancy. Gleeson, *Privilege and Scandal,* 205–208.
11. Lady Spencer was an ever-present force in her children's lives. She expected obedience and proper decorum. She also expected regular correspondence and complained when she did not receive it. See Foreman *Georgiana*, 52.
12. Gleeson, *Privilege and Scandal*, 206.
13. Ibid., 327.
14. Ibid., 368–369.
15. Ibid., 255–256.
16. Tomalin, *Mrs Jordan's Profession*, 136.
17. Bowes, *The Confession of the Countess Strathmore,* 23.
18. Moore, *Wedlock*, 99–100.
19. Bowes, *The Confession of the Countess Strathmore,* 23.
20. Ibid., 89.
21. Hicks, *Improper Pursuits*, 175–176.
22. Bowes, *The Confession of the Countess Strathmore,* 6.
23. Ibid., 88.
24. Ibid., 89.
25. Moore, *Wedlock,* 116.
26. Ibid., 188.
27. Ibid., 193.

Chapter Fourteen

1. Stone, *Road to Divorce*, 239–240.
2. Ibid., 272.
3. Rubenhold, *Lady Worsley's Whim,* 81–82.
4. Dodwell, *Adultery Trial in the Court of King's Bench*, 5.
5. Horace Bleackley, *The Story of a Beautiful Duchess: Being an Account of the Life & Times of Elizabeth Gunning, Duchess of Hamilton & Argyll* (London: John Lane, 1927), 288.
6. Donkin, *The Trial with the Whole of the Evidence*, 3–4.
7. Mary Sokol *Bentham, Law and Marriage: A Utilitarian Code of Law in Historical Contexts* (London: Bloomsbury, 2013), 107.
8. Dodwell, *Adultery Trial in the Court of King's Bench*, 2–3.
9. Rubenhold, *Lady Worsley's Whim*, 91–95.
10. Donkin, *The Trial with the Whole of the Evidence*, 8.
11. *Morning Herald* as quoted in Rubenhold, *Lady Worsley's Whim*, 124.
12. Donkin, *The Trial with the Whole of the Evidence*, 13.
13. Ibid.
14. Ibid.
15. Ibid.
16. Ibid., 14.
17. Joanne Major and Sarah Murden, *An Infamous Mistress: The Life, Loves and Family of the Celebrated Grace Dalrymple Elliott* (Barnsley: Pen & Sword, 2016), 103.
18. Donkin, *The Trial with the Whole of Evidence*, 11.
19. For instance, James Gillray's *Sir Richard Worse-than-Sly, exposing his wife's bottom – o fye!* (1782). Speaking about the notoriety of the trial, Cindy McCreery states that there were dozens of unflattering caricatures made following the trial. Cindy McCreery, 'Breaking All the Rules: The Worsley Affair in Late-Eighteenth-Century Britain', in *Orthodoxy and Heresy in Eighteenth-Century Society: Essays from the DeBartolo Conference* edited by Regina Hewitt and Pat Rogers (Lewisburg: Bucknell University Press, 2002), 74.
20. Donkin, *The Trial with the Whole of Evidence*, 11.
21. Ibid.

22. Dodwell, *Adultery Trial in the Court of King's Bench*, 17.
23. Ibid.
24. Ibid.
25. Ibid., 18.
26. Ibid., 15.
27. Ibid., 16.
28. Ibid.
29. Ibid., 24–25.
30. Ibid., 25.
31. Ibid., 22–23.
32. Ibid., 25.
33. Sokol, *Bentham, Law and Marriage*, 107.
34. Stone, *Road to Divorce*, 234.
35. Manning, *Lady Scandalous*, 84.
36. Rubenhold, *Lady Worsley's Whim*, 181.

Bibliography

Newspapers and Magazines

The Gentleman's Magazine
The Lady's Magazine
The New Bon Ton; Magazine; or, Telescope of the Times
The Rambler's Magazine
The Tatler
The Town and Country Magazine

Printed Sources

Akamatsu, Junko. 'Revisiting Ecclesiastical Adultery Cases in Eighteenth-Century England'. *Journal of Women's History*. 28, 1 (Spring 2016): 13–37.

Ambrose, Tom. *Prinny and His Pals: George IV and His Remarkable Gift of Friendship*. London and Chester Springs: Peter Owen Publishers, 2009.

Andrew, Donna T. *Aristocratic Vice: The Attack on Duelling, Suicide, Adultery, and Gambling in Eighteenth-Century England.* New Haven & London, 2013.

Andrew, Donna T. 'Adultery à-la-monde:' Privilege, the Law and Attitudes to Adultery 1770–1809', *History*. 82 (January 1997): 5–23.

Andrews, John. *Letters to a Young Gentleman, on His Setting Out for France: Containing a Survey of Paris, and a Review of French Literature; with Rules and Directions for Travellers, and Observations and Anecdotes Relating to the Subject*. London: J. Walter, 1784.

Anon. *Character of a Town-Miss*. London: Rowland Reynolds, 1680.

Anon. *A View of the Beau Monde: or, Memoirs of Celebrated Coquetilla. A Real History in which interspersed the Amours of Several Persons of Quality and Distinction.* London: A. Dodd; J. Jolyfee, 1731.

Anon. *Tryal of a Case for Criminal Conversation, between Theophilus Cibber, Gent., Plaintiff, and William Sloper, Esq., Defendant*. London: T. Trott, 1739.

Anon. *The Midnight Ramble, Or, The Adventures of Two Noble Females: Being a True and Impartial Account of their Late Excursion through the Streets of London and Westminster.* London: B. Dickson, 1754.

Anon. *Prostitutes of Quality; or Adultery à-la-monde. Being Authentic Memoirs of Several Person of the Highest Quality.* London: J. Cook & J. Cootes, 1757.

Anon. *Nunnery for Coquettes*. London: T. Lowndes, 1771.

Anon. *The Adulteress*. London: S. Bladdon, 1773.

Anon. *The Case and Memoirs of the Late Rev. Mr James Hackman, And of His Acquaintance with the Late Miss Martha Reay: with a Commentary on His Conviction ... And Also, Some Thoughts on Lunacy and Suicide*. London: Printed for G. Kearsley, 1779.

Anon. *Trials for Adultery: or the History of Divorces. Being Select Trials at Doctors Commons, For Adultery, Cruelty Fornication, Impotence, &c. From the year 1760, to the present time. Including the Whole of the Evidence on Each Cause*, Vol. 3. London: S. Bladdon, 1779.

Anon. *The Man of Pleasure's Pocket-Book or the Bon Vivant's Vade Mecum, for the year 1780. Being the Universal Companion in Every Line of Taste Gallantry and Haut Ton.* London: S. Bladdon, 1779.

Anon. *Harris's List of Covent-Garden Ladies: Or, Man of Pleasure's Kalendar, For the Year 1789 Containing The Histories and Some Curious Anecdotes of the Most Celebrated Ladies now on the Town, or in Keeping, and also many of their Keepers.* London: H. Ranger, 1789.

Anon. *The Evils of Adultery and Prostitution with an Inquiry into the Causes of their Present Alarming Increase.* London: T. Vernon, 1792.

Anon. *Trial of J. Hacket, Esquire for Adultery with Mrs Mansergh in the Irish Court of Exchequer on December 10th 1807.* London: J. Day, 1807.

Anon. *The Trial of R. Fergusson, Esq. For Crim. Con. with the RT. Hon. Lady Elgin, Before R. Birchall, Esq. Under-Sheriff, In the Sheriffs Court, Tuesday, Dec. 22, 1807.* London: J.B. Bell and J. De Camp, 1807.

Anon. *The Book of Gentility; or the Why and Because of Polite Society: By a member of 'The Beef Steak Club'.* London: W. Kidd, 1835.

Anon. *An Account of the Life of that Celebrated Actress, Mrs Susannah Maria Cibber with Interesting and Amusing Anecdotes. Also the Two Remarkable and Romantic Trials Between Theophilus Cibber and William Sloper.* London: Reader, 1887.

Anon. *The Life of Miss Anne Catley, Celebrated Singing Performer of the Last Century: Including an Account of Her Introduction to Public Life, Her Professional Engagements in London and Dublin, and Her Various Adventures and Intrigues with Well-Known Men of Quality and Wealth.* London: 1888.

Ashenburg, Katherine. *The Dirt on Clean: An Unsanitized History.* Toronto: A. A. Knopf, 2007.

Askwith, Betty. *Piety and Wit: A Biography of Harriet, Countess Granville, 1785–1862.* London: Collins, 1982.

Astell, Mary. *Some Reflections Upon Marriage.* London: R. Wilkin, 1706.

Austen, Jane Austen. *Emma: A Novel.* London: John Murray, 1816.

Bailey, Joanne. *Unquiet Lives: Marriage and Marriage Breakdown in England, 1660–1800.* Cambridge: Cambridge University Press, 2003.

Barker, Hannah. *Newspapers, Politics and English Society 1695–1855.* London: Longman, 2000.

Barker, Hannah and Elaine Chalus eds. *Gender in Eighteenth-Century England: Roles, Representations and Responsibilities.* London & New York: Longman, 1997.

Beckett, John V. *The Aristocracy in England 1660–1914.* Oxford: Basil Blackwell, 1986.

Berg, Maxine. *Luxury and Pleasure in Eighteenth-Century Britain.* Oxford: Oxford University Press, 2005.

Berg, Maxine and Elizabeth Eger, eds. *Luxury in the Eighteenth Century: Debates, Desires and Delectable Goods.* Basingstoke: Palgrave Macmillan, 2003.

Bermingham, Ann and John Brewer, eds. *The Consumption of Culture 1600–1800: Object, Image and Text.* London: Routledge, 1995.

Berry, Helen. 'Rethinking Politeness in Eighteenth-Century England: Moll King's Coffee House and the Significance of "Flash Talk": The Alexander Prize Lecture'. *Transactions of the Royal Historical Society* 11 (2001): 65–81.

Black, Jeremy. *The British Abroad: The Grand Tour in the Eighteenth Century.* Stroud: Alan Sutton, 1992.

Bleackley, Horace. *The Story of a Beautiful Duchess: Being an Account of the Life & Times of Elizabeth Gunning, Duchess of Hamilton & Argyll.* London: John Lane, 1927.

Bleackley, Horace. *Ladies Fair and Frail.* London: Lane, 1925.

Nor, Margot and Lamond Clelland. *Still the Lark: A Biography of Elizabeth Linley.* London: Merlin Press, 1962.

Boswell, James. *The Journals of James Boswell, 1762–1795.* Edited by John Wain. New Haven: Yale University Press, 1991.

Boucé, Paul Gabriel, ed. *Sexuality in Eighteenth-Century Britain.* Manchester: Manchester University Press, 1995.

Bowes, Mary Eleanor, The Countess of Strathmore. *The Confessions of the Countess of Strathmore; Written by Herself. Carefully Copied from the Original Lodged in Doctor's Common.* London: W. Locke, 1793.

Brauer, George. *The Education of a Gentleman: Theories of Gentlemanly Education in England.* New Haven: College & University Press, 1959.

Brewer, John. *The Pleasures of the Imagination: English Culture in the Eighteenth Century.* London: Harper Collins, 2000.

Brewer, John and Roy Porter, eds. *Consumption and the World of Goods: Consumption and Culture in the Seventeenth and Eighteenth Centuries.* London: Routledge, 1994.

Brewer, John. *Sentimental Murder: Love and Madness in the Eighteenth Century.* London: Harper Collins, 2004.

Broadley, Alexander Meyrick. *The Beautiful Lady Craven.* London: John Lane, 1914.

Browne, George Lathom. *Nelson; the Public and Private Life of Horatio, Viscount Nelson: As Told by Himself, His Comrades, and His Friends.* London: T. Fisher Unwin, 1891.

Burford, E.J. *Wits, Wenchers and Wantons: London's Low Life: Covent Garden in the Eighteenth Century.* London: Robert Hale, 1986.

Cannadine, David. *The Pleasures of the Past.* Harmondsworth: Penguin, 1997.

Canon, John. *Aristocratic Century: The Peerage of Eighteenth-Century England.* Cambridge: Cambridge University Press, 1984.

Catley, Ann. *A Brief Narrative of the Life of the Celebrated Miss Catley. Containing the Adventures of that Lady in her Public Character as a Singer, and Private one of a Courtezan.* London, 1780.

Cecil, David. *The Young Melbourne & Lord M.* London: Bello 2017.

Chalus, Elaine and Perry Gauci eds. *Revisiting the Polite and Commercial People: Essays in Georgian Politics, Society, and Culture in Honour of Professor Paul Langford.* Oxford: Oxford University Press, 2019.

Charke, Charlotte. *A Narrative of the Life of Mrs Charlotte Charke: Youngest Daughter of Colley Cibber*. London: Hunt and Clarke, 1827.

Chilvers, Allan. *The Berties of Grimsthorpe Castle.* Bloomington: AuthorHouse, 2010.

Clarke, W. *The Authentic and Impartial Life of Mrs Mary Anne Clarke: Including Numerous Original Letters and Anecdotes of Persons Deeply Interested, Never Before Published. With a Compendious View of the Whole Proceedings, Both Public and Private, Illustrative of the Late Important Investigation of the Conduct of His Royal Highness, the Duke of York, &C., &C.* London: T. Kelly, 1809.

Coke, Mary Campbell. *The Letters and Journals of Lady Mary Coke.* J. A. Home, ed. Vols. 1–4 (Edinburgh: David Douglas, 1889–1896).

Coke, Lady Mary. *The Letters and Journals of Lady Mary Coke.* J. A. Home, ed. Vols. 1–4. Bath: Kingsmead, 1970.

Constantine, David. *Fields of Fire: A Life of Sir William Hamilton.* London: Weidenfeld & Nicolson, 2001.

Coleman, Terry. *Nelson: The Man and the Legend.* London: Bloomsbury, 2002.

Coleman, Terry. *The Nelson Touch: The Life and Legend of Horatio Nelson.* Oxford: Oxford University Press, 2002.

Creevey, Thomas. *Thomas Creevey's Papers, 1793–1838,* John Gore, ed. Harmondsworth: Penguin Books, 1985.

Curtis, Edith Roelker. *Lady Sarah Lennox, An Irrepressible Stuart, 1745–1826*. London: W.H. Allen, 1947.

David, Saul. *Prince of Pleasure: The Prince of Wales and the Making of the Regency*. London: Abacus, 1999.

Davis, I.M. *The Harlot and the Statesman: The Story of Elizabeth Armistead & Charles James Fox*. Bourne End: The Kensal Press, 1986.

Dodwell, Edward. *Adultery Trial in the Court of King's Bench Before Lord Kenyon, And a Special Jury, Between Edward Dodwell, Esq. Plaintiff, And The Rev. Henry Bate Dudley, Defendant, For Crim Con* Second Edition. London: H. D. Symonds, 1789.

Dolan, Brian. *Ladies of the Grand Tour: British Women in Pursuit of Enlightenment and Adventure in Eighteenth-Century Europe.* New York: Harper Collins, 2001.

Donkin, Robert Pye. *The Trial with the Whole of the Evidence between the Right Hon. Sir Richard Worsley, Bart, and George Maurice Bissett, Esq. Defendant for Criminal Conversation with the Plaintiff's Wife*, 5th Edition. London: G. Kearsley, 1782.

Douglass, Paul. *Lady Caroline Lamb: A Biography.* New York: Palgrave Macmillan, 2004.

Druett, Joan. *She Captains: Heroines and Hellions of the Sea.* London: Simon & Schuster, 2001.

Ekirch, A. Roger, *Birthright: The True Story that Inspired Kidnapped.* New York and London: W.W. Norton & Company, 2010.

Erskine, Beatrice Caroline. *Lady Diana Beauclerk: Her Life and Her Work.* London: T. F. Unwin, 1903.

Farquhar, Michael. *Behind the Palace Doors: Five Centuries of Sex, Adventure, Vice, Treachery, and Folly from Royal Britain.* New York: Random House Trade Paperbacks, 2011.

Felus, Kate. *The Secret Life of the Georgian Garden: Beautiful Objects and Agreeable Retreats.* London: I. B. Tauris & Co., 2016.

Ferguson, William. *Scotland's Relations with England: A Survey to 1707*. Edinburgh: Saltire Society, 1994.

FitzGerald, Brian ed. *Correspondence of Emily, Duchess of Leinster.* Vols. 1–3. Dublin: Stationary Office, 1949.

FitzGerald, Brian. *Emily Duchess of Leinster, 1731–1814; A Study of Her Life and Times*. London: Staples Press, 1949.

Fletcher, Anthony. *Gender, Sex, and Subordination in England 1500–1800*. New Haven and London: Yale University Press, 1995.

Foot, Jesse. *The Lives of Andrew Robinson Bowes, Esq. and the Countess of Strathmore, written from thirty-three years professional attendance, from letters, and other well authenticated documents*. London: Becket and Porter, 1810.

Foote, Maria and Joseph Hayne. *Fairburn's Edition of the Trial Between Maria Foote, the Celebrated Actress, Plaintiff and Joseph Hayne, Esq. Defendant, for a Breach of Promise of Marriage; including the Evidence at the Full length, Speeches of Counsel, &c. And the Whole of the Lover Letters*. London: John Fairburn, 1825.

Foster, Vere. *The Two Duchesses: Georgiana, Duchess of Devonshire, Elizabeth, Duchess of Devonshire*. London: Blackie & Son, 1898.

Fothergill, Brian. *The Strawberry Hill Set: Horace Walpole and His Circle*. London: Faber and Faber, 1983.

Foreman, Amanda. *Georgiana: Duchess of Devonshire*. New York: The Modern Library, 1998.

Fraser, Antonia. *King Charles II*. London: Phoenix, 2002.

Fraser, Flora. *Beloved Emma: The Life of Emma Hamilton*. London: Weidenfeld and Nicolson, 1986.

Fraser, Rebecca. *Story of Britain; From the Romans to the Present: A Narrative History*. New York: W.W. Norton & Company, 2006.

Fyvie, John. *Tragedy Queens of the Georgian Era*. London: Methuen, 1909.

Gleeson, Janet. *Privilege and Scandal: The Remarkable Life of Harriet Spencer, Sister of Georgiana*. New York: Crown Publishers, 2006.

Gillen, Mollie. *The Prince and His Lady: The Love Story of the Duke of Kent and Madam de St Laurent*. New York: St Martin's Press, 1970.

Glover, Katharine. *Elite Women and Polite Society in Eighteenth-Century Scotland*. Woodbridge: Boydell & Brewer, 2011.

Goldsmith, Sarah. *Masculinity and Danger on the Eighteenth-Century Grand Tour*. London: University of London Press, 2020.

Grant, Nisbet Hamilton. *The Letters of Mary Nisbet of Dirleton, Countess of Elgin.* London: J. Murray, 1926.

Grieg, Hannah. *The Beau Monde: Fashionable Society in Georgian London.* Oxford: Oxford University Press, 2013.

Grosley, P.J. *A Tour to London, or New Observations on England and Its Inhabitants*. London: Lockyer Davis, 1772.

Gross, Jonathan David. *Byron's 'Corbeau Blanc' Life and Letters of Lady Melbourne.* Texas A&M University Press, 1998.

Grove, Joseph. *The Lives of All the Earls and Dukes of Devonshire, Descended from the Renowned Sir William Cavendish: To Which Is Added a Short Account of the Rise, Progress, and Present State of the High Court of Chancery*. London, 1764.

Hadlow, Janice. *A Royal Experiment: The Private Life of King George III.* New York: Henry Holt and Company, 2014.

Hall, Monica. *A Visitor's Guide to Georgian England.* Barnsley: Pen & Sword History, 2017.

Haslam, Sir Samuel. *The Exemplary Mr Day, 1748–1789, Author of Sandford and Merton.* London, Faber & Faber, 1935.

Harvey, A.D. *Sex in Georgian England: Attitudes and Prejudices from the 1720s to the 1820s.* London: Phoenix Press, 2001.

Hay, Douglas and Nicholas Rogers *Eighteenth-Century English Society.* Oxford: Oxford University Press, 1997.

Hertzler, James R. 'Who Dubbed It 'The Glorious Revolution?'' *Albion: A Quarterly Journal Concerned with British Studies* 19,4 (Winter, 1987): 579–585.

Hibbert, Christopher. *The Grand Tour*. London: Thomas Methuen, 1987.

Hibbert, Christopher. *Nelson: A Personal History.* Reading: Mass: Addison-Wesley, 1994.

Hibbert, Christopher. *Queen Victoria: A Personal History.* London: Harper Collins, 2000.

Hickman, Katie. *Courtesans: Money, Sex and Fame in the Nineteenth Century.* New York: William Morrow, 2003.

Hicks, Carola. *Improper Pursuits: The Scandalous Life of an Earlier Lady Diana Spencer.* New York: St Martin's Press, 2001.

Hilton, Lisa. *Mistress Peachum's Pleasure: The Life of Lavinia, Duchess of Bolton.* London: Phoenix Press, 2006.

Hitchcock, Tim. *English Sexualities, 1700–1800.* New York: St Martin's Press, 1997.

Hitchcock, Tim and Michèle Cohen, eds. *English Masculinities, 1660–1800.* London: Longman, 1999.

Hobhouse, John Cam, Lord Broughton. *Recollections of a Long Life: With Additional Extracts from His Private Diaries,* Lady Dorchester, ed. Vol. 1. London, John Murray, 1910.

Hobhouse, John Cam, Lord Broughton. *Recollections of a Long Life, 1816–1822.* Charlotte Hobhouse Carleton, ed. Vol. 2. Cambridge: Cambridge University Press, 2011.

Holloway, Sally. *The Game of Love in Georgian England: Courtship, Emotions, and Material Culture.* Oxford: Oxford University Press, 2019.

Hume, Robert D. 'The Value of Money in Eighteenth-Century England: Incomes, Prices, Buying Power – and Some Problems in Cultural Economics'. *Huntington Library Quarterly.* 77,4 (Winter, 2014): 373–416.

Hunt, Margaret. *The Middling Sort: Commerce, Gender and the Family in England, 1680–1780.* Berkeley and London: University of California Press, 1996.

Inglis, Lucy. *Georgian London: Into the Streets.* London: Viking, 2013.

Jaeger, Muriel. *Before Victoria: Changing Standards and Behaviour 1787–1837.* London: Chatto and Windus, 1956.

James, Edward Boucher. *Letters, Archaeological and Historical: Relating to the Isle of Wight.* 2 Vols. London: Henry Frowde, 1896.

James, Douglas. 'Parliamentary Divorce, 1700–1857', *Parliamentary History.* 31,2 (2012): 169–189.

Johnstone, Julia. *Confessions of Julia Johnstone: Written by Herself in Contradiction of the Fables of Harriette Wilson.* London: Benbow, 1825.

Jones, Robert W. *Gender and the Formation of Taste in Eighteenth-Century Britain: The Analysis of Beauty.* Cambridge: Cambridge University Press, 1998.

Jones, Vivien, ed. *Women in the Eighteenth Century.* London: Routledge, 1990.

Keir, James. *An Account of the Life and Writings of Thomas Day, Esq.* London: John Stockdale, 1791.

Kelly, Ian. *Beau Brummell: The Ultimate Man of Style.* New York: Free Press, 2006.

Kinservik, Matthew J. *Sex, Scandal and Celebrity in Late Eighteenth-Century England.* Basingstoke: Palgrave, 2007.

Langford, Paul. *A Polite and Commercial People: England 1727–1783.* Oxford: Oxford University Press, 1992.

Larman, Alexander. *Byron's Women.* London: Head of Zeus, 2016.

Lascelles, Edward Charles Ponsonby. *The Life of Charles James Fox.* London: Oxford University Press, 1936.

Laughton, John Knox. *Nelson and His Companions in Arms.* London: George Allen, 1896.

Laurence, Anne. *Women in England 1500–1760. A Social History.* London: Weidenfeld & Nicolson, 1994.

Lemmings, David. 'Marriage and the Law in the Eighteenth Century: Hardwicke's Marriage Act of 1753'. *The Historical Journal.* 39,2 (June, 1996): 339–360.

Leneman, Lena. *Alienated Affections: The Scottish Experiences of Divorce and Separation, 1684–1830.* Edinburgh: Edinburgh University Press, 1998.

Lennox, Sarah, Henry Fox, Baron Holland, Mary Eleanor Anne Dawson, Countess Ilchester, Giles Stephen Holland Fox-Strangways, Earl of Ilchester, Henry Edward Napier, *The Life and Letters of Lady Sarah Lennox, 1745–1826: Daughter of Charles, 2nd Duke of Richmond, and Successively the Wife of Sir Thomas Charles Bunbury, Bart., and of the Hon. George Napier; Also a Short Political Sketch of the Years 1760 to 1763 by Henry Fox, 1st Lord Holland.* London: J. Murray, 1901.

Leveson-Gower, Sir George and Iris Palmer, eds. *Hary-O: The Letters of Lady Harriet Cavendish, 1769–1809*. London: John Murray, 1940.

Lewis, Judith S. *In the Family Way: Childbearing in the British Aristocracy 1760–1860.* New Brunswick: Rutgers University Press, 1986.

Lewis, Judith S. *Sacred to the Female Patriotism.* London: Routledge, 2003.

Lewis, Judith S. 'When a House Is Not a Home: Elite English Women and the Eighteenth-Century Country House'. *Journal of British Studies.* 48,2 (April, 2009): 336–363.

Linnane, Fergus. *Madams: Bawds & Brothel Keepers of London.* Stroud: The History Press, 2009.

Linnane Fergus. *The Lives of the English Rakes.* London: Piatkus, 2010.

Lock, F.P. *Edmund Burke. Volume 1, 1730–1784.* Oxford: Oxford University Press, 2007.

Mackie, Erin. *Market a la Mode: Fashion, Commodity and Gender in the Tatler and Spectator.* Baltimore: Johns Hopkins University Press, 1997.

Major, Joanne and Sarah Murden. *An Infamous Mistress: The Life, Loves and Family of the Celebrated Grace Dalrymple Elliott.* Barnsley: Pen & Sword, 2016.

Major, Joanne and Sarah Murden. *All Things Georgian: Tales from the Long Eighteenth-Century.* Barnsley: Pen & Sword, 2019.

Malcomson, A.P.W. *The Pursuit of the Heiress: Aristocratic Marriage in Ireland, 1750–1820.* Belfast: Ulster Historical Foundation, 1982.

Manning, Jo. *My Lady Scandalous: The Amazing Life and Outrageous Times of Grace Dalrymple Elliott, Royal Courtesan.* New York: Simon & Schuster, 2005.

Masters, Brian. *The Dukes: The Origins, Ennoblement and History of 26 Families.* London: Pimlico, 2001.

Mayne, Ethel Colburn. *A Regency Chapter: Lady Bessborough and her Friendships.* London: Macmillan, 1939.

McCreery, Cindy. 'Keeping up with the *Bon Ton*: The Tête-à-Tête series in the *Town and Country Magazine*'. In *Gender in Eighteenth-Century England: Roles, Representations and Responsibilities.* Hannah Barker and Elaine Chalus, eds. London & New York: Longman, 1997.

McCreery, Cindy. 'Breaking All the Rules: The Worsley Affair in Late-Eighteenth-Century Britain'. In *Orthodoxy and Heresy in Eighteenth-Century Society: Essays from the DeBartolo Conference.* Regina Hewitt and Pat Rogers, eds. Lewisburg: Bucknell University Press, 2002.

McCullagh Torrens, W.T. *Memoirs of the Right Honourable William, Second Viscount Melbourne*. 2 Vols. London: Macmillan, 1878.

Meynell, Esther. *Nelson's Lady Hamilton*. London: Methuen & Company, 1907.

Miller, John. *James II*. New Haven and London: Yale University Press, 2000.

Moore, Wendy. *Wedlock: The True Story of the Disastrous Marriage and Remarkable Divorce of Mary Eleanor Bowes, Countess of Strathmore*. New York: Three Rivers Press, 2009.

Moore, Wendy. *How to Create the Perfect Wife: Britain's Most Ineligible Bachelor and His Quest to Train the Ideal Mate*. New York: Basic Books, 2013.

Morris, Marilyn. *Sex, Money and Personal Character in Eighteenth-Century British Politics*. New Haven and London: Yale University Press, 2014.

Morrison, Alfred, ed. *The Collection of Autograph Letters and Historical Documents: The Hamilton and Nelson Papers*. United Kingdom: Private Circulation, 1894.

Morrison, Robert. *The Regency Years: During Which Jane Austen Writes, Napoleon Fights, Byron Makes Love, and Britain Becomes Modern*. New York: W.W. Norton & Company, 2019.

Murray, Frances. *Memoirs of the Celebrated Miss Fanny Murray. The Second Edition*. London: J. Scott, 1759.

Murray, Venetia. *An Elegant Madness: High Society in Regency England*. London: Viking, 1999.

Nash, Mary. *The Provoked Wife: The Life and Times of Susannah Cibber*. Boston and Toronto: Little, Brown and Company, 1977.

Nelson, Horatio. *Nelson: The New Letters*. Colin White, ed. Woodbridge: Boydell Press, 2005.

Nicolaou, Maria. *Divorced, Beheaded, Sold: Ending an English Marriage, 1500–1847*. Barnsley: Pen & Sword, 2014.

Normington, Susan. *Lady Caroline Lamb: This Infernal Woman*. London: House of Stratus, 2001.

Nussbaum, Felicity. *Rival Queens: Actresses, Performances and the Eighteenth Century*. Philadelphia: University of Pennsylvania Press, 2010.

Oliver, Neil. *A History of Scotland.* London: Weidenfeld & Nicolson, 2010.

O'Toole, Fintan. *A Traitor's Kiss: The Life of Richard Brinsley Sheridan.* New York: Farrar, Straus and Giroux, 1998.

Peakman, Julie. *Lascivious Bodies: A Sexual History of the Eighteenth-Century.* London: Atlantic Books, 2005.

Phillips, Teresia Constantia. *An Apology for the Conduct of Mrs T.C. Phillips: More Particularly, That Part of It Which Relates to Her Marriage with an Eminent Dutch Merchant*. London: G. Smith, 1761.

Phillips, Nicola. *The Profligate Son; Or A True Story of Family Conflict, Fashionable Vice, and Financial Ruin in Regency Britain.* New York: Basic Books, 2013.

Phillips, Roderick. *Untying the Knot: A Short History of Divorce.* Cambridge: Cambridge University Press, 2004.

Plumb, J.H. *England in the Eighteenth Century.* Harmondsworth: Penguin, 1950.

Pocock, Tom. *Horatio Nelson.* New York: Alfred A. Knopf, 1988.

Pocock, Tom. *Nelson's Women.* London: André Deutsch Limited, 1999.

Poovey, Mary. *The Proper Lady and the Woman Writer: Ideology as Style in the Works of Mary Wollstonecraft, Mary Shelley, and Jane Austen*. Chicago: University of Chicago Press, 1985.

Pope, Dudley. *The Great Gamble.* London: Weidenfeld and Nicolson, 1972.

Porter, Roy. *English Society in the Eighteenth Century.* London: Penguin Books, 1990.

Porter, Roy. *London: A Social History.* Cambridge: Harvard University Press, 1998.

Porter, Roy and Lesley Hall. *The Facts of Life: The Creation of Sexual Knowledge in Britain, 1650–1950.* New Haven: Yale University Press, 1995.

Poser, Norman S. *The Birth of Modern Theatre: Rivalry, Riots, and Romance in the Age of Garrick.* London: Routledge, 2018.

Rowland, Peter. *The Life and Times of Thomas Day, 1748–1789, English Philanthropist and Author, Virtue Almost Personified.* New York: Lampeter, 1996.

Rubenhold, Hallie. *Lady Worsley's Whim: An Eighteenth-Century Tale of Sex, Scandal and Divorce.* London: Chatto & Windus, 2008.

Runciman, Walter. *Drake, Nelson, and Napoleon.* New York and London: G.P. Putnam's, 1920.

Sherrard, O.A. *The Life of Emma Hamilton.* London: Sidgwick & Jackson, 1927.

Shoemaker, Robert. *Gender in English Society 1650–1850: The Emergence of Separate Spheres.* London & New York: Longman, 1998.

Sichel, Walter. *Memoirs of Emma, Lady Hamilton, the Friend of Lord Nelson and the Court of Naples: With a Special Introduction and Illustrations*. New York: P.F. Collier, 1910.

Simpson, Colin. *Emma: The Life of Lady Hamilton.* London: The Bodley Head, 1983.

Smail, John. 'Credit, Risk, and Honor in Eighteenth-Century Commerce'. *Journal of British Studies.* 44,3 (July 2005): 439–456.

Smith, Hannah. *The Georgian Monarchy.* Cambridge: Cambridge University Press, 2006.

Smith, Woodruff D. *Consumption and the Making of Respectability 1600–1800.* London: Routledge, 2002.

Smuts, Malcolm R. *Court Culture and the Origins of a Royalist Tradition in Early Stuart England.* Philadelphia: University of Pennsylvania Press, 1999.

Sokol, Mary. *Bentham, Law and Marriage: A Utilitarian Code of Law in Historical Contexts.* London: Bloomsbury, 2013.

Spencer, Charles, Earl Spencer, *The Spencers: A Personal History of an English Family.* New York: St Martin's Press, 2000.

Steele, Elizabeth. *The Memoirs of Mrs Sophia Baddeley: Late of Drury-Lane.* 3 Vols. Dublin: Printers for Messrs. Colles, Moncrieffe, Gilbert, Exshaw, Wogan [and 9 others], 1787.

Stocks, Huge. *The Devonshire House Circle.* London: Herbert Jenkins, 1917.

Stone, Lawrence. *The Family, Sex and Marriage in England 1500–1800* Abridged Edition. New York: Harper, 1979.

Stone, Lawrence. *Road to Divorce: England 1530–1987.* Oxford: Oxford University Press, 1990.

Stone, Lawrence. *Broken Lives: Separation and Divorce in England 1660–1857.* Oxford: Oxford University Press, 1993.

Stone, Lawrence and Jeanne C. Fawtier Stone. *An Open Elite? England 1540–1880.* Oxford: Clarendon, 1986.

Styles, John. *Dress of the People: Everyday Fashion in Eighteenth-Century England.* London: Yale University Press, 2007.

Tague, Ingrid H. '*Women of Quality: Accepting and Contesting Ideals of Femininity in England, 1690–1760*. Woodbridge, Suffolk; Rochester, NY: Boydell & Brewer, 2002.

Tague, Ingrid H. 'Love, Honor, and Obedience: Fashionable Women and the Discourse of Marriage in the Early Eighteenth Century'. *Journal of British Studies*. 40, 1 (January 2001): 76–106.

Thompson, Andrew C. *Britain, Hanover, and the Protestant Interest, 1688–1756.* Woodbridge: Boydell Press, 2006.

Thompson, Andrew C. *George II: King and Elector.* New Haven and London: Yale University Press, 2011.

Thompson, E.P. *Making the English-Working Class*. New York: Vintage Books, 1966.

Thompson, Francis M.L. *English Landed Society in the Nineteenth Century.* London: Routledge, 1961.

Tillyard, Stella. *Aristocrats: Caroline, Emily, Louisa and Sarah Lennox, 1740–1832*. London: Chatto & Windus, 1994.

Timbs, John. *Clubs and Club Life in London.* London: Chatto and Windus, 1899.

Tomalin, Claire. *Mrs Jordan's Profession: The Story of a Great Actress and a Future King.* London, Penguin Books, 1995.

Tours, Hugh. *The Life & Letters of Emma Hamilton: The Story of Admiral Nelson and the Most Famous Woman of the Georgian Age.* Havertown: Pen & Sword, 2020.

Trumbach, Randolph. *The Rise of the Egalitarian Family: Aristocratic Kinship and Domestic Relations in Eighteenth-Century England.* New York: Academic Press, 1978.

Turner, David M. *Fashioning Adultery: Gender, Sex, and Civility in England, 1660–1740.* Cambridge: Cambridge University Press, 2002.

Turner, E.S. *Amazing Grace: The Great Days of Dukes.* Stroud: Sutton Publishing, 2003.

Van der Kiste, John. *William and Mary: Heroes of the Glorious Revolution.* Stroud: The History Press, 2008.

Vickery, Amanda. *The Gentleman's Daughter: Women's Lives in Georgian England.* New Haven: Yale University Press, 2003.

Vickery, Amanda. *Behind Closed Doors: At Home in Georgian England.* New Haven: Yale University Press, 2009.

Vincent, Edgar. *Nelson: Love & Fame.* New Haven & London: Yale University Press, 2003.

Wahrman, Dror. *Imagining the Middle Class: The Political Representation of Class in Britain c. 1780–1840.* Cambridge: Cambridge University Press, 1992.

Walker, Capt. Charles. *Authentic Memoirs of the Life, Intrigues and Adventures of the Celebrated Sally Salisbury.* London, 1723.

Waller, Maureen. *Sovereign Ladies: The Six Reigning Queens of England.* New York: St Martin's Press, 2007.

Waller, Maureen. *The English Marriage: Tales of Love, Money and Adultery.* London: John Murray, 2009.

Williams, Robert Folkestone. *Memoirs of Sophia Dorothea, Consort of George I: Chiefly from the Secret Archives of Hanover, Brunswick, Berlin, and Vienna; Including a Diary of the Conversations of Illustrious Personages of those Courts, Illustrative of Her History, with Letters and other Documents. In Two Volumes.* London: Henry Colburn, 1845.

White, Barbara. *Queen of the Courtesans: Fanny Murray.* Stroud: The History Press, 2014.

White, T.H. *The Age of Scandal: An Excursion through a Minor Period.* Harmondsworth: Penguin Books, 1962.

Williams, Kate. *England's Mistress: The Infamous Life of Emma Hamilton.* New York: Ballantine Books, 2006.

Wilson, Harriette. *The Interesting Memoirs and Amorous Adventures of Harriette Wilson; One of the Most Celebrated Women of the Day, Etc.* London: W. Chubb, 1825.

Wilson, Harriette. *Memoirs of Harriette Wilson*. United Kingdom: W. Dugdale, 1825.

Wohlcke, Anne. *The 'Perpetual Fair' Gender, Disorder, and Urban Amusements in Eighteenth-Century London*. Manchester: Manchester University Press, 2014.

Wolfram, Sybil. 'Divorce in England 1700–1857'. *Oxford Journal of Legal Studies*. 5,2 (Summer, 1985): 155–186.

Wollstonecraft, Mary. *A Vindication of the Rights of Woman: Abridged, with Related Texts*. Phillip Barnard and Stephen Shapiro, eds. Indianapolis: Hackett, 2013.

Worsley, Lucy. *The Courtiers: Splendor and Intrigue in the Georgian Court at Kensington Palace*. New York: Walker & Co., 2010.